The Path to Inner Calm. Stories of Transforming
Fear into Faith for a Fulfilling Life

PRAY

DON'T PANIC

HANNA OLIVAS
Along with 25 Inspiring Authors

© 2025 ALL RIGHTS RESERVED.

Published by She Rises Studios Publishing **www.SheRisesStudios.com.**

No part of this book may be reproduced or transmitted in any form whatsoever, electronic, or mechanical, including photocopying, recording, or by any informational storage or retrieval system without the expressed written, dated and signed permission from the publisher and co-authors.

LIMITS OF LIABILITY/DISCLAIMER OF WARRANTY:

The co-authors and publisher of this book have used their best efforts in preparing this material. While every attempt has been made to verify the information provided in this book, neither the co-authors nor the publisher assumes any responsibility for any errors, omissions, or inaccuracies.

The co-authors and publisher make no representation or warranties with respect to the accuracy, applicability, or completeness of the contents of this book. They disclaim any warranties (expressed or implied), merchantability, or for any purpose. The co-authors and publisher shall in no event be held liable for any loss or other damages, including but not limited to special, incidental, consequential, or other damages.

ISBN: 978-1-964619-95-8

TABLE OF CONTENTS

INTRODUCTION 7

The Power of Prayer: Embracing Faith Over Panic
   By Hanna 9

It Was No Accident
   By Tracy Kyler 15

Overcoming Isn't a Straight Line, It's *The Lion King*
   By Dr. Breanna BOSS James 24

Trust, Hope, Persevere
   By Cynthia Piccini 34

Leap of Faith
   By Teresa Monaghan 42

Faith in the Storm's Shadow
   By Yvonne Bacon 48

Embracing Life Beyond Stress and Trauma: A Journey of Transformation and Healing
   By Victoria L. Sanchez 62

No Wrong Way to Pray: How to Underthink Prayer When You Suffer from Panic Disorder
   By Kenya E. Aissa, MS 72

Divine Lessons
   By Ayesha Amjad Faizi 85

Faith in Action: Transformative Power of Prayer
   By Shraddha Chandwadkar 99

Faith in the Storm: A Mother's Journey of Strength, Loss, and Divine Reassurance
    By Shaniqua Gibbs..113

From Fear to Faith: My Journey of Healing
    By Kim Castrillon..122

Breath as Prayer: Connecting to God's Life Force
    By Alison Levine..131

Between Forceps and Faith
    By Dr. Josette Ga-an...140

Overcoming in the Midst of Challenges
    By Angela Chademunhu...145

Challenges Propelled My Growth
    By Loretta Lee...155

From Shadows to Light: Transforming Fear into Freedom
    By Dr. Elizabeth Pritchard..169

Faith, Fear, and the Call to Lead
    By Anastasia Mouzina...179

Flourishing by Design: Finding Healing in God's Original Blueprint
    By Antonette Jeske..192

The Unseen Strength: From Sanctuary to Advocacy
    By Virginia Walters...202

A Love Tap
    By Gabrielle Burton..214

Moments of Impact
    By Carmen Maendel..218

The Wisdom Tree
    By Debra Hillard...238

Praise and Gratitude: The Most Powerful and Effective Tag Team
  By Hiedi Emily 248

From Grief to Gift
  By Quennie Marie Rose 258

Everything is "Up2UGod"
  By Anna Barboza Lugo 269

INTRODUCTION

Welcome to *Pray, Don't Panic: The Path to Inner Calm. Stories of Transforming Fear into Faith for a Fulfilling Life.* This anthology is a heartfelt collection of wisdom, strength, and personal stories from a diverse group of women who have faced life's toughest moments and learned to transform fear into faith. Their journeys, shared with raw vulnerability and courage, offer you a roadmap to navigate the uncertainties of life with grace and trust.

In a world where anxiety and stress often seem to reign, the pages of this book serve as a reminder that we have the power to choose a different path. By embracing prayer over panic, we can foster a sense of inner peace and spiritual resilience, no matter what life throws our way. The contributors to this anthology have walked different roads, but they all share one common truth: trust in a higher power can guide us through even the darkest times, leading to lives filled with purpose, joy, and fulfillment.

As you read, let each chapter be a beacon of hope. Allow these stories and reflections to inspire you to quiet your mind, soothe your heart, and find the calm you seek. Through prayer, trust, and unwavering belief, we can overcome our fears, embrace our strengths, and step into a future brimming with peace and possibility.

Pray, Don't Panic is more than just a book; it is an invitation to step into a life of faith, resilience, and inner calm.

Hanna Olivas

Founder and CEO of SHE RISES STUDIOS

https://www.linkedin.com/company/she-rises-studios/
https://www.facebook.com/sherisesstudios
https://www.instagram.com/sherisesstudios_llc/
www.SheRisesStudios.com

Author, Speaker, and Founder. Hanna was born and raised in Las Vegas, Nevada, and has paved her way to becoming one of the most influential women of 2022. Hanna is the co-founder of She Rises Studios and the founder of the Brave & Beautiful Blood Cancer Foundation. Her journey started in 2017 when she was first diagnosed with Multiple Myeloma, an incurable blood cancer. Now more than ever, her focus is to empower other women to become leaders because The Future is Female. She is currently traveling and speaking publicly to women to educate them on entrepreneurship, leadership, and owning the female power within.

The Power of Prayer: Embracing Faith Over Panic

By Hanna

In the journey of life, we often find ourselves at a crossroads, facing challenges that can feel overwhelming. At these pivotal moments, we have two choices: we can pray, or we can panic. But we cannot do both simultaneously. Choosing to pray invites peace into our hearts, while choosing to panic only serves to magnify our fears. As I reflect on my own journey, I have come to understand that prayer is not just a practice; it is a profound lifeline that can transform our experiences and empower us to navigate even the most turbulent times.

The Beauty of Prayer

Prayer is a beautiful act of surrender. It allows us to lay our burdens at the feet of God, trusting that He hears our cries and cares for us deeply. It is a moment when we connect with the Divine, seeking guidance, strength, and comfort. In my life, prayer has been a source of solace during my darkest hours, a reminder that I am not alone in my struggles.

I recall a particularly challenging period in my life when I faced a series of unexpected trials. I felt as if I were drowning in uncertainty, and the weight of my circumstances threatened to crush me. In those moments, I turned to prayer as my refuge. I would sit quietly, close my eyes, and pour out my heart to God, expressing my fears, anxieties, and hopes. It was in those vulnerable moments that I felt an indescribable peace wash over me, a reassurance that I was being held by a loving Creator.

Prayer has a way of shifting our focus from the chaos around us to the unwavering strength within us. It provides clarity in moments of confusion and offers comfort when we feel lost. When we pray, we invite God into our situations, acknowledging that we cannot face our challenges alone. It is a humbling act that opens our hearts to receive His grace.

The Choice Between Prayer and Panic

In life, we often encounter situations that ignite panic. Whether it's facing a health crisis, financial instability, or relational turmoil, our instinct may be to react out of fear. However, when we choose to panic, we allow our worries to cloud our judgment and drain our energy. Panic can lead to rash decisions, heightened anxiety, and a sense of hopelessness.

Conversely, when we choose to pray, we shift our perspective. We acknowledge that while we may not have control over our circumstances, we have control over our response. In those moments of prayer, we can find the strength to navigate our challenges with grace and courage.

One of my favorite prayers embodies this spirit of surrender:

"Lord, I surrender my worries to you. Help me to trust in your perfect plan and to find peace in your presence."

This prayer serves as a reminder that we don't have to carry our burdens alone. By entrusting our worries to God, we open ourselves to His guidance and wisdom.

The Transformative Power of Prayer

Prayer is transformative. It has the power to change our hearts, perspectives, and circumstances. When we pray, we invite God into our lives, allowing Him to work in ways that exceed our understanding. Throughout my journey, I have witnessed the profound impact of prayer on my own life and the lives of others.

During one of my most trying times, I faced a daunting diagnosis that left me feeling vulnerable and afraid. As I grappled with the uncertainty of my health, I turned to prayer as a source of strength. I prayed not only for healing but also for the courage to face whatever lay ahead. In my darkest moments, I would recite another prayer that resonated deeply within me:

"God, grant me the serenity to accept the things I cannot change, the courage to change the things I can, and the wisdom to know the difference."

This prayer has become a mantra in my life, reminding me that while I may not control every aspect of my journey, I can control how I respond to it. Through prayer, I found the serenity to accept my circumstances, the courage to seek healing, and the wisdom to navigate the unknown.

Finding Courage Through Prayer

Prayer is a source of courage. It empowers us to face our fears head-on and to take steps toward the life we desire. When we surrender our worries to God, we receive the strength to act in faith. We become warriors equipped with the knowledge that we are supported by a higher power.

One of the most profound lessons I've learned through prayer is that it is not merely about asking for what we want; it is about aligning our hearts with God's will. In moments of uncertainty, I have found solace in praying for clarity and guidance, trusting that God knows what is best for me.

As women, we often carry the weight of our responsibilities, juggling various roles and expectations. It can be easy to feel overwhelmed and question our abilities. However, through prayer, we can release that burden and find the courage to step into our power. Prayer reminds us that we are equipped with the tools we need to thrive, even when faced with adversity.

Prayer as an Uplifting Force

Prayer can be an uplifting force in our lives, infusing our days with hope and joy. It allows us to express gratitude for the blessings we often take for granted. In the midst of challenges, it is essential to remember that there is always something to be thankful for.

I encourage you to incorporate gratitude into your prayer life. Each day, take a moment to reflect on the gifts that surround you, no matter how small. Thank God for the love of family and friends, for the beauty of nature, and for the opportunities that lie ahead. By cultivating a spirit of gratitude, we open ourselves to experiencing joy and abundance.

Moreover, prayer fosters a sense of community and connection. When we share our prayer requests with others, we invite them to walk alongside us in our journey. There is immense power in collective prayer, as we lift one another up and support each other through life's challenges.

Grace and Forgiveness in Prayer

Prayer is also a gateway to grace and forgiveness. It encourages us to let go of grudges and release the burdens of resentment. When we approach God with a humble heart, we recognize our need for His forgiveness and the importance of extending that forgiveness to others.

In my journey, I have encountered moments when I struggled to forgive those who had hurt me. It was through prayer that I found the strength to release those burdens and move forward. I learned that forgiveness is not about condoning the actions of others but about freeing myself from the shackles of anger and pain.

One prayer that resonates deeply with me is:

"Lord, help me to forgive those who have wronged me. Grant me the strength to let go of the past and to embrace a future filled with love and compassion."

This prayer serves as a reminder that forgiveness is a process—a journey that requires patience and grace. By choosing to forgive, we create space for healing and restoration in our lives.

Embracing Life's Journey Through Prayer

Life is a journey filled with ups and downs, and through it all, prayer can be our guiding light. It empowers us to embrace each moment, whether joyous or challenging, with grace and gratitude. When we choose to pray, we acknowledge that we are part of a greater story—one that is woven with purpose and meaning.

As you navigate your own journey, I encourage you to make prayer a central part of your life. It can be as simple as whispering a prayer of gratitude in the morning, seeking guidance before making decisions, or turning to prayer during moments of uncertainty. The more we engage in prayer, the more we cultivate a deeper relationship with God and ourselves.

Conclusion: The Power of Choice

In conclusion, we have a powerful choice in life: to pray or to panic. I encourage you to choose prayer as your response to the challenges you face. In doing so, you will find solace, strength, and courage to navigate the storms of life.

Prayer is a beautiful act of faith that invites God into our experiences, offering us grace, forgiveness, and hope. By embracing the power of prayer, we empower ourselves to face life's uncertainties with resilience and joy.

Let us remember that no matter what we encounter, we are never alone. God is with us, guiding our steps and holding our hearts. Choose to pray, and watch how it transforms your life into a beautiful tapestry of faith, love, and purpose.

Tracy Kyler

CEO of Glow Coach LLC

https://www.linkedin.com/in/tracy-kyler-4121a4153/
https://www.facebook.com/tracy.kyler.5/
https://www.instagram.com/glowcoachtracy/
https://glowcoachtracy.com/

Tracy Kyler is the Published Author of Glowing Through the Chakras and an Intuitive Business Coach teaching Holistic Healers how to charge their worth and go full time in their own business.

Early in life, Tracy was a teenage mother who grew up with trauma and emotional struggles. She had a passion to succeed and pursued a career in Human and Social Services to help other kids going through the same in life. She then stepped into her calling as a Spiritual Coach helping others overcome limiting beliefs, developing their spiritual gifts and now coaches intuitive healers how to have a successful business.

A mother of two and a grandmother of three living in Omaha, Nebraska with her high school sweetheart, Rich. At the age of 57, Tracy is enjoying her life continuing to help others as well as beginning to travel with her husband as they enter retirement years.

It Was No Accident

By Tracy Kyler

February 11, 2006, is a day I will never forget. It was the day my life ended, only to begin again. Remembering the night before, I was angry with God. I regretted the words as soon as they came out of my mouth and even appeared in my head. I broke down, "Why have you abandoned me? Why have you made my life so damn hard? I don't BELIEVE IN YOU anymore! If YOU existed, my life wouldn't be so horrible!" The night before my car accident, I had given up on life and fell into a deep hole, and there was no consoling me as my husband tried to make me think rationally. It was the second time in my life that I had considered taking my own life. The first being in high school, my junior year, feeling lost, struggling from sexual abuse, and having no self-confidence or direction. As if my life couldn't get worse then, I became pregnant; however, it saved my life. This particular night was one of the ones where I normally would pull the sheet over my head and want everyone to leave me alone. I cried myself to sleep.

I quit my 15-year career and followed my passion to open a restaurant. When I bought one from a friend in 2004, I realized there was no income coming in, and the last two years of owing it drained us financially. I quickly realized the ruins I had put my family in, and this weighed heavily on my mind. I cried uncontrollably and let God have it as I pleaded, "Why would you open those doors for me just to close them so harshly?" I was, once again, a failure, and it reminded me of all the negative things I already thought of myself. I was tired, defeated, and didn't even know why I continued to try because nothing was easy in my life. I prayed I just wouldn't wake up to make it easier on my family than taking my own life, leaving them feeling abandoned.

The Accident

The next day was super unpleasant for my husband and me. My daughter realized there was no way she was going on this trip with a grumpy mom and asked to stay with a friend. I had no energy to argue with her. Boy, my poor husband had to deal with this swollen-eyed and angry woman. Honestly, I was angry that morning because I woke up. Another disappointment with God. I felt a knot in my stomach for saying the words I had to HIM ... that Big Guy I had prayed to my entire life! We headed on the road that early morning, and I was so rude to my husband. He was the NICEST man, my rock since high school, and always trying to console me. As I bossed him around on how to drive, he said, "Can you let me drive?" and I responded, "Can you put your seatbelt on?" Click, he put his seat belt on, and he asked, "Happy?" and I responded, "Drive away!"

We passed the ice truck laying sand on the Iowa Interstate a few miles back. Honestly, the road didn't seem icy at all. The snow had just begun to fall, and it was so pretty, but I refused to acknowledge it. We had made the trip from Nebraska to Kansas many times. We had committed to seeing our friends' new home and baby in Kansas months in advance due to canceling twice before. As I further stewed and felt sorry for myself, my husband suddenly screamed and extended his arm to protect me, "Tracy, Tracy, Tracy!"

I remember hitting the side of the road and the first roll of the vehicle. Waking up, which felt like minutes, I found myself looking at my husband through the broken windshield and him crying and panicking. "Get me out of here!" I demanded but quickly saw the panic on his face. "I can't," with full-on tears, he responded. It was then I quickly realized I was trapped! The truck had rolled 300 feet into a cornfield, hopping a fence along the way, and I was trapped with the vehicle lying on the passenger side and my leg partially out of the window and under the vehicle. The roof was caved in on my left shoulder, pinning me back as well as putting pressure on my head. My arm rested against my face, my face was to the dirt, the seatbelt was across my eye, and I felt the blood dripping down my face. As my husband cried seeing me and feeling helpless, I felt my soul coming away from my body and realized that *God had listened,* and *this was it*. "Please tell our children I love them and goodbye. You are a fantastic daddy, so take good care of them!" My husband refused to let me go, and he began screaming, "DON'T YOU LEAVE ME!"

The BIG GUY

My soul pulled away from my body effortlessly as my husband's pleas to me to stay got louder. As I floated above the scene and saw his sadness, I felt guilty about how I had treated him that morning. Many days, actually, he was always there for me and such an amazing husband and father. I wasn't always too kind and felt the need to control EVERYTHING. I then realized I was moving toward heaven and I was excited to get the chance to be with my mama. Another thing I was angry with God about—taking my mama away from me when we only had just begun to have a relationship. When she passed away, I felt robbed of the opportunity to finally be close to her and get the closure needed between us. And there he was ...

Standing right in front of me with his arms outstretched, God looked like I always imagined him. Loving, ready to embrace me warmly, and with the kindest eyes and smile. He said to me, plain and simple, *"You have a choice!"* I could see my mama behind Him awaiting to embrace me excitedly, as well as glimpses of others standing behind her without faces, just shadows. As I looked down at my husband, sobbing uncontrollably, all alone in the field with my body, I made a decision quickly and without reservation. "I can't leave him. Please tell my mom I will see her again one day." As soon as I said those words, I was back in my body gasping with air. My husband lifted his head in shock! "You died!" he exclaimed. I reassured him God gave me a choice to stay and demanded he leave me and go get help. He felt distraught at the thought of leaving me, and I reassured and bossed him (as always), "God told me I could stay, so go get help!" He ran to the road, and I could hear his screams for help. The ice truck we passed had pulled up along the road and already called 911. I could hear the sirens in the distance as I sat, thinking of what just happened.

Just Pray, Don't Panic

Now, anyone who knows me knows that I DO NOT like to be cold, and the immediate freezing started as soon as I was in my body. The cold air hitting my face and the feeling of the warm blood from my face sent me into panic. For years, I struggled with panic attacks and not being "in control" of everything since childhood. If I could control things, then no longer would I be a victim to anyone ever again. At this time, I had no control, so I started to pray the Catholic prayers I said over the years, and it calmed me down until the true rescuers showed up. When they did, they were not forthcoming with me on what the situation was and tried to pacify me with comforting words. Taking control as usual, I said to them, "Look—I'm not someone you can BS! I'm a straight shooter, so tell me what is going on!" The poor rescuer who climbed in the window was assessing the damage, and he replied, "Okay, Tracy, I'm gonna tell you what's going on, but you need to not panic. The vehicle is lying on its passenger side, and your leg is underneath. You are pinned from the roof, so we cannot remove you. It will take about two hours to cut you out of here and roll the vehicle back upright."

I was ready for this and assured him to get going. But I asked him to do me a favor as he promised to stay inside the vehicle with me as best he could ... "Pray with me?!" He told me he was embarrassed to say that he had forgotten his prayers. I reassured him I knew them well and would say them for the two of us. Looking past him, I saw my husband on the telephone, making all the calls needed to keep him supported, and he looked so miserable. Beginning with the 'Our Father,' I went through many prayers as the hours ticked on. The rescuer began to say the prayers with me as if he remembered them instantly. The rescuers working above me were praying as well, and I could hear them all in unison. I was amazed and feeling so blessed as I remained calm. About ten minutes from my ultimate freeing of the vehicle, my breathing became labored, and I stopped praying out loud. All rescuers immediately stopped what they were doing to check on me. "It's okay, keep going, I'm just having a hard time breathing, so I'm praying to myself."

As the truck rolled off of my leg and upright, quick scattering started to occur all around me. I was lifted onto the stretcher, and I wondered, "Did I lose a shoe? Thank goodness I had on clean underwear and a new bra as my mama always taught me to do when traveling." I giggled to myself but quickly felt pain in my wrist but nothing in my leg. In the ambulance, I went as the rescuers cut my clothing off, "There is a better way to see a girl naked," I joked. Repeated questions about health, medications, illnesses, and allergies barraged me, and I asked where my husband was. The driver responded, "He is up front with us." "Are you okay, honey?" I asked and only heard sobs and a faint "yes". I continued to joke, "Well, if he isn't driving then let's go." Realizing quickly it wasn't the best joke to make. Rich was feeling so guilty at the moment and in fear. I reassured him once again, "It's okay, honey, God told me I could stay!"

The Recovery

My injuries were more severe than the little town in Iowa could manage, and the weather became bad in order to transport me back to Omaha by helicopter. We were back on the road in an ambulance to travel on the roads that brought us to this situation. Rich refused to stay at the little hospital in order to get checked out himself, and the ambulance made its journey, with Rich insisting to be with me. My husband shared with me when we passed the scene of the accident and informed me there were other cars off the road in the same spot that had hit black ice themselves. I prayed for their safety and continued to say my Catholic prayers. It was then I expressed gratitude to God for giving me this chance to LIVE AGAIN. I learned later that many people died that day in accidents all across Nebraska and Iowa.

This energy in my hand was interesting, and I began to feel electricity shooting from it. At the hospital, they quickly assessed me, and I learned I had the following injuries: broken left collar bone, broken right wrist, fracture to left temple, cut eyelid from seatbelt, broken right femur, and my spleen was torn and bleeding. The doctors put my leg in retraction to address the spleen's ability to heal itself immediately before surgery could be performed. They drugged me up with morphine and waited for the spleen's decision. The hospital staff insisted my husband go home, and he reluctantly listened as I reassured him again, "It's okay, God told me I can stay!"

The spleen healed, and the surgery was successful. The hospital, unfortunately, kicked me out due to the insurance company refusing to keep paying. I remember a sweet nurse's aide coming in and asking if there was ANYTHING she could do for me. "Yes, can you please wash the blood and glass from my hair that has been here a week?" She comforted me as she gently washed my hair and body. They released me to go home, and a hospital bed was waiting for me in our living room. For six months, I became fully dependent on my family to bathe me and assist me in going to the bathroom. I was usually a very private girl, and did I mention IN CONTROL? I reluctantly released that control during my recovery and relied on my restored faith in God. The energy in my hand was still present, and I couldn't understand it. As I googled it, I learned about Reiki and the ability to heal your own body. I grew up with a strong Catholic faith and had abandoned it when the church did not want to marry me due to having a child out of wedlock. As I dove into my spirituality and the "gifts" that opened throughout my life, my faith in God remained. I began to lay my hands on my body and prayed, "In your name I heal, in your name I heal, <u>in</u> YOUR NAME I <u>heal</u>." Quick progress was made in these six months at home while my business took a back seat.

Not a Coincidence

The months of recovery were the most difficult for my husband. He was maintaining the home, and my daughter watched us struggle through the trauma of the accident. Our son was away in college, and we later learned he struggled quietly by himself. Although we had a lot of support from friends and family, I watched daily as Rich stared intently at me, struggling to walk or do anything. He would begin crying and apologizing daily, often multiple times a day. I prayed for his peace and felt troubled by the fact that all I was feeling was joy and gratitude while he suffered. It was then I asked God for the answer to relieve him of his pain, and it came to me. I knew this much, since knowing Rich at the age of 15—all he has ever wanted to do was take care of me and for me to be happy. It clicked!

The next opportunity I got, I took it. We were having dinner for the first time at the dining room table alone. He had cooked an amazing meal, as always, and I struggled to use my fork resulting in me dropping food all over my shirt. He began to cry and apologize. "That's IT!" as I threw my fork down angrily (I was good at this acting). "What? What do you need?" he pleaded. "Well, God gave me this gift, and I can't even enjoy it if you are gonna cry and feel guilty!" He looked at me in shock, not understanding. It was then it flowed from me ...

> *"Do you remember the night before our car accident, Rich? When I was angry and the saddest I've ever been? Well, do you think it is a coincidence that I was hurt in that rollover and you weren't? Can you explain that to me because I see this as a blessing? I no longer feel guilty about my past or feel the need to be in control. This is the*

MOST JOY I have ever felt in my entire life. I feel God blessed me that day, and I have found the courage to forgive myself and others like never before. I know I have a purpose now, and that is to take all that pain I experienced and help others find their purpose. But, if I can't even enjoy it because you are feeling guilty, well, then I don't want it!"

He was in disbelief, "I never looked at it like that!"

We cried together as we held hands and shared how special we were to each other. It was the most beautiful moment, by far, between us. We knew our life was only going up from here.

IT WASN'T AN ACCIDENT

Many times I've thought about those days before the accident. I know I was bound unnecessarily for so many years by the trauma that made me feel unworthy. I went on to own that restaurant for another twelve years and sold it for double my investment. I then jumped into writing the book I always wanted, *Glowing Through The Chakras*, where I share how I released blocks to further open up my spiritual gifts to help others while sharing my stories. I then went on to be a Transformation Coach, helping healers open their own gifts and shed the emotional barriers holding them back.

Today, I am an Intuitive Business Coach helping holistic healers build a business in order to help others transform their lives. Rich and I have raised our beautiful children, who are now married and enjoying the true love of having children themselves. We love to spend time with our two granddaughters and one grandson. We will be celebrating thirty-five years of marriage in January of 2025 and we are so excited to start traveling when he retires soon. We are both faithful and in gratitude for our love and life together.

Life is good ... but it wasn't always this way!

Dr. Breanna BOSS James

Founder and CEO of She BOSSIN' Up | P31X

https://www.linkedin.com/in/breannajames/
https://www.facebook.com/msjames637
https://www.instagram.com/bossupmylife
http://www.bossupmylife.com/
https://www.unleashthebosswithin.com/

I'm Dr. Breanna BOSS James, AKA, Dr. BOSS, living my God-designed purpose empowering women to break free from the chains that hold them back. Having faced struggles like fear, lack of confidence, procrastination, low self-esteem, poor credit, and debt, I intimately understand these battles. Through my personal transformation, I've discovered the keys to freedom and empowerment. I have a doctorate in business and over 14 years of HR, coaching, and training experience. I've authored two books and have been featured in magazines. I envision impacting one million women through She BOSSIN' Up and P31X Global Enterprises, offering coaching and financial solutions. Through SBU, we guide women to redefine themselves and start businesses using biblical principles. With P31X, we help people see wealth differently with life/health insurance and homeownership. Beyond work, I enjoy cake decorating, reading, painting, target shooting, volunteering, and nurturing my plants.

Overcoming Isn't a Straight Line, It's *The Lion King*

By Dr. Breanna BOSS James

Are you starting my chapter with a little confusion or maybe even a tiny bit of intrigue? I'm almost sure you're wondering what Simba and Mufasa have to do with prayer and your ability to overcome in your life. Stick with me through the end and not only will you understand, but you'll also be referencing the movie.

I love movies, and my favorite line in the movie Forest Gump truly characterizes what I believe is the reality of our human condition. "Life is like a box of chocolates, you never know what you're gonna get." Life is extremely unpredictable. Things are going great, then life switches up on you. You make plans and have everything perfect, then boom. Your plans take a long detour into a deep quicksand-filled sinkhole. Yet, even with this reality, hope is never lost, and you're not alone in whatever you're facing. This is us. We're here together. It might seem like you're on an island alone, and no one understands what you're going through. Others might not be going through exactly what you're facing, but everyone has faced something. Everybody, at one point or another, is either in the middle of a storm, has just come out of a storm, or is about to enter a storm. You are not alone!

Life's challenges, struggles, and setbacks visit everyone. No one escapes the responsibility of having to navigate through unplanned negative circumstances. The question is, how do you choose to handle negative circumstances? Do you react to them with worry, anxiety, fear, and complaints, or do you respond to them with concern, contemplation, and a determination to not crumble under the pressure and weight of the circumstances?

I know what it feels like to face many challenges, most of them at the same time. I don't usually have the pleasure of life being considerate and only throwing me one curveball at a time. I get most of the ball in the basket, either thrown at the same time or right behind each other. I've found that it's easy to fall apart and give up, yet that method has never helped fix anything. That only made them worse. When looking back over the different challenges, they were all longer and more consuming than they needed to be. I didn't understand that hope never dies, and all is not lost. I needed to change my perspective on how I viewed negative circumstances and how I chose to handle them.

The phrase "Circle of life," as expressed in the movie *The Lion King*, has stuck with me all these years. Anything that loops back around, I call it 'The Lion King' because I see it as a circle of repeated things and events in life. The need to continuously overcome throughout life is not a straight line, it's 'The Lion King.' It's a part of the circle of life. Everyone will face challenges that they need to overcome. Those challenges don't usually create a picture of a beautiful diamond-encrusted golden circle laced with elegant flowers. No, it's an ugly, rugged, dark, dried-up, crooked circle that gives the illusion that it will never go away. But there is hope during all this, and that hope is anchored in prayer.

Prayer is the key to altering your perspective on how 'The Lion King' (circle of life) looks for you. You might have the habit of allowing life's challenges to be all-consuming, but that shouldn't be your response. Prayer should be all-consuming. Prayer must be your first response, intermediate action, and your last resort. Prayer is the answer for all circumstances, bad and good.

Lifestyle Vibes: Offensive vs. Defensive Prayer

What is your prayer life like? Do you pray daily, several times a day, or just when you're in a bind? What are your honest thoughts about prayer? Do you believe prayer changes things or do you undercover think it's sort of a waste of time? Wherever you stand, there is room for an upgrade today.

Seeing that you've picked up this book I believe you're at least interested in learning more about prayer. Let's cover how to integrate prayer as a lifestyle and not just a knee-jerk response to negative circumstances. Now, before we get started you need to know that I pray to the God of Abraham, Isaac, and Jacob (Israel), Jesus' daddy. When I refer to prayer and things thereof, I'll reference God, the Lord, and the Word (Bible).

There are two approaches to praying that one can take, offensive and defensive. Offensive prayer is praying proactively. When praying offensively, you're looking to keep yourself covered no matter what. You want to make sure that you're protecting your life and being in a consistent state of gratitude before negative circumstances arrive. Considering panic, offensive praying is about being intentional with your life. You understand the concept of 'The Lion King.' You know that different forms of life's dramas circle, so you anticipate challenges and confront them head-on with faith through prayer.

The Word says, "Rejoice always and delight in your faith; be unceasing and persistent in prayer; in every situation [no matter what the circumstances] be thankful and continually give thanks to God; for this is the will of God for you in Christ Jesus" (1 Thessalonians 5:16-18, AMP). We're called to pray in and through everything and to be joyful about prayer. Praying offensively as a lifestyle helps you prepare for obstacles while being able to focus on living life and trusting God instead of focusing on problems. Offensive praying helps you face difficulties from a position of confidence rather than fear.

On the flip side, defensive praying is reactive. This type of praying usually arises in response to crises. When unexpected obstacles or challenges come, your instinctual reaction is to pray. With this lifestyle approach, you're only praying because you're struggling, and you want it to stop. Relying solely on prayer when you're having problems can lead to a cycle of panic that accompanies every problem. Praying only when problems arise also creates an extra sense of urgency that leads to feelings of overwhelm and anxiety. You're not inviting the Lord into your whole life, you're only letting Him in when you have problems and need help. Think about your relationships with people. Do you only want people calling you when they are in trouble and need something from you, or would you prefer they call you because they enjoy interacting with you and when they need help? God desires our attention and devotion just like we do with other people. We're created in His image and likeness, so we reflect His nature.

He desires to connect with you continually through daily prayer, and also during difficult times. If you find yourself in defensive prayer mode, I'm encouraging you to take a hybrid approach and do both. Praying to God regularly will help you decrease panic mode when challenges arise. As you spend more time with God, you create an intimate relationship with Him. This will help you build your trust in Him. You will have faith-filled confidence in Him and His Word. It's here that you learn to pray through negative circumstances instead of panic. This shift allows you to remain calm and give every concern to the Lord when faced with adversity.

A Serious 'Lion King' Experience

In May of 2022, I tested positive for COVID-19, and my life was flipped upside down, and it's still flipped today. Unfortunately, I'm one of the chosen ones who suffer from long-haul COVID. I have lingering consistent issues with breathing and chest pain, fatigue, body aches, migraines, memory loss, and brain fog. It would have been easy to panic in the situation. I didn't know what was going on or when it would stop, and my doctors were no help. I thought I was slowly dying. All I knew to do was pray and seek God's wisdom. I engage in hybrid prayer. I pray all the time, yet I do double down when problems arise. I was a praying little something. Even though I thought I was slowly dying, I trusted that one way or the other, God would see me through this mess just like the others.

This has been the craziest experience yet. For the first year and a half, every other month, I experienced episodes that mimicked COVID. I would test negative, yet I was sick for 10 days, each episode with all the symptoms. The most trying part of this was that I had to press to maintain my contracted job while working to launch my new business. Since it was a contract position, I only had three days of sick time and zero PTO. I wasn't in a position to take time off work without being paid, so I had to get creative with my at-home work setup. I couldn't sit up straight for long periods, so I had to unplug my laptop and lay on my side with a heating pad on my chest several times a day. This is the part where I give the Lord praise, as I worked remotely, and my manager was the best. As long as I got my work done, he didn't care about the how. If I needed to take extra breaks he was good with it. I prayed for help and favor, and God gave me just what I needed, even though He didn't take the problem away.

I couldn't walk much nor barely breathe or think most of the time, but I wasn't scared. I was calm and yet very angry that this was happening to me. Again, another one of life's ugly crooked circle moments had come to torment me and decided to take up residence for the long haul. No one else that I know who contracted COVID got stuck with it, just me. No one understood what I was going through. During that short moment of utter frustration, I began to pray and asked the Lord to comfort me and help me give everything to Him, so I could rest. I asked Him to show me Him, to heal me, and to help with my job and business. With tears in my eyes, I asked Him to have His way and for His will to be done, no matter what that is. Then I turned on praise and worship music and sang and danced around until I quickly started coughing and needed to lie down. I laughed as I lay down and continued to listen to the music with a smile on my face and thanksgiving in my heart.

To date, over two years later, I'm still suffering from the pain, discomforts, and setbacks that long-haul COVID is having in my life. Yet here's 'The Lion King' blessing that prayer and previous life struggles have given me. Back in 2009, I suffered serious medical problems dealing with consistent, unending headaches and migraines. It wasn't pleasant, but now, I thank God that I went through that period of struggle. Grit and resilience were forged. I'm able to function today with these health problems. I had to learn how to work through the pain. I had to pray and seek guidance to create systems and processes to help me function, and it worked.

Panic Tried to Creep In With a Compound Hit

Prayer and studying the Word are a part of my lifestyle, and sometimes abrupt problems still shake me. Let's be real. It's one thing to face sickness while the other areas of your life are good, yet it's another thing to be consistently sick and struggling financially. I'm sure you'll agree that sick and broke just don't mix.

In May of 2023, while still suffering from all those symptoms, I took a serious financial hit. A short call from my boss changed everything. My job assignment was ending sooner than we thought. My business launch was again put on hold since my job ended abruptly. I had to survive off a fifth of what I used to earn. Then every time I thought I was starting to get better, I would experience one of those 10-day COVID episodes. Those symptoms compounded my issues, limiting my ability to seek and accept certain types of employment. My bills began to pile up as my resources steadily and rapidly decreased. I struggled with lots of self-doubt. I spent so much time wondering if my dream of launching my business was futile. I've poured my heart and soul into this venture for years, yet struggles and setbacks keep hindering my plans.

At that point, uncertainty, frustration, and depression were quickly trying to take over. Yet, it was the frustration of not being able to launch that reminded me that I needed to shift my focus and give everything to God in prayer. It's prayer through faith that changes things, not whining, complaining, panicking, or focusing on the problems. I had to stop myself from a downward spiral. I took a few days and spent time praying, reading the Word, and sitting quietly in God's presence. I didn't know what to do, but pray and seek the Lord's help.

Upward and Onward, No Matter What

Since then, I've had to update my processes to continue to work on building my business. Most days, it's a struggle to remember what I need to get done for the day, even with writing it down, let alone having the energy to get things done. My hope is in the Lord, and I take each day as it comes. I might move slower than I used to, but as long as there is breath in my body and I can think even a little bit, I will be persistent until I succeed. The key is prayer and keeping messages of hope and faith before me. I praise God for who He is, no matter my circumstances. I read to keep my mind sharp and to grow myself. The vital part is that I give myself the patience and grace to create new norms that allow me to keep life moving. It's so easy to fall apart because I can't do the things I was once able to do. I'm still alive, so that means my God-designed purpose is still needed, and I'm not stopping until I've satisfied it, then on to the next. I do what needs to be done when it needs to be done, no matter how I feel or how long it takes, period!

Let prayer be the anchoring foundation for every area of your life. Allow prayer to guide you through 'The Lion King,' crooked circle moments. God is amazing, and He's here for you in and through everything. Don't cubbyhole your prayers. No matter what is happening in life, the good, the bad, the ugly, the beautiful, and the indifferent, prayer is the answer. In times of hurt and doubt, don't just pray for peace, courage, wisdom, and help, offer up prayers of thanksgiving and gratitude.

When I cast my cares, fears, and burdens to Christ through prayer, peace covers me. Instead of dwelling on my struggles and setbacks, I focus on the promises of God and choose to walk in faith. I've embraced my calling and God-designed purpose to empower others through my business, and I won't allow negative circumstances to stop me, and they shouldn't stop you, either. I help women BOSS up! To Boldly Overcome Struggles and Setbacks as they positively transform themselves Body, Occupation, Soul, and Spirit. BOSSin' up has become more than a simple statement, it's a testament to resilience and peace through prayer and work. It's a reminder that even in the darkest moments, prayer and faith help us conquer the crooked circle detours of life.

Thank the Lord for what He's done for you in the past, what He's already doing now, and what He will do in your future. Trust that prayer is necessary for navigating and overcoming obstacles, struggles, and setbacks. It's been difficult keeping everything together, but through prayer, I've been able to make life work. God is using every struggle I've faced to help me now, and I believe everything I'm struggling with today will help me later in life. I believe the same is true for you. Overcoming isn't a straight line, it's 'The Lion King.'

When Shadows Fall, Pray Boldly

When the world feels dark and cold,
And whispers of doubt, make your faith grow old,
Let not your heart retreat in depression, anxiety, worry, or fear,
But lift your prayers up to heaven, for God is always near.

With courage drawn from depths unknown,
Cry out to God before His abundant throne.
Not with a vague, doubting, timid, or a trembling plea,
But come before His throne boldly, knowing you are already free.

In the midst of the struggle, in shadows that creep,
Let prayer be your anchor, your joy, and your peace.
For with faith like a fire and a heart open wide,
In every bold prayer, the Lord our God will abide.

So, pray fervently with strength, declaring your trust,
In the one true God who is faithful, good, and just.
Let not your soul and spirit bend or sway—
Be bold, have faith, kneel down, raise your hand, and pray.

Pray with relentless fire, might, and grace,
Claim your God-ordained courage with haste.
For when you pray, with faith so deep and wide,
You'll find that His strength and your needs collide.

For in your time of prayer, there lies a key,
To peace, to strength, to your predetermined victory.
So, when life's tests and trials press their claim,
Pray boldly and without ceasing, in Jesus Christ's holy name.

You may be dealing with a consistent and seemingly unending challenging life situation but don't give up on yourself. Although you may want to, yet there is rest that comes even in the greatest of storms.

Need someone to chat with? Let's talk! Visit https://linktr.ee/drboss to schedule your FREE *Ignite the BOSS Within Discovery Session* and learn how to navigate obstacles.

Let's BOSS Up!

References

The Holy Bible, Amplified Bible. (2015). *1 Thessalonians 5:16-18*. Zondervan.

Cynthia Piccini

Founder and Owner of Breathe Easy Therapy Services

https://www.linkedin.com/company/breathe-easy-therapy-services-llc/
https://www.facebook.com/BreatheEasyTherapyServices
https://www.instagram.com/breatheeasy_therapy/
https://breatheeasytherapy.com/
https://breatheeasytherapy.com/cynthia-piccini/

Cynthia Piccini is a Licensed Marriage and Family Therapist and Founder of Breathe Easy Therapy Services LLC in Pennsylvania. Once she submitted her life to Christ, God has been the author of her life story and vision. Breathe Easy Therapy Services was a vision God gave me several years ago. My experiences and how God has used them are the key to understanding his vision in my life.

She obtained a Bachelor's of Arts Degree from East Stroudsburg University in Sociology. Then studied at Capella University for her Masters in Marriage and Family Therapy. Her goal is to help keep families together. She has been working with couples and individuals surrounding communication within relationships, healing from past hurts, and recapturing the beauty of connection. Breathe Easy Therapy Services promotes health and well- being both inside and outside the workplace.

Trust, Hope, Persevere

By Cynthia Piccini

In the words of 1995 Gwen Stefani, "I'm just a girl in the world." And this girl's life has been filled with ups and downs, twists and turns, hidden surprises, and in-your-face nightmares. This story changed the trajectory of my career from pursuing deep sea diving with whales to studying the human psyche and fulfilling my God-given purpose. This story is about a comforting, warm person, with a special spirit, who is welcomed everywhere she goes. To give some background to what this person is like, imagine a warm fire on a cold night, or a cool kiss on the cheek on a hot day. She is a comforter, a compassionate ear, and a kind-hearted person, who willingly shares her love with everyone. This chapter is about what happened to her that inevitably affected my life and, in turn, many others. This chapter is about My Mom.

It was a hot summer day in 2002. I was getting ready to begin my pool cleaning duties at the place I was a lifeguard. I chatted with my friend Matt who was always a kind soul, and let him know I was getting ready to head out. We were best friends, so I am sure we were making some plans for the night. When I got home, my Mom was very quiet, which wasn't always unusual. She was sometimes stressed from long days of doing Mom's duties. She was cleaning the house when I asked a question, and she snapped at me. Now, in my Mom's case, this is not normal to snap, but she did have her moods. To give you some background: my Mom is the middle of seven children, exact middle. She has always been the sweetest. All of my aunts and uncles agree. She is kind, soft-spoken, the kind of Mom who thinks it's fun to bake chocolate chip cookies with her four children, all under the age of 10, and maybe even a few cousins. She is a faithful woman who has taught us all to love the Lord above all else, even in the difficult seasons. Her faithfulness always extended to people she met. This is what I have been taught as a person. To love people and God with all my heart, to forgive and, in many cases, forget. But she is from Brooklyn, NY, so there are times she will not be forgetting.

She has always lent a listening ear to anyone who has needed it. As her eldest daughter, I always looked up to her in ways that she may not have known. The way she could exude kindness to all people was a gift. I myself have always been more feisty, a bit of a firecracker, not always speaking truth in love, but still speaking truth. She has taught me so much about faith, hope, and love.

Back to that night. My Dad knew things about emergency situations. At the time he volunteered at the ambulance services as well as his normal everyday life skills he got from also growing up in NYC in the 70s. They have been together since they were teenagers. He came over to Mom and asked her how she was doing, and she snapped at him, but he found it odd and started investigating. He asked her where she was, what she was doing, and what her name was and she couldn't respond. He knew immediately something was wrong and took her to the hospital. I stayed home with my three sisters that night as instructed by my Dad.

He told us we could go to work as they were only keeping Mom for observations overnight, and he would pick her up in the morning with my little sisters. She had a mini-stroke and they would be releasing her in the morning. That next morning, my sister and I were lifeguarding together, so we went to work. We were only there for about 30 minutes when we got a call from Dad that Mom was not coming home, and we had to get to the hospital as soon as possible. I drove fast, and it was so scary because we did not know what was happening. When we got to the hospital, my two younger sisters, Anita and Katie, were holding each other upset, and my Dad was crying. I asked what happened and was told by Dad that Mom had brain cancer. Her body was riddled with cancer, and it was causing these strokes. The last one was massive, she was completely unconscious. In the doctor's words, she died for a few minutes in front of my sisters and my Dad. When she came to, she could not speak or move and was very confused and scared, not knowing who anyone was except Dad. My sisters were beside themselves and Dad was also so upset. At that moment, I couldn't let myself cry because I knew the tears wouldn't stop, I had to be strong and do what was needed. Mom always held the family together. Driving everywhere, making dinner, doing laundry, keeping us in line, and having the talks that comforted and encouraged us as people. She was an incredible human, and now she was unrecognizable, as if trapped in her own body.

Finding out at twenty-one that my Mom had brain cancer and being the oldest of four, I felt the responsibility of managing the day-to-day routine for my siblings. I became the ride to and from school, practices, church events, and such. I became a nurse to my Mom. My Dad, sisters, and I shared the responsibility. But because I was of driving age and was the oldest, I felt a lot of responsibility. To give you background on me, I never much liked responsibility or staying in one place for too long. I liked exploring, learning about new cultures and people, and trying new things. Before the event, I was looking at teaching English abroad in the Orient and then moving West through Europe. I had no desire to marry or have children. My relationship with the Lord was always one of intensity, but my flesh was also strong, and my anger and frustration were the strongest of all. The reasons for this lie in another story.

So now here I am, taking care of everyone. My spirit of freedom, fun, and exploration was put on hold due to obligation and compassion for everyone in my family who was dealing with this, especially my Mom.

During this time, I watched as the people from the church that Mom and younger sisters belonged to came to worship in my Mom's hospital room. They started a food train, making dinner for all of us since we were all in the hospital or running around throughout the day. Someone from the prayer team would pray over her daily. My Mima, Papa (her parents) and my Titi's and Uncles would pray as well and visit. So many prayers. We continued to get bad news from the doctor, "it spread", "she doesn't have much time", and "say your goodbyes soon." She didn't know who anyone was still except Dad. She always made a fist when she saw me, I don't know if it was because she thought I was strong or she wanted to hit me. I will go with the first one. She did not recognize my younger siblings, which affected my baby sister the most. She was the closest to Mom at that time, and she was only twelve years old.

One night as we were preparing for bed, the doctor called. It wasn't a welcomed call since all the rest were bill collectors, as she had written bad checks during the mini-stroke period or doctors calling to say death was at the door. But tonight was different, The doctor sounded different. He said, "Gary," that's my Dad, "I cannot believe I am saying this, but I have both results in hand, and one shows the cancer and the other has none." "I ordered more tests to confirm, and the cancer is gone." My Dad told us right away. But the doctor said it still didn't mean she was out of the weeds. He said she most likely would never walk again, or talk again, and would be wheelchair-bound. It was a hard pill to swallow, but she would still be here, and we would still have her. She is still there. That was the day my family and I learned about ambiguous grief. I didn't have a name for it until later in my life, but that is what it was. Learning to accept Mom for who she is, not comparing her to who she was, and grieving what we cannot have. I found myself often during school hours at the hospital bed by my Mom, reading her the Bible and praying with her as I knew she loved spending time with the Lord. At this point, she was in the hospital for a good month.

I remember always feeling drawn to hurting people and wanting to help them so much. Not realizing at the time it was my purpose, I would pray over Mom's feet and touch them. One day with just us two there, she moved them, and we were so excited and laughed and kept praying, and in the same moment, she moved her right leg. It was the hope we needed. She still couldn't speak, but it was an incredible thing to see. As the days continued, it was obvious Mom was regaining movement, so she was moved to a rehab facility within the hospital.

She shared as much as she could with me, trying her best to speak, but it didn't make much sense. We would laugh a lot together not to make fun, but just because I was trying so hard and when you cannot cry anymore you laugh. At that point I still didn't cry or let my emotions out. I felt that was being strong, boy, has that changed now.

Eventually, Mom was well enough to come home. She was going to get occupational therapy, speech therapy, and physical therapy at home. We had to prepare the downstairs for her hospital bed, commode, and other things she needed. One of us would have night duty if she needed help. Through this time, I began to realize how important having people around you who love you, would sacrifice for you, and would invest their time into you is. Not just family but also friends, people in the community, and church she belonged.

Mom would always hold her hand up to the sky when worship was happening, praising the Lord in the hospital bed. Watching this was so strange to me. She truly loved the Lord and knew him. No matter what happened to her, she would always praise his name.

She eventually was able to share with us, that when she died, she went through a long tunnel and followed a light, when she came out, the light was Jesus. She saw his hands and feet and his blue eyes and knew it was him. She desperately wanted to go with him, but he told her it was not her time. And she was then returned to her body in the hospital bed. Watching her go through that strengthened my faith in a way I didn't know it would. She modeled an ultimate commitment in a way I never was able to witness before.

Today Mom has full use of her right leg and right arm, partial use of her left leg. She can speak, read, and write again. She is able to cook, clean, and take care of people, which brings her joy. She may move slower, but she moves with purpose. My sisters and Dad have memories that have stuck out to them as well, as we each were affected in different ways.

Because of everything I saw with Mom, friends, family, Dad, and my siblings, my trajectory from world traveler and studying marine life changed shortly after finishing a degree in psychology and continuing my education to become a Marriage and Family Therapist. I ended up meeting someone who I wanted to marry, and we have a child now. I also have a company where I provide these types of services to help other families learn how to get through different situations in their lives.

With everything that has happened, I have learned that ambiguous grief is about learning how to live and love the person today without giving up the memories of the person whom we had in the past. It is about holding onto and sharing the stories at the same time as making new ones. I learned it's okay to cry sometimes when I want my Mom to come to help with my kids or come over for a quick visit, watch our child play sports, or just go to lunch, and recognizing it will not always be possible as she cannot drive and cannot physically do certain things. My Dad is also disabled now, but again that is another story. My sisters and I have learned to be strong in ways that we would not have, but we are also compassionate and kind human beings, not taking life for granted. I often live like there is no tomorrow, showing love, and doing my best to let bygones be bygones, as I learned life is short. I have also learned to let things go, as sometimes you have to move forward alone.

Dad also gave his heart to the Lord as his love for Mom had him driving her to church and reading her the Bible. Eventually, his heart was touched, and he accepted the Lord into it again. During one of these trips to church, my Mom danced in a choreographed human worship video for the church. At that point, I cried watching her still dance to her fingertips with her one arm, as she was a dancer when she was young and would always share to dance to your fingertips. My Dad had tears as well. Right there again, the Lord touched me and gave me a vision. He showed me both of my parents running through tall grass in a beautiful field, young, healthy, and happy. I know in eternity, this will be them, and I thank God for that vision. I thank him for life, and now every day, I speak with him, and he speaks to me. For I am who I am, He is who he is, He is Abba Father.

Teresa Monaghan

https://www.linkedin.com/in/teresa-monaghan-25287342/
https://www.facebook.com/loveasmuse/
https://www.instagram.com/teresa_monaghan_author/
http://www.teresamonaghan.ca/

Teresa Monaghan is a highly respected educator of children and youth of all ages, who's been seen on Global News. She started her teaching career in the remote community of Fort Chipewyan, Alberta, on the edge of the Canadian Shield, where it is not uncommon to have a black bear visit the playground.

Teresa's experiences working directly with children and their families have convinced her that emotional regulation and the ability to find calm in all circumstances is the clearest pathway to making sense of our lives and finding the highest possible level of personal fulfillment.

Today, when she's not hiking in the high alpine meadows of Kananaskis Country Provincial Park, you'll often find her teaching Spanish to children or coaching parents in emotional education for their kids (and themselves).

To learn more about Teresa Monaghan and how she can help you to explore mindfulness with your child,
visit http://www.teresamonaghan.ca/

Leap of Faith

By Teresa Monaghan

There are few things more tiring in life than extended legal battles with ex-spouses. Endless bills, endless stress, endless paperwork, more bills... and all that with a seven-year-old son caught in the middle. I sat down with him one afternoon after a court session and explained the situation to him as best I could. And then, utterly exhausted, I hid in my bedroom and had a big cry. I didn't want him to have to witness that.

Of course, from that point, the day could only get better—just kidding! When I went to check the mail after mopping up the waterworks, I found a legal bill for 1100 dollars! I wasn't expecting it; I'd thought the previous bill was the last one. Standing at the mailbox, the bill in hand, I felt a wave of despair hit me because I knew that I had absolutely no room in the budget to pay it. My next payday wasn't for three months.

I deliberated. I don't know why I didn't consider asking the lawyer for more time to pay or asking friends or family for a loan, either of which may have worked. Instead, I decided, on faith, that I would pay the bill and trust God to help me work it out. I wrote out a check for $1100 and change, put it in an envelope, and tucked it into the tiny left front pocket of my jeans to mail while I was out with friends that evening.

It was to be a 'fun, girls' night out,' though I wished I wasn't going. In the aftermath of the court date, I was emotionally worn out and wished I was spending a quiet night at home with my son. I convinced myself that it was 'important for emotional health' to go out and be social, so I stuck to plans, fixed my face, and prepared to leave.

I headed off on the usual milk run to pick up my girlfriends, Simona, Caitlin, and Liv. Because I lived the furthest, I was always the designated driver and chauffeur for our evenings out. Though I intended to mail the check along the way, there was no mailbox anywhere along our route. The event was taking place at the local university—and I knew there would be a mailbox on campus. As we paid for our entry tickets, Simona urged me to buy a ticket for the 50-50 draw as well. "Teresa, buy a ticket, it's for charity." So, I did and tucked it into my other puny pocket, forgetting about it immediately.

Uncomfortable about carrying a rather large check in my pocket, especially in such a big, busy event, I headed off alone, confident in my mission to place the envelope safely in a mailbox. I wandered through the basement of the Students' Union building of my alma mater and finally found the mailbox. To my dismay, it was securely chained up for the weekend. Good grief, was there no way to offload this envelope? Feeling both amused and defeated, I resigned myself to carrying the check around in my pocket for the remainder of the evening. I folded the envelope smaller and pushed it to the deepest depth of my insufficient pocket.

The event was the World Police and Fire Games pub night, and there were probably a couple of thousand mingling, mostly singles. My friends and I were continuously losing each other in the crowd. At one point, we met and were chatting with two firemen from a different part of the country. They were charming, one married and one very flirtatious, single firefighter. My girlfriends and I were having quite a bit of fun, despite being continuously lost from one another or maybe in part, because we were continually being lost and found.

After a couple of hours, I left the main ballroom to call the babysitter and check on my young son. Re-entering the vast ballroom, I heard my name being called over the sound system. They were paging me to come up to the stage. Somewhat dazed, I made my way up to the stage, where I was told I had won the 50-50 draw! Next, I was led out of the ballroom, down a hallway, to a small office where I was presented with a cheque for $1100, the proceeds of the 50-50 draw prize. I was awestruck. As I folded the envelope containing the check and stuck it in my right front pocket, I could scarcely believe that I had just won nearly the exact amount needed to cover the check in my left pocket!

In due time, I found and reconnected with my friends and shared my news. We were giddy with excitement. The first of the two firemen, the married one, came over and congratulated me as soon as I told him of my win. When the flirty firefighter found us again in the crowd, I repeated my news. He assumed I was kidding and said that there was no way he would believe me unless I showed him the check, which I promptly did. I was immediately reminded of the story of the apostle Thomas in the Bible, who doubted reports by his fellow apostles of Jesus' return and told them that he would not believe unless he saw and could feel Jesus' wounds. The second firefighter was behaving just like a 'Doubting Thomas'. Knowing they were both Christian and not wanting to insult him, I kept this thought to myself. Eventually, we all headed our separate ways, and I arrived home late, tired, and still amazed.

It had been such a spiritually powerful evening that I couldn't quite call it a night. I wanted to know if there was more that God wanted to show me that night. After all, something amazing had just happened in my life. I went to my Bible and looked up the first and second readings for that week. There was nothing that jumped out at me. Finally, I turned to see the gospel reading for that weekend. To my amazement, the reading was the story of Doubting Thomas. Now, I was completely certain. It was no coincidence that I won the draw in the exact amount that I needed. It was no coincidence that we had been chatting with those particular firefighters.

Somehow, when I decided to pay the bill and trust God that I would be provided with what I needed, the wheels were set in motion to meet my needs. It was the Leap of Faith that I had only read about. It was the step forward in faith that allowed for a miracle to happen. I was filled with gratitude for the gift of this beautiful lesson of faith with which God had gifted me. What a powerful way to teach me that the way through my difficulties was through faith, in this instance, through a very bold leap of faith. What a comfort to know that even when I am wandering, lost, and uncertain through a crowd of strangers, my God is my constant companion, aware of my every thought, feeling, and action.

I carry this lesson with me to this day and have shared it many times. It's a reminder to me to have faith, even when I cannot see God's presence in my life. It comforts me that God is always there to dry my tears in my low and lonely moments. He calls me to be brave, to live my faith, and to trust that things are working their way out, though it may get messy before it gets better. It's this understanding that has allowed me to accept challenges that seemed beyond my capacity and to succeed beyond my expectations both personally and in my profession as a teacher.

Just in case I was tempted to doubt the whole experience, there on the front page of our local newspaper the next morning was an article highlighting the success of the Fire Police event. Front and center in full color and chosen to represent the firefighters in the article was my buddy, 'The Doubting Firefighter' from the evening before. And I wondered, was it a coincidence, or was God just really showing off?

Yvonne Bacon

Certified Life Coach, Certified Holistic Health Coach, Speaker, Author

https://www.linkedin.com/in/yvonne-bacon-clc-hhc-54aa1314
https://m.facebook.com/yvonne.bacon/
https://m.instagram.com/yvonne.bacon/
https://www.instagram.com/lilliesteacakes/
https://www.instagram.com/nourishe1210/

Yvonne Bacon is the Founder of Nourishe. Nourishe' is a Wellness Lifestyle community for women over fifty. We are here to nourishe' your MIND, BODY & SPIRIT, with nutriments that will bloom and help propel you forward in life. Activating your light to live more brilliantly, boldly, and bodaciously your dreams being the best Y.O.U. (your own universe) Do not allow complacency to rob you of years of engagement and fulfilling contribution. Midlife Mentor, Certified Life Coach, and Personal Development Coach. Her mission centers on helping women navigate challenging life seasons, empowering them to unlock possibilities in their personal and professional lives.

As an Empowerment Speaker, Yvonne inspires audiences through humorous stories and a fresh perspective, demonstrating that anything is possible.

Literary Contributions

Yvonne is a co-author of four books:

- Stand Up, Be Heard Vol. II
- Moments in Life, The Caregiver Story
- Fear to Freedom
- Awaken to Wellness

Entrepreneurial Ventures

She is also the founder and owner of:

- Lillie's Tea Cakes
- S.I.S.T.E.R. Connection
- "See It, Believe It, Be It, Dream Big" Vision Board Workshops

Her core philosophy resonates with her powerful personal motto: "I believe we are all brilliant and extraordinary - we just sometimes forget. I'm here to remind you that you have everything in you, and I will help you unpack and understand the applications toward you living your best life. YOU owe it to yourself."

Faith in the Storm's Shadow

By Yvonne Bacon

The Storm Within

The rain fell in relentless sheets, each dropping a hammer against the window, echoing the turmoil that churned within me. I had settled into my evening routine, the soft glow of my laptop illuminating the dim room, when the phone rang. The shrill sound cut through the air like a siren, and I instinctively knew that it was not just any call. I answered, my heart pounding as I recognized my dad's voice on the other end. It was loud and shaky, a jarring contrast to his usual calm demeanor. "It's Mama," he said, his words crashing over me like the storm outside. "She's in the hospital… she may not make it through the night." A chill ran down my spine, freezing me in place. My mind raced with images of her laughter, her warm smile, and her unwavering support. I could hardly process what he was saying. "What happened?" I managed to ask, my voice barely above a whisper. "It appears she had a heart attack and renal failure," he replied, his voice cracking. "Can you come home?" The urgency in his tone ignited a fire of panic in my chest. Home was a two-hour flight away, but time felt like it was slipping through my fingers like water. I glanced out the window; the rain lashed against the glass as if warning me to stay put, but I couldn't bear the thought of not being there for her. "I'll be there," I said, my voice steadier than I felt. I hung up and called the airline to book a flight, then ran to the garage to grab my suitcase. I began frantically shoving my essentials and clothing items inside as I was leaving in three hours on a two-hour flight. The world outside seemed darker and more threatening as I stepped into the storm.

The Drive

The roads glistened under the downpour, slick and treacherous. My headlights cut through the darkness like a knife, illuminating fleeting glimpses of trees swaying violently in the wind. Each mile felt like an eternity as dread gnawed on my insides. My thoughts spiraled—what if this was it? What if I didn't make it in time? I turned up the radio, desperate for distraction, but all that filled the airwaves were ominous news reports about flooding and accidents on the very route I was taking. My grip tightened on the steering wheel as I maneuvered through puddles that threatened to swallow my car whole. Suddenly, a flash of lightning illuminated the night sky, followed by an earth-shattering clap of thunder that rattled my bones. The rhythmic drumming of rain on the windshield set a frantic pace as I navigated the slick roads toward the airport. Each drop felt like a countdown, reminding me that time was slipping away.

I gripped the steering wheel tightly, as I fought against the growing anxiety that churned in my stomach. The visibility was poor; the headlights barely pierced through the sheets of rain cascading down like a curtain. It was as if the sky had opened, unleashing its fury just as I needed to be on my way. "Why now?" I muttered to myself, glancing at the clock on the dashboard.

As I approached a particularly treacherous stretch of highway, a flash of lightning illuminated the landscape for just a moment—a stark reminder of how quickly things could change. I took a deep breath and focused on the road ahead, trying to block out thoughts of what awaited me in the sky. The radio crackled, breaking through my spiraling thoughts with an urgent weather report. "Severe thunderstorms are moving through the area, with possible delays at local airports," the announcer's voice warned. My stomach dropped at the mention of delays; it felt like bad news piled upon bad news. "Just keep moving," I told myself, trying to drown out my worries with determination. I turned up the volume on my favorite playlist, hoping that familiar tunes would soothe my nerves and keep me grounded.

Airport Arrival

Finally, after what felt like an eternity battling both the storm and my anxiety, I pulled into the airport's parking lot. The rain was relentless now, pounding against my car roof like a thousand tiny fists demanding entry. I glanced at my watch—there was still time, but it was slipping away fast.

The minutes ticked by with agonizing slowness, each second a reminder that I might miss my flight. My heart raced not just from the pressure of time but from the thought of flying in this weather. I had always been uneasy about flying, but storms intensified that fear into something almost paralyzing. Turbulence felt like being tossed around in a washing machine, and I could still recall the last flight where we hit a patch of rough air that sent my heart into my throat. The thought of being airborne during a storm made my palms sweat. My flight was scheduled to leave in less than an hour, and the storm outside mirrored the turmoil inside me.

I dashed through the downpour toward the terminal entrance, clutching my bag tightly against my side to shield it from the rain. Each step felt heavy as I navigated through puddles that threatened to soak my shoes. The wind whipped around me, chilling me to the bone despite my hurried pace. Once inside, I was met with a cacophony of sounds: announcements blaring over loudspeakers, travelers rushing past with frantic expressions, and children crying in frustration over canceled flights. My heart raced as I approached the check-in counter. "Flight 237 to Tucson?" I asked breathlessly when it was finally my turn. The attendant looked up from her screen with an unreadable expression. "That flight is still scheduled to depart on time," she said, though there was an edge of uncertainty in her voice that didn't reassure me. "Still?" I pressed, searching her face for any sign of hope. "Yes," she replied curtly before turning back to her computer screen. With boarding passes in hand, I hurried toward security, weaving through crowds of travelers who seemed oblivious to my urgency. The line moved slowly—too slowly for my liking—as anxiety clawed at me from within. Every beep of a scanner and shuffle of feet heightened my sense of dread about what lay ahead. Finally, through security, I glanced at the departure board; it still showed "On Time." A small flicker of hope ignited within me as I made my way toward Gate 12. But as I walked down the terminal corridor, another flash of lightning lit up the sky outside through large glass windows—followed by a low rumble of thunder that seemed to vibrate through the very ground beneath me. My flight was leaving, and of course, I was nervous as the storm was picking up and I don't like flying when it's storming. As I settled into one of the hard plastic chairs near Gate 12, I tried to calm myself by focusing on deep breaths—inhale… exhale…

The thought of being stuck here while knowing there might be no flights out for hours—or worse—made me restless. I stood up abruptly and walked toward a nearby window, where rain continued to pour down in sheets outside. Lightning flickered again across the sky—a stark reminder that nature had its own plans tonight. Suddenly, I began to pray. I had been praying all along, but at this point, I did a full-on prayer, calling out to my God.

The Hospital

Finally, after what felt like an eternity trapped in that storm both outside and within me, I arrived in Tucson and went straight to the hospital. The building loomed ahead cold, sterile, and calm against the backdrop of chaos inside of me. As I rushed through the sliding doors of the emergency room, adrenaline coursed through me like electricity. The sterile scent of antiseptic filled my nostrils as nurses rushed past me with urgency. "Where is she? Where's my mom?" I gasped at a receptionist who looked up at me with sympathetic eyes. "Room 204," she replied gently. With every step toward that room, dread coiled tighter around my heart. What awaited me beyond those doors? Would it be hope or despair? As I pushed open the door to Room 204, bracing myself for whatever lay ahead, one thing became clear: this storm was far from over.

A Prayer in the Eye of the Storm

Dear Lord, as I stand before this threshold, my hands trembling on the door to room 204, I come to you with a heavy heart with uncertainty. The storm raged both outside and within me, each raindrop echoing the beat of my anxious heart. In this moment of fear and hope intertwined, I seek Your strength and guidance. Father, grant me the courage to face whatever lies beyond this door. If it be hope, let me embrace it with gratitude; if it be despair, give me the fortitude to endure. I pray for Your healing touch upon my mama, for Your comforting presence to surround her. Let Your light shine in this darkest hour, illuminating a path through this tempest. Lord, I know this storm is far from over, but I trust in Your infinite wisdom and love. Help me weather the challenges ahead and find peace in the eye of this hurricane. Grant me the serenity to accept what I cannot change, the strength to change what I can, and the wisdom to know the difference. In Jesus' name, I place my fears and hopes, knowing that You walk beside me through every trial and tribulation. AMEN.

Scriptures

In a world filled with uncertainty and fear, we often find ourselves in a state of panic, searching for ways to ease our worries and doubts. But what if I told you that there is a powerful tool right at your fingertips, one that can transform your fear into faith? Yes, the incredible power of prayer. Within the pages of "Pray Don't Panic: Transforming Fear into Faith for a Fulfilling Life," you will discover how to tap into this strength, find courage in the face of adversity, and ultimately, experience a transformative journey of faith to live a fulfilling life.

Fear is a natural human emotion, but as believers, we have the power to transform fear into faith through the power of prayer. I want to provide you with Bible scriptures that will encourage you to turn to prayer, seeking God's guidance and strength in times of fear. Let these verses remind you of God's promises, His presence in your life, and the faith that can overcome any fear.

2 Timothy 1:7
"For God has not given us a spirit of fear, but of power and of love and of a sound mind."

Psalm 56:3
"When I am afraid, I put my trust in you."

Isaiah 41:13
"For I am the Lord your God who takes hold of your right hand and says to you, do not fear; I will help you."

Joshua 1:9
"Have I not commanded you? Be strong and courageous. Do not be afraid; do not be discouraged, for the Lord your God will be with you wherever you go."

Psalm 23:4
"Even though I walk through the darkest valley, I will fear no evil, for you are with me; your rod and your staff, they comfort me."

1 John 4:18
"There is no fear in love. But perfect love drives out fear because fear has to do with punishment. The one who fears is not made perfect in love."

Matthew 10:31
"So don't be afraid; you are worth more than many sparrows."

Psalm 27:1
"The Lord is my light and my salvation— whom shall, I fear? The Lord is the stronghold of my life— of whom shall I be afraid?"

Philippians 4:6-7
"Do not be anxious about anything, but in every situation, by prayer and petition, with thanksgiving, present your requests to God. And the peace of God, which transcends all understanding, will guard your hearts and your minds in Christ Jesus."

Matthew 6:25-27
"Therefore, I tell you, do not worry about your life, what you will eat or drink; or about your body, what you will wear. Is not life more than food, and the body more than clothes? Look at the birds of the air; they do not sow or reap or store away in barns, and yet your heavenly Father feeds them. Are you not much more valuable than they? Can any one of you by worrying add a single hour to your life?"

Psalm 55:22
"Cast your cares on the Lord and he will sustain you; he will never let the righteous be shaken."

1 Peter 5:7
"Cast all your anxiety on him because he cares for you."

Isaiah 41:10
"So do not fear, for I am with you; do not be dismayed, for I am your God. I will strengthen you and help you; I will uphold you with my righteous right hand."

Psalm 46:1-3
"God is our refuge and strength, an ever-present help in trouble. Therefore, we will not fear, though the earth give way and the mountains fall into the heart of the sea, though its waters roar and foam and the mountains quake with their surging."

Matthew 11:28-30
"Come to me, all you who are weary and burdened, and I will give you rest. Take my yoke upon you and learn from me, for I am gentle and

humble in heart, and you will find rest for your souls. For my yoke is easy and my burden is light."

Expansion

By consciously shifting from a mindset dominated by fear to one anchored in faith, you can experience greater fulfillment, resilience, and joy in your life. The transformation is not necessarily easy or quick, but it can lead to profound changes that enhance your overall well-being and outlook on life.

Here's an elaboration on how this shift in mindset and perspective can take place:

Recognizing Fear: The first step in this transformation is acknowledging the presence of fear. By recognizing and accepting fears as a natural part of life, individuals can begin to understand their origins and the triggers that cause anxiety.

Challenging Negative Thoughts: Fear often stems from negative thoughts and beliefs. A key part of transformation involves questioning these thoughts and replacing them with more positive, empowering beliefs. This mental reframing can help alleviate the intensity of fear.

Shifting Focus: Taking the focus away from fear and redirecting it toward faith involves concentrating on trust, hope, and positive outcomes. This can be achieved through practices such as prayer, meditation, or affirmations, which reinforce a sense of faith in oneself and a higher power.

Embracing Vulnerability: Accepting vulnerability is essential. It allows individuals to confront their fears head-on rather than avoid them. Embracing vulnerability makes it easier to lean into faith, promoting growth and resilience.

Finding Purpose: Fear can often feel overwhelming, but connecting with a sense of purpose or a deeper calling can provide motivation and direction. When individuals find meaning in their experiences, it fosters faith that their struggles can lead to greater fulfillment.

Building a Support System: Surrounding oneself with supportive friends, family, or faith communities can be instrumental in transforming fear into faith. Sharing fears openly and seeking guidance can create a sense of belonging and reduce feelings of isolation.

Practicing Gratitude: Cultivating an attitude of gratitude shifts focus away from fear-based thinking. By recognizing and appreciating the positive aspects of life, individuals can create a more optimistic mindset that nurtures faith.

Learning from Challenges: Viewing challenges as opportunities for growth can transform fear into faith. Understanding that difficulties often lead to valuable life lessons reinforces the belief that one can overcome obstacles and emerge stronger.

Reinforcing Beliefs: Regularly engaging with faith—whether through prayer, reading sacred texts, or participating in community worship—can deepen one's spiritual connection and reinforce a belief in a greater purpose, providing strength during times of fear.

Take Action: Fear often leads to inaction. By facing fears and taking deliberate steps forward, individuals can cultivate confidence and trust in themselves and their abilities. This proactive approach reinforces faith in one's capacity to navigate life's uncertainties.

Celebrating Progress: Recognizing and celebrating small victories along the journey can keep individuals motivated. Every step taken to confront fear and embrace faith is a testament to personal growth and resilience.

Cultivating Mindfulness: Practicing mindfulness can help individuals stay grounded in the present moment, reducing anxiety about the future. This awareness fosters a sense of calm and trust in the unfolding of life.

Find Solace in these Quotes

"Prayer is not asking. It is a longing of the soul. It is daily admission of one's weakness." —Mahatma Gandhi

"Faith is taking the first step even when you can't see the whole staircase." —Martin Luther King Jr.

"Prayer is simply talking to God like a friend and should be the easiest thing we do each day." —Joyce Meyer

"Faith and prayer are the vitamins of the soul; man cannot live in health without them." —Mahalia Jackson

"Prayer is the key of the morning and the bolt of the evening." —Mahatma Gandhi

"Prayer does not change God, but it changes him who prays." —Søren Kierkegaard

"To be a Christian without prayer is no more possible than to be alive without breathing." —Martin Luther King Jr.

"Faith is about trusting God when you have unanswered questions." —Joel Osteen

"Prayer is the exercise of drawing on the grace of God." —Oswald Chambers

Prayer

Fear and panic have become all too common. It's important to acknowledge these emotions and their impact on our lives. Taking a moment to pause, breathe, and center ourselves can help us navigate through these difficult times with more clarity and calmness. Remember, it's okay to feel afraid, but it's also important to find ways to cope and find moments of peace amidst the chaos.

The concept of transformation through faith and prayer for achieving inner calm is rooted in the belief that spiritual practices can bring about a sense of peace and tranquility. However, for many, it serves as a source of hope, comfort, and peace in navigating the challenges of life and the storm within.

Addressing fear and anxiety through prayer and faith can be significant for several reasons: incorporating prayer and faith into the approach to fear and anxiety can provide individuals with tools for coping, healing, and personal growth, enhancing their overall well-being.

Provides Comfort: Prayer can be a source of comfort during difficult times. It allows individuals to express their fears and anxieties, providing a cathartic release that can lighten emotional burdens.

Promotes Inner Peace: Engaging in prayer can help cultivate a sense of inner peace, enabling individuals to cope with stress and uncertainty more effectively.

Strengthens Faith: Trusting in a higher power can help people feel more secure and less alone in facing their fears. Faith can provide reassurance that there is a greater plan at work.

Encourages Reflection: Prayer invites introspection, helping individuals identify the root causes of their fears and anxieties, and enabling them to address these issues more consciously.

Fosters Community Support: Many faith traditions encourage communal prayer and support, which can help individuals feel connected and supported by others who share similar beliefs.

Inspires Hope: Faith can instill hope in challenging situations, motivating individuals to maintain a positive outlook and work through their fears rather than succumbing to them.

Encourages Resilience: Regular prayer can build emotional resilience, equipping individuals with the tools to navigate adversity and bounce back from setbacks.

Offers Perspective: Prayer can help put fears in context, allowing individuals to see the bigger picture and understand that many challenges are temporary or manageable.

Cultivates Gratitude: Focusing on gratitude through prayer can shift attention away from fear and anxiety, fostering a more positive mindset.

Facilitates Forgiveness: Prayer can help individuals let go of grudges and resentments that may contribute to anxiety, promoting emotional healing and liberation.

Conclusion:

Remember: In times of fear and panic, prayer is a powerful tool to find peace and strength. As you meditate on these scriptures and seek God through prayer, may you find comfort, guidance, and the assurance that He is with you. Trust in His promises, cast your anxieties upon Him, and experience the peace that surpasses all understanding. Pray, don't panic.

Victoria L. Sanchez

PHD (Peace and Harmony Doctor)
Author, Influencer, Podcaster, Virtual MC and Producer Speaker,
TREE (Trauma Reversal Education Expert)

https://www.linkedin.com/in/victoria-sanchez-71442765/
https://www.facebook.com/vsanchez552?mibextid=ZbWKwL
https://www.instagram.com/vsanchez552
https://ridewithvictoria.com/
https://ezwaywalloffame.com/members/vsanchez55212/

Victoria L. Sanchez, PHD (Peace and Harmony Doctor), is a passionate author, influencer, podcaster, speaker, and Trauma Reversal Expert, recognized for her heart-centered healing approach. A certified practitioner in Hypnosis and NLP (Neuro-Linguistic Programming), she has triumphed over incredible adversity, including surviving a rare flesh-eating bacterium and enduring the heartbreaking loss of her son, Cody, in 2020.

Her healing journey included a transformative 10,000-mile ATV ride of prayer and meditation. After a profound death experience in 2019, Victoria harnessed NLP and biohacking to elevate her physical and mental well-being. With steadfast determination, she guides others using tapping, meditation, sound bowl healing, and vibrational techniques to unlock their potential and transform grief into gratitude.

Victoria's mission is to empower individuals to heal deeply and thrive. Through her impactful books, courses, engaging podcasts, and motivational speaking engagements, she serves as a beacon of hope, transforming trauma into triumph for those seeking healing.

Embracing Life Beyond Stress and Trauma: A Journey of Transformation and Healing

By Victoria L. Sanchez

Mission Statement

"In my journey, I have discovered the extraordinary power of healing beyond our physical senses—a profound ability to connect with the heart, spirit, and body through sound, breath, and intentional transformation. My mission is to support those struggling with trauma, grief, and stress, offering a path toward inner peace, emotional resilience, and personal rebirth. I aim to bring a loving, calming impact to traumatized souls, uniting people worldwide to discover their healing truths and to walk with courage, love, and balance as they step beyond pain into a life of purpose and joy."

Introduction: The Journey Beyond Trauma

Have you ever wondered where you go when you die? Or perhaps you've felt the creeping toll of relentless stress, how it slowly erodes your peace, like death by a thousand paper cuts? I am Victoria L. Sanchez, often referred to as the "Peace and Harmony Doctor" (PHD). My journey has been marked by incredible transformation, resilience, and the discovery of powerful tools to heal, not just survive.

I am an author, influencer, podcaster, speaker, virtual MC, producer, and certified Hypnosis and Neuro-Linguistic Programming (NLP) practitioner. But these titles only skim the surface of a life filled with trials and triumphs. My journey has been a tapestry woven with both darkness and light, from surviving mucormycosis—a rare, flesh-eating bacteria that required multiple surgeries—to experiencing the profound loss of my son, Cody, in 2020. Through it all, I have dedicated myself to discovering, embodying, and teaching powerful techniques that have allowed me to transform grief into gratitude, adversity into resilience, and trauma into empowerment.

In 2019, after surviving mucormycosis, I had a profound death experience. Emerging from this moment, I felt called to heal deeply, not just for myself but for others as well. This journey took me over 10,000 miles on my ATV in meditation and prayer, exploring the depths of ancestral trauma, biohacking techniques, and personal empowerment. Now, I share these insights through techniques like tapping, meditation, sound healing, and vibrational frequency alignment, helping others to unlock their potential, find purpose amidst pain, and thrive in the face of adversity.

Section 1: The Physical and Emotional Impact of Trauma

My journey to becoming a Trauma Reversal Expert began with my own need to heal. My experience with mucormycosis—a rare, invasive fungal infection—transformed my life overnight. This illness led to multiple surgeries, during which I lost my palatal plate and septum, essential structures for basic functions like eating, breathing, and even speaking. It felt as though I was losing pieces of myself with each surgery, and each day became a struggle to simply exist in my own body.

Imagine the challenge of eating and drinking when every sip of water or bite of food could potentially be fatal. Food would often enter, and exit through my eye, creating fear around even the most basic of actions. Physically, this daily ordeal was exhausting. Emotionally, the toll was even greater. I felt trapped in a body that I no longer recognized, disconnected from the vibrant person I once was.

But perhaps the most profound layer of this trauma was the emotional isolation that followed. The people I believed would support me—my family—did not understand or acknowledge my pain. Their distance created an emotional void, leaving me with a sense of abandonment that compounded my suffering. As I grappled with the loneliness of this experience, I began searching for connection in new ways, eventually discovering TEDx talks and personal stories from others who had experienced near-death journeys.

These voices became my solace. Their stories mirrored my own pain and, more importantly, offered hope. Through their journeys, I learned about the healing power of sound and frequency, the transformative effects of meditation, and the strength that comes from self-discovery. These tools were not just aids for coping; they became a lifeline, a way to rediscover the power within myself and reconnect with my spirit.

Section 2: The Science of Sound, Vibration, and Frequency

As I embarked on my healing journey, I began to delve into the science behind sound, frequency, and vibration. This exploration led me to the work of Dr. Robert Gilbert, a pioneer in understanding how sound frequencies impact the brain, emotions, and even our cellular health. His studies, along with those of visionaries like Dr. Joe Dispenza, demonstrate that sound isn't just something we hear—it's something that permeates and transforms us at a cellular level, down to our DNA.

The concept of using sound frequencies, specifically solfeggio tones, became an integral part of my healing practice. Each solfeggio tone within the ancient musical spectrum resonates with a specific energy center in the body, encouraging release, healing, and recalibration. The 396 Hz tone, known for helping to release guilt and fear, allows us to shed emotional weights we may have carried for years. The 528 Hz frequency, often referred to as the "love frequency," is believed to facilitate DNA repair and cellular regeneration, promoting both physical and emotional healing.

Science now shows that sound can synchronize brainwave patterns, creating harmony and coherence within the mind. One way this occurs is through binaural beats—a technique that introduces slightly different frequencies to each ear, creating a "third frequency" in the brain that brings the two hemispheres into harmony. This synchrony induces states of relaxation, clarity, and even profound healing. Research has shown that binaural beats can help reduce anxiety, improve focus, and aid in processing unresolved trauma.

But perhaps the most exciting discovery is sound's ability to influence our DNA. Traditionally, DNA was thought to be a fixed blueprint, but we now know that our environment, thoughts, and even sounds can influence gene expression, effectively "reprogramming" us at a cellular level. This was a revelation for me, opening a door to transformation I hadn't thought possible. Sound wasn't just soothing—it was a vehicle for rewriting the stories held within my cells. It allowed me to confront the trauma that had embedded itself deep within my body and mind, helping me to release and heal at an extraordinary level.

Section 3: The Elements and Senses as Healing Tools

While sound and frequency were transformative, they were only one layer of the healing journey. The next level of discovery was learning to work with the five elements—earth, water, fire, air, and spirit—and their connection to our five senses. Each element offered a unique pathway to grounding, reconnection, and deep healing, helping me realign with nature's wisdom and remember my place in the larger universe.

Earth: Stability and Grounding

The earth element, connected to our sense of touch, represents stability, strength, and grounding. It reminds us to feel rooted, solid, and held, especially during times of adversity. In my healing journey, the earth became my anchor, allowing me to ground myself when emotions felt overwhelming. Grounding exercises, such as visualizing roots extending from my feet deep into the earth, created a stabilizing force that held me in moments of vulnerability.

Incorporating physical grounding practices—like walking barefoot on natural surfaces (earthing)—helped me re-establish a connection with the earth's healing energy. Research shows that earthing can reduce inflammation, promote better sleep, and alleviate stress, aligning us with the earth's frequencies. Additionally, using grounding crystals such as hematite and red jasper provided an additional layer of stability, helping me hold onto strength during moments of inner turmoil.

Water: Flow and Emotion

Water, linked to our sense of taste, embodies qualities of adaptability, emotional depth, and fluidity. It teaches us to move gracefully with life's changes, releasing resistance and embracing flow. For me, water became a guide, reminding me to honor and release my emotions without judgment. Spending time near rivers, lakes, or oceans has a calming effect on the nervous system, reminding us of the power of surrender.

Incorporating water into my healing practices allowed me to process and release emotions that had been buried for years. Whether through a mindful bath, sitting quietly by a body of water, or simply drinking water with intention, water's energy helped me connect with my emotional depths, allowing feelings of grief and sadness to flow through me naturally. Water not only cleanses our physical bodies but purifies our spirits, allowing us to embrace life with renewed openness.

Fire: Transformation and Passion

Fire, associated with our sense of sight, is the element of transformation, energy, and inner light. Fire embodies both destruction and creation, the ability to burn away the old and bring forth the new. In my journey, fire served as a beacon of resilience, lighting my path as I learned to turn pain into purpose.

Connecting with the fire element became an empowering practice. Lighting candles, visualizing flames during meditation, or spending time by fire helped me tap into my inner strength and passions. Fire teaches us to look at ourselves honestly, to confront our fears, and to let go of what no longer serves us. This process of transformation is at the core of healing, allowing us to grow from adversity. Fire also ignites our inner motivation, fueling us to pursue our dreams and purpose with courage.

Air: Clarity and Communication

Air, tied to our sense of hearing, represents clarity, communication, and freedom. It is the element that reminds us to think clearly, connect with our inner wisdom, and express our truths. Practicing breathwork or pranayama, a yogic breath-control technique, became essential in aligning with the air element. This practice helped me release mental clutter, embrace a sense of calm, and connect more deeply with my inner voice.

Pranayama has a profound effect on the nervous system, helping to calm the mind and body, improve focus, and foster a sense of clarity. Other air-related practices—like journaling, speaking our truths, and practicing active listening—encourage us to be present, process our thoughts and emotions, and release limiting beliefs. Through the air element, I found the freedom to express myself and the clarity to understand my own journey on a deeper level.

Spirit: Connection and Unity

The spirit element, connected to intuition, invites us to connect with something greater than ourselves. It represents unity, purpose, and the space where the physical and spiritual worlds intersect. Through practices like meditation, prayer, and creative expression, I began to connect with spirit, gaining a sense of peace, purpose, and belonging.

Spirit reminds us that we are not isolated beings but part of a vast, interconnected web. Through spirit, we find our sense of meaning and purpose. Meditation, mindfulness, and creative pursuits—such as painting, music, or writing—allow us to tap into the spirit element, aligning our energy with universal consciousness. Embracing spirit allowed me to trust my intuition, connect with my inner wisdom, and find peace in the understanding that we are all one.

Each of these elements offers unique pathways to healing, balance, and transformation. By working with them intentionally, I was able to reconnect with my senses, align with the natural world, and find profound inner peace and clarity. The elements remind us that we are part of a larger whole, rooted in nature's rhythms and cycles, empowered by our connection to the universe.

Section 4: Holistic Practices for Self-Regulation and DNA Restructuring

In addition to working with the elements, I found that self-regulation and biohacking techniques were essential in my journey. Self-regulation is the ability to manage our emotions, thoughts, and physical responses, keeping us centered and balanced even in the face of intense adversity. These practices empowered me to release stress, process trauma, and embrace a new level of health and resilience.

Balancing Biorhythms and Circadian Rhythms

The human body follows natural cycles, such as our biorhythms and circadian rhythms. Aligning with these rhythms helps promote optimal health, mental clarity, and emotional balance. Practices like maintaining a consistent sleep schedule, spending time in natural light, and incorporating physical activity into daily life support our body's natural cycles, promoting resilience against stress and enhancing mental and physical well-being.

Balancing my biorhythms was one of the most transformative aspects of my healing journey. By aligning my lifestyle with natural cycles—sleeping at regular times, waking up with the sunrise, and eating nourishing foods—I found that my body and mind were better equipped to manage stress, anxiety, and physical pain.

Meditation and Breathwork

Meditation and breathwork, particularly pranayama, were foundational tools for self-regulation. Meditation creates a space for the mind to rest and reconnect with the present, while pranayama enables us to calm the nervous system, process emotions, and cultivate inner peace. Each breath in pranayama becomes a tool for healing, helping us return to ourselves and let go of stored stress and tension.

By practicing these techniques consistently, I developed a strong foundation for mental clarity, emotional resilience, and self-awareness. The effects were profound, allowing me to experience not only greater calm but a deeper connection to my inner wisdom and purpose.

Sound Therapy for Cellular Transformation

Incorporating sound healing techniques, particularly solfeggio tones, proved to be a powerful tool for cellular transformation. Each frequency within the solfeggio spectrum resonates with different energy centers, encouraging cellular repair, emotional release, and inner balance. Listening to these frequencies daily provided a profound shift in my overall resilience, mood, and physical well-being.

Sound became more than just a practice—it became a portal for transformation, a means of rewriting the stories held within my cells. Sound therapy helped me not only cope with physical and emotional pain but also created a new, healthier narrative of self-empowerment, resilience, and peace.

Section 5: Reflections on Resilience and Transformation

Through sound healing, elemental wisdom, and self-regulation practices, trauma has transformed from a limitation to a source of resilience and strength. Resilience, I've learned is not just about surviving, but about growing through challenges, embracing them as invitations to evolve, and using pain as fuel for self-discovery and growth.

I now see life from a higher vantage point, recognizing the interconnectedness of all things. This perspective has allowed me to see my journey not only as my own but as part of a collective human experience—a journey that reflects our shared path toward healing, resilience, and personal transformation.

Conclusion: Embracing a Harmonious Life

Healing is not a destination, it is an ongoing journey of growth, self-awareness, and transformation. By reconnecting with sound, the elements, and your inner wisdom, we find purpose, peace, and harmony. I invite you to explore these tools, to unlock the healing potential within yourself, and to embark on your journey toward balance, clarity, and fulfillment.

Kenya E. Aissa, MS

Owner of Ruby Envy Wellness LLC

https://www.linkedin.com/in/kenya-e-aissa-ms-91463bb6
https://www.facebook.com/ruby.envy.1
https://www.instagram.com/rubyenvy/
https://www.patreon.com/everythingkenya
https://www.rubyenvywellness.com

Kenya E. Aissa, MS, is an author and the owner of Ruby Envy Wellness LLC. After earning her Master's Degree in Counseling Psychology, she chose to serve the children and families of her community by working as a counselor and social worker for over 20 years before leaning into her true entrepreneurial spirit. Kenya is a yoga teacher and trainer (E-RYT, RYT-500, YACEP), workshop facilitator, and dancer specializing in healing through movement. Kenya's experience as a women's trauma counselor and spirituality group facilitator led to her first book, "Sacred Girl: Spiritual Life Skills for Conscious Young Women", and her second book, "Independent Wife", is scheduled to be released in 2025. Kenya is the co-host of the San Francisco Bay Area radio show, "The Anything Can Happen Show" on 96.9 KGPC.

No Wrong Way to Pray: How to Underthink Prayer When You Suffer from Panic Disorder

By Kenya E. Aissa, MS

It was during my junior year of college when my first panic attack struck. I remember sitting in the library, surrounded by the quiet rustle of pages turning and the fervent whispers of my fellow students. Suddenly, the air felt thick, suffocating. My heart raced as if it were trying to escape my chest, and a wave of fear crashed over me. It was disorienting; I was supposed to be studying for my midterms, but all I could think about was the overwhelming sense of dread and the urge to escape immediately. I had never experienced anything like it before, and in that moment, I felt trapped, confused, and utterly alone.

As the weeks rolled on, the panic attacks became a recurring nightmare. They somehow redirected themselves to occur only when I was driving, specifically, on the freeway. I had no choice but to commute almost an hour to school in my beat-up 1980 Toyota Corolla. In an attempt to combat my rapid heartbeat and fear of passing out, I made sure to drive in the slow lane the entire distance. I took to wearing rubber bands on my wrists, popping them against my skin when I felt my panic rise. I felt like I was in a hot, windowless closet, with no way to escape. Desperate for answers, I sought guidance from my favorite psychology professor, a wise man who had a well-earned reputation for his humorous yet compassionate approach to teaching. He listened patiently as I cried, sharing my confusion and fears. Being a psychology major came in handy, and I was able to devote a lot of my time to researching the causes and symptoms of anxiety and panic disorders. As my symptoms continued, I learned some healthy coping skills that didn't result in wrist rash. My professor suggested that I share what was happening to me with my study group. He also said that since he was my Psychopharmacology teacher, it would be inappropriate for him to suggest that I consider meds—wink wink. I heard his not-so-subtle insinuation loud and clear, but I wasn't ready to go that route just yet. I did ponder what one of my classmates said, though: he asked if I had any kind of spiritual practice. I admitted that it was hit or miss. He recommended that I consciously set aside time for prayer, and, when I felt a panic attack come on, to welcome divine intervention. I had always found peace in the stillness of both prayer and meditation, like a sense of calm enveloping me in a warm blanket. In those moments, I felt held by divine protection, my Creator wrapping me in love, assuring me that I was safe.

Inspired by my professor's encouragement, I dove into books and articles, learning about the physiological and psychological aspects of what I was experiencing. Knowledge became my most powerful tool; it transformed my fear into understanding, and my self-criticism into self-compassion. I discovered breathing exercises, grounding techniques, and mindfulness practices that helped me manage my symptoms. Each time I felt the familiar dizziness and shallow breathing come on, I would pause, breathe deeply, and remind myself of the strength I was cultivating through my connection with the divine. This connection was my superpower, and it gave me the strength and confidence to believe that I could indeed overcome these "irrational" feelings.

As I continued to pray and meditate, I noticed a shift within me. The panic attacks didn't disappear overnight, but I began to feel more in control. I learned to embrace the stillness, using it as a refuge rather than a battleground. My prayers became a dialogue, a way to express my fears and hopes, and in return, I felt a growing sense of strength and resilience.

By the time I graduated, I had transformed my relationship with anxiety. As life will have it, I still experience panic attacks occasionally, and I've accepted them as an annoying part of my reality. However, unlike the prayers that I was taught in childhood, the language and intentionality of my personal prayers became my unique conduit to the divine. It also became a source of empowerment, reminding me that even in the face of fear, I could find peace. The journey hasn't been easy, but through prayer, therapy, education, and self-discovery, I've emerged stronger, ready to face whatever life has in store for me. Anxiety was and is a part of my story, but it doesn't define me.

For many women who are navigating the challenges of panic disorder, the experience can feel isolating and overwhelming. The sudden onset of panic attacks can disrupt daily life, creating a cycle of fear and avoidance. In these moments, prayer can offer a sense of peace, connection, and hope. However, the pressure that was put on many of us to "pray the right way" can sometimes add to our anxiety. Women who felt rejected or disconnected from their faith due to religious persecution, childhood trauma, or fear of showing up in the world as their authentic selves due to their sexual orientation or gender identity have a greater chance of retreating from their faith. This illustrates the controlling and patriarchal nature of many religious belief systems, and the extraordinary power that these systems wield on us and the very root of our spiritual existence. Conflating our religious experience with our spiritual experience can create a barrier between us and the Divine, and impede our ability to view faith, prayer, and spiritual connection as something that is "meant for us". If, therefore, prayer isn't meant for us, then how can we feel safe integrating it into our lives during periods when panic makes us feel scared and untethered?

Understanding Panic Disorder

Panic disorder is characterized by recurrent panic attacks—sudden episodes of intense fear or discomfort that might include physical symptoms like heart palpitations, shortness of breath, dizziness, and feelings of impending doom. My panic attacks include all of the above, and my "impending doom" is the fear that I will faint, particularly while driving. Women are statistically more likely to experience panic disorders than men, and societal pressures, hormonal fluctuations, and life transitions often contribute to this disparity. For women who experience Postpartum Depression, or, like myself, Postpartum Psychosis, the hormonal chaos often partners with panic disorder to create a train wreck of emotional dysregulation.

The impact of panic disorder extends beyond the individual; it affects relationships, work, and overall quality of life. As women navigate these challenges, many turn to their doctors for guidance and support. It can be so confusing, and it makes sense to seek answers from a professional. Panic disorder often requires a multifaceted approach that may include therapy and lifestyle changes. This could mean using prescription medications, depending on the severity of the symptoms. Some women choose to seek both professional help and divine intervention. Either way, the questions some women ask themselves are, "Am I too damaged to pray? Am I worthy of receiving divine grace? Is there a right way to pray?"

The Essence of Prayer

At its core, prayer is a form of communication—a way to connect with something greater than ourselves, whether that be a higher power, the universe, or our inner selves. Prayer can take many forms, and each woman's experience with it is unique. Let's explore the beauty of personalizing prayer, and letting go of perfectionism.

Personal Connection

I've known many people who struggle with prayer as a personal practice. I was raised Catholic and come from a very church-going extended family. Making a public show of your relationship with God or your higher power was the expectation when I was growing up, and there was a lot of emphasis put on being physically present at church. It didn't matter that my grandmother slept through the entire service, at least she was there! It wasn't until I was in the 8th grade that I really began to see my relationship with my Creator as deeply personal. Prayer can occur in a community, of course, and that community is exactly what many women need. My former colleague Charlotte was a mom of two who experienced debilitating panic attacks that affected her ability to work. We were both social workers and experienced a great deal of vicarious trauma and compassion fatigue. Knowing that I was also a yoga teacher, sometimes she would come to my cubicle and say, "Can we meditate for a few minutes?" Sharing moments of calm with another person was very helpful and healing for her. After attending a community prayer group, she found that the power of collective prayer resonated with her. The support she received from others who understood her struggles motivated her to confront her growing anxiety head-on, ultimately leading to significant improvements in her mental health. She began to take "prayerful pauses" at work, which helped ease her stressful days. She told me that she no longer feels guilty for carving out small moments for prayer since she was overall a happier, more balanced, and more productive person.

No matter what our support system looks like, the true essence of prayer occurs between the individual and their higher power. Some women find comfort in structured prayers, or stories and songs found in or inspired by religious texts, while others prefer spontaneous, heartfelt conversations with the Divine. My friend Sarah, a woman in her early 30s, struggled with panic attacks for years. She began incorporating prayer into her daily life. Initially hesitant, she found that petitioning for peace during moments of panic provided her with immediate comfort. Over time, she developed a deeper connection with her faith, which helped her manage her anxiety more effectively.

The key is to find what resonates with you. There is no need for eloquent language or formal rituals; sincerity is what matters most. Charlotte and Sarah each found what worked for them, and each way, though different, was their version of perfect. Come as you are, vulnerable, scared, or however you're feeling at the time. Just be real, and know that you're enough. We should never get caught up on the hamster wheel of perfection.

Embracing Imperfection

We as women often hold ourselves to impossibly high standards, striving for perfection in various aspects of life, even in how we connect with the divine. Striving for perfection in anything can lead to frustration and feelings of inadequacy. However, embracing imperfection in prayer can be liberating, can help us to accept ourselves as we are, and can allow us to embrace our authenticity. If you can only muster a word or two, or a simple thought, or you find your mind wandering, acknowledge that this is part of your process, today. It may not always manifest in the same way, and that's okay. Your intention, not your technique, is what matters. Perfectionism is the enemy of authentic connection, but it's definitely one of anxiety's best friends.

No Wrong Way to Pray

The beauty of prayer lies in its flexibility and adaptability. When suffering from panic disorder, it's essential to "underthink" prayer instead of overthinking it, and approach it with an open heart and mind. Here are some approaches to prayer that can help you find your way.

Breath as Prayer

It was decades after my first panic attack that I became a registered yoga teacher (RYT-500) and a certified trauma-informed instructor. Learning about how connecting to the breath can ground us and provide a sense of peace and stability was life-changing. In moments of panic, the breath itself can become a type of prayer. Breath can also be a gateway to a deeper connection to the Divine. Inhale deeply, envisioning calmness and light entering your body, and exhale, releasing tension and fear. This practice of mindful breathing can ground you and help you connect with a sense of stillness. Consider this rhythmic breathing as a part of your prayer process, a way to invite tranquility into your life. When we practice breathwork, we are still. When we are still, we are better able to quiet our minds. And when we quiet our minds, we can hear the messages from our higher power, loud and clear. We can ask for our prayers to be answered, but we have to be ready to receive those answers. Breathwork helps prepare us for whatever the message may be.

Gratitude Practice

One of the undeniable signs that I had a serious problem with anxiety was that my hair started falling out. Not a light shedding throughout my scalp, but a 1-inch chunk fell out, leaving me with a bald spot as smooth as an egg. Horrified, I would make a little comb-over on top of my head, securing it with a bobby pin and praying for days with no wind. One day, my hairstylist Janice broke it down for me in no uncertain terms. "You don't have a face for baldness," she said bluntly. "You need to get a handle on this immediately." She explained that I had alopecia areata, also known as "spot baldness", which is often brought on by stress or illness. I read up on this condition and decided to launch a very focused, personal campaign against alopecia. I began a meditation practice, which was very difficult at first, and usually resulted in me sitting at my altar, alone with my thoughts, crying. I reconnected to dancing, my first love, and went on walks in my neighborhood. I took long, luxurious bubble baths, usually with a cheesy romance novel and a glass of wine. I prayed. As I began to gain clarity about my anxiety and my response to stressors, as well as the importance of setting boundaries in my life, a natural progression was to start a gratitude journal. I had spent so much time feeling aggravated and hopeless about my inability to "fix" myself, that I had forgotten to focus on everything that I had to be grateful for.

Gratitude is a practice all by itself, and in time, it can shift your focus from anxiety to appreciation. Take a few moments each day to express gratitude for the small things—sunshine, a comforting bubble bath, a supportive friend. Acknowledging what you are thankful for can not only serve as a powerful element of prayer but also as a way to shift your mind from a state of panic to peace.

Prayer Through Movement

For some, prayer is not confined to kneeling, sitting, or even stillness. Engaging in movement, whether it's walking, dancing, lifting weights, or something else, can be a form of prayer in motion. As a young mom, my friend Cori suffered from debilitating panic attacks after the birth of her third child. She hadn't experienced this after the birth of her older twins; she jokingly attributed that to being too busy and exhausted to feel much of anything. However, after giving birth to Jadah, she found that she was "jumpy", distracted, and unable to sleep. Even short trips away from home became too difficult. Formerly a long-distance runner, she slowly began jogging, bringing Jadah along in her jogging stroller. She realized that she could go for several blocks if she was in "deep conversation with God." She said that her style of prayer felt like talking to a good friend: she expressed her fears, and sometimes even laughed out loud at something she said. Despite getting plenty of funny looks from passersby, she continued her unique practice of prayer through movement, and although Jadah is now 15 years old, Cori still prays while she runs. She also discovered the power of gratitude, making it a daily practice to list three things she was thankful for during her run. This creative approach gradually reduced her anxiety. While prayer can be a powerful tool, it is important to remember that some women may benefit from medical intervention. Strong hormonal shifts, like Cori and I experienced postpartum, can have a profound impact on women's mental health, and should not be taken lightly. Panic disorders often require a multifaceted approach that may include therapy, medication, and lifestyle changes. Seeking professional help alongside spiritual practices is an option, and should be considered in some cases.

Affirmations of Faith

Many years ago, I created and facilitated a spirituality group for adolescent girls who were residents of a substance abuse rehabilitation program. I encouraged the girls to make up positive affirmations that were specific to their own needs and experiences. One of the girls was very reluctant to participate in this exercise due to her strict, fear-based, religious upbringing. In fact, it was rare that she felt comfortable engaging in any of our activities because she had been raised to believe that any activity that involved independent thought would "invite demons" into her spirit.

Liz was a painfully anxious and curiously hypervigilant seventeen-year-old girl from a small town. She was a devout Christian, raised in a family that took the phrase "spare the rod, spoil the child" to the extreme. Her days were filled with Christian school, church activities, and chores, much like her peers. Her few social activities were heavily monitored by her parents. She was a good student and never caused any trouble. However, amidst her devotion, Liz carried a heavy burden: fear of the unknown. Oddly, these fears included fear of her own thoughts, ideas, and opinions. Liz's mind bore the weight of her anxiety, and she eventually began abusing alcohol to ease the pressure. She felt guilty every time she tried to talk herself down from her heavy feelings since her family and larger community espoused that one should only talk to God. They believed that any type of self-talk or reflection could be the Devil's way of tricking you into communicating with him, and, therefore, must be avoided.

Liz learned about affirmations for the first time in our spirituality group. I described affirmations as "verbal acknowledgments of people, things, or ideas". We spoke about how positive affirmations could change someone's life, boost their confidence, and, ultimately, help them achieve their dreams. For Liz, however, the idea of affirmations was enveloped in fear. As the other girls excitedly shared the affirmations that they created, Liz chose to separate herself during group, which I and the other girls respected. Liz confessed to "ear hustling"—listening secretly to the other girls—and that their heartfelt words made her emotional. Liz's best friend Claire encouraged her to consider a different perspective. Claire believed that affirmations could be framed within the context of faith. "What if you used affirmations as a way to strengthen your prayers?" she suggested. Liz was hesitant but intrigued. The idea of merging affirmations with her existing faith felt like something that she could safely explore.

That night, Liz began to write down affirmations based on her faith. "I am loved by God," "I am strong in my beliefs," and "I am capable of achieving great things" flowed onto the page. As days turned into weeks, Liz continued to incorporate affirmations into her prayers. Slowly, she noticed a change within herself. Her confidence began to grow, and the fear that once consumed her started to dissipate. She felt empowered, and her faith deepened. Liz realized that these affirmations did not invite negativity; rather, they were a declaration of her belief in God's promises.

However, not all was smooth sailing. Liz faced challenges that tested her newfound strength. A family crisis caused worry and fear to creep back into her heart. Did she cause the trouble because of her new practice? She had been raised to believe that her God was a punitive God. She feared that her original concerns were being justified, and her faith was being tested. As Liz struggled to affirm her faith, she leaned into her prayers and affirmations with the support of her group, reminding herself of God's unwavering love.

As her counselor, Liz shared with me that her journey of faith was difficult and scary. By incorporating affirmations into her prayers, she had discovered strength, resilience, and a deeper connection to her higher power than she had ever imagined. She chose faith over fear, and the change in her demeanor was obvious. Transforming into a much more peaceful young woman, she stepped into her future with a newly acquired faith in herself, and belief that she deserved to be happy.

Prayer can be a powerful ally in your journey toward managing panic disorder. By underthinking prayer and allowing yourself to express your spirituality authentically, you can cultivate a sense of peace, connection, and hope. Remember that you are not alone—countless women can relate to what you're going through and are also struggling with ways to effectively navigate the healing journey. As you explore the relationship between panic and prayer, may you find strength in vulnerability, comfort in connection, and joy in your successes along the journey. Celebrate the process, not just the progress, and know that every prayer is a powerful and beautiful step toward living your most authentic and fulfilling life.

Ayesha Amjad Faizi

Owner and CEO of ANIAS CLOSET LLC

https://www.linkedin.com/in/ayesha-a-faizi-ba63718/
https://www.facebook.com/ashfaizi01
https://www.instagram.com/ashtothepower_2
https://www.aniascloset.com/

Ayesha Faizi is an entrepreneur, certified spiritual counselor and a passionate advocate for women's empowerment. Her journey, marked by resilience and transformation, showcases the profound impact of faith and surrender. In this book, Ayesha shares her personal experiences of navigating life's challenges, from overcoming heartbreak and loss to discovering a deeper sense of purpose and peace.

Originally from Pakistan, Ayesha has always regarded spirituality as a guiding force in her life. The unexpected passing of her father in 2018 became a pivotal moment that intensified her connection to God and transformed her perspective on life. Through her writing, she imparts the invaluable lessons she has learned—how every setback presents an opportunity for growth and how faith and trust in the Divine can foster inner strength and transformation.

Beyond her writing, Ayesha is committed to empowering women through spiritual guidance and entrepreneurship. She firmly believes in the strength of women supporting women, using her platform to inspire others to uncover their purpose and live authentically. Her life's work is centered around nurturing spiritual growth, self-discovery, and personal empowerment.

Ayesha's deep connection to spirituality and her dedication to helping others lead fulfilling lives make her an inspiring figure for those seeking guidance, strength, and purpose. Through her book, counseling, and entrepreneurial endeavors, she continues to motivate others to embrace faith, surrender to the unknown, and find true contentment.

Currently residing in Dallas, Ayesha owns a successful online lingerie company and is devoted to creating spaces that empower women to embrace their authentic selves. Her mission is to inspire others to live authentically and discover strength in their faith and personal journeys.

Divine Lessons

By Ayesha Amjad Faizi

Introduction

I was born in Pakistan to a moderately liberal family where Islam wasn't just our faith; it was the backbone of our lives. My father was an airline captain who had also served in the Air Force, and my mother, an extraordinary homemaker, had a calming yet firm influence over our family. We weren't wealthy, but we lived in an environment full of love, discipline, and encouragement to grow. In a household where education and exploration were valued deeply, my parents instilled in my siblings and me an unquenchable thirst for knowledge.

Traveling was one of the biggest blessings of my childhood, thanks to my father's airline career. We visited the United States for summer holidays, took trips across Europe, and journeyed through Asia during his work stints. These experiences opened my eyes to the richness of various cultures and people. I quickly realized that the world was much bigger than the small bubble we occupied in Pakistan. Travel became not only an enjoyable activity but also an education that broadened my worldview and deepened my appreciation for diverse cultures and ways of life.

Yet despite the worldly exposure, the cornerstone of our household was Islam. Our faith was not something limited to rituals or holidays; it was integrated into every aspect of our lives. I grew up learning how to pray five times a day, fasting during the holy month of Ramadan, recite the Quran, and observe Islamic traditions. Like most Pakistani children, I was taught to read and memorize the Quran in Arabic from an incredibly early age, without really understanding its meaning. I remember sitting on the prayer mat, dutifully repeating the words I had been taught, feeling a sense of accomplishment, without truly grasping the weight of the words I was reciting.

By the time I was a teenager, I started questioning certain aspects of our faith. It wasn't that I doubted Islam, but more so that I realized I didn't fully understand it. One afternoon, as I stood on the prayer mat at the age of fifteen, I had an epiphany. I was saying the words I had memorized from the Quran, but I didn't know their meaning. *How could I connect with God, I wondered, if I didn't understand the language I was using to speak to Him?*

This realization created a quiet internal rebellion. I remember asking my mother, "Why can't we pray in our own language? How are we supposed to truly connect with God if we don't understand what we're saying?"

Her answer, though simple, was profound. "You can read the Quran in its original form because that's how it was revealed, but you should also read the translation to understand the message."

While her advice made sense, it also left me feeling conflicted. I felt like I wasn't fulfilling my duties as a Muslim properly, and I began to doubt whether my prayers had any real meaning. This inner conflict gradually grew over the years, and as I entered my late teens, I began drifting away from the regular practice of Islam. I still identified as a Muslim, but I had lost the personal connection to my faith. I prayed less often, and when I did, it felt more like an obligation than a spiritual practice.

Despite this, life continued, and by the time I was twenty-nine, I found myself living in the United States and married. In our culture, getting married at that age was considered "late," and there was a great deal of pressure to settle down, start a family, and fulfill the traditional roles expected of a woman. I thought I was ready for marriage, but it became clear early on that I hadn't anticipated the challenges that lay ahead.

My husband had two sons from a previous marriage, and blending our families proved more difficult than I had ever imagined. We struggled to find common ground, and over time, the emotional distance between us grew. Our relationship became strained, and the marriage began to unravel. Divorce, which I had once feared as an unthinkable outcome, suddenly became an unavoidable reality. In retrospect, I see now that God was guiding me out of an unhealthy environment, even though it was incredibly painful at the time.

Prelude to the Journey

Life has a way of breaking us down only to rebuild us stronger, and even in the darkest moments, there are glimpses of light. One of those moments for me came through travel, which had always been a passion of mine. My job as a buyer for our furnishing stores took me to trade shows around the world, providing me the opportunity to explore unfamiliar places and cultures.

One such trip took me to Cologne, Germany. It was a cold, rainy afternoon, and after a long day of meetings, I decided to explore the city. As I walked through the streets, I found myself standing in front of the famous Cologne Cathedral. The towering structure, with its intricate Gothic architecture, exuded a sense of peace and reverence that drew me in. I stepped inside, seeking refuge from both the rain and my turbulent thoughts.

For the first time in years, I felt a genuine urge to pray—not the kind of prayer I had memorized as a child but a heartfelt plea. As I prayed in that massive cathedral, surrounded by strangers, I prayed for peace, strength, and clarity. I asked God to guide me out of the darkness that was my marriage.

That simple prayer in the Cologne Cathedral marked the beginning of my journey back to faith. As I left the cathedral, I felt lighter, as if a weight had been lifted off my shoulders. I realized that prayer isn't confined to a language or ritual; it's a conversation between the soul and the Divine. In that moment, I reconnected with a part of myself that had been dormant for too long.

Moment of Realization: Divine Intervention or Dire Circumstances?

After my divorce, I was left with nothing: no savings, no assets, and no financial security. The fear of uncertainty was overwhelming. I had no professional experience outside of working in our family business, and my college degree had long since lost its relevance. I was terrified. How was I going to survive? Where would I go? What would I do?

It was during this time of desperation that I realized life often presents us with unexpected opportunities—doors we hadn't even considered. For me, that door opened in 2012, in the form of a job opportunity I never thought I would consider. While searching for work across the United States, I stumbled across a listing for a marketing manager position with an international QSR (Quick Service Restaurant) brand based in Dubai.

At the time, I was on my way to Pakistan to inform my parents about my divorce. I made a spontaneous decision to stop in Dubai and rent an apartment for three months while I searched for jobs. It felt like a bold move, but in hindsight, I see it as divine intervention. Within weeks of arriving, I landed the job, and my life took a completely different trajectory.

The position took me across the Middle East, and for the first time in my life, I was truly independent. I thrived in my new role, and for the first time in years, I felt like I was back in control of my life. I was in my early forties, single, and living life on my terms. It was liberating, but I had no idea that more challenges were on the horizon.

In October 2015, I was unexpectedly laid off from my job. The stability I had fought so hard to create was shattered in an instant. I found myself once again facing the uncertainty of the future, and the fear of the unknown came rushing back vigorously.

Months passed, and despite my best efforts, I couldn't find another opportunity. The fear that had once been a quiet whisper in the back of my mind grew into a deafening roar. I felt like I was drowning in my own anxiety.

Synchronicity: The Breaking Point and the Beginning of Change

On New Year's Eve of 2015, I hit my breaking point. Overwhelmed by stress, I ended up in the emergency room, convinced I was having a heart attack. Lying in that hospital bed, I realized fear had taken over my life.

Looking back, the timing felt like synchronicity—a wake-up call from the universe urging me to reflect. In my relentless quest for control over my career and future, I had lost sight of trusting God's plan. Fear had overshadowed my faith, but that night marked the beginning of change.

The Divine Lessons: Omer "The Teacher"

On January 1, 2016, an old childhood friend named Omer reached out to me unexpectedly. We hadn't spoken in years, but he somehow sensed I needed help. Over coffee, I poured out my fears and frustrations, and when I finished, Omer said something that changed everything: "Ayesha, you do realize you're not in control—God is."

His words struck me deeply, aligning perfectly with my New Year's Eve realization just hours earlier. In hindsight, the timing felt like synchronicity—a divine orchestration of events designed to guide me back to faith. For years, I had been trying to control every detail of my life—relationships, career, and future. But in that moment, I saw the futility of my efforts. I wasn't in control—God was, and He always had been.

From that day, my perspective shifted. I stopped resisting life's uncertainty and started embracing it. Omer became my mentor, guiding me through a spiritual awakening. He taught me to meditate more meaningfully, provided tools for spiritual growth, and reminded me that life's "tests" are blessings from God. Through his wisdom, I learned to shed fear and embrace faith, recognizing that synchronicity often carries the lessons we most need to hear.

Atiya "The Healer"

During one of the darkest times in my life, my younger sister, Atiya, emerged as one of my greatest pillars of strength. Her name, which means "gift," couldn't have been more fitting. In every sense, she embodied the emotional support and wisdom I desperately needed. Throughout my spiritual journey, she was always by my side, offering more than just sisterly love—she became my anchor.

Atiya is a healer by profession, and it was through her that I rediscovered the balance I had been missing in my life. Her calming presence, her patience, and her gentle strength functioned as the perfect antidote to the chaos I was battling internally. It wasn't just her soothing words, but her whole attitude toward life that gave me courage. Atiya's resilience inspired me to push through my own fears, and her unwavering patience gave me the strength to endure my struggles.

What's remarkable about Atiya is that she has always been there as my sister, my confidante, and my friend. But during this phase of my life, she transformed into something more—a teacher. She taught me invaluable lessons about trust and surrender, helping me see the beauty in letting go of fear. She showed me that faith isn't about belief but also about releasing control and embracing the unknown with open arms. Atiya reinstated in me the power of prayer and belief in Him.

Atiya played a pivotal role in every step of my spiritual transformation. She was and still is my guide, encouraging me to rediscover the strength I had within myself. Her influence continues to shape my life, and for that, I am eternally grateful. The unwavering love, compassion, and wisdom she brought into my life are gifts I carry with me every day.

Iram "The Logical One"

Another key figure during this time was my friend Iram. She was a sounding board for me, offering wisdom and guidance that helped me move from a place of fear to a place of faith. Iram had a unique ability to simplify life's biggest challenges into profound lessons. When I once asked her, "Why me?" she laughed and said, "Have you ever heard of someone being tested by God and not making it through?" Her words were a reminder that God never gives us more than we can handle.

Iram also taught me the importance of asking God for what I wanted. Up until that point, I had been praying for guidance and strength, but I hadn't been specific about what I wanted from life. Iram encouraged me to be bold in my prayers and to trust that God would provide for me in ways I couldn't even imagine.

Rauf "The Insightful One"

After my father's passing, I believe God knew I needed another soul to help guide me through the next chapter of my life. That's when Rauf entered my world. Initially, he came in a different capacity, but he ended up being the most genuine well-wisher and friend I could have ever hoped for.

Rauf introduced me to a new perspective on spirituality. He was deeply immersed in his own spiritual journey, and through our friendship, he challenged me to rethink my preconceived notions. He quietly nudged me toward becoming a better version of myself, all while bringing joy back into my life—the kind of joy that makes you laugh so hard you're lying on the floor.

Rauf's wisdom was not loud or forceful; it was a gentle, guiding light. He showed me that spirituality is not just about rituals or structured beliefs but about trusting the flow of life with a heart full of faith. His ability to embrace uncertainty with unwavering trust in the Divine inspired me to do the same. Through him, I learned that faith isn't about knowing the answers, but about being willing to move forward without them, trusting that the journey itself will reveal what we need.

He didn't just fill the void of friendship in my life; he became a mirror reflecting the strength and grace I had within myself. His unwavering belief in the unknown taught me to surrender to the sacredness of faith and to live with a deeper purpose. Rauf didn't just help me rediscover laughter—he helped me rediscover life.

Lessons of Faith and Surrender

This journey has taught me that fear and faith cannot share the same space. While fear holds us back, faith sets us free. Trusting in God's plan gives us the courage to move forward, even when we can't see what's ahead. Letting go of control and surrendering to the Divine has been the most profound lesson of my life.

I came to understand that life's challenges aren't meant to break us but to guide us back to who we truly are and strengthen our connection with God. Each obstacle, setback, and heartache became an opportunity for growth and transformation.

In 2018, when I unexpectedly lost my father, my world was turned upside down. He was more than just a father to us—he was a giant, touching the lives of many. His sudden passing left me in turmoil. I was outwardly strong, but inside, I felt completely shattered. I found myself angry with God, questioning why He had taken my father so abruptly, and why I couldn't be there in his last moments.

In time, I realized that life's impermanence and death's certainty were truths we must all come to accept. My father's passing forced me to confront my faith in a way I never had before. I struggled to find strength within, and the idea of moving forward seemed impossible. But I came to see that we are all here with a purpose, and in discovering that purpose, we find a sense of peace. Isn't that what we're all seeking? Peace and contentment in this world?

Six years later, I still carry the scar of his absence. The void left behind can never truly be filled. But I've learned how to live with it, how to manage the grief a little better each day. The one thing that continues to bring me solace is praying for his soul, trusting that he is in a better place now.

Lessons Learnt

The Power of Prayer

Over time, I had distanced myself from prayer. I had forgotten the transformative power of simply asking for help. I had convinced myself that I had to handle everything on my own—that my strength and independence were enough to overcome any challenge. But as I reconnected with my faith, I realized how misguided I had been. Prayer wasn't just a ritual or obligation—it was a lifeline.

Through prayer, I rediscovered that I didn't have to carry the weight of the world on my shoulders. I didn't need to have all the answers. Reaching out to God reminded me that I was never alone. By surrendering my struggles to Him, I felt a deep sense of relief, knowing that the Divine was always there to guide, support, and carry me through even the darkest times.

Don't Let Fear Overcome Faith

Fear is a subtle but powerful force that can quietly creep into our lives, often without us realizing it. It can paralyze us, make us doubt ourselves, and rob us of the joy we deserve. For years, fear dominated my life—fear of the unknown, fear of failure, fear of being alone. But as I rediscovered my faith, I learned a profound truth: fear and faith cannot coexist. While fear limits us, faith frees us.

Faith provides a way out of the darkness. It gives us the strength to face our challenges, knowing we never face them alone. By placing our trust in God, even when the path ahead seems unclear, we are guided by something far greater than our fears. I learned that trusting God means acknowledging that no matter how difficult the circumstances, with faith as my anchor, I could rise above them.

Trust the Process

Life rarely goes as we imagine. We set goals, map out our dreams, and plan for our future, only to find the journey is full of unexpected twists and detours. In my life, I had meticulously planned everything—my career, marriage, and future. When those plans fell apart, I was left questioning why.

Over time, I realized there is always a reason for the challenges we face. Obstacles are not placed in our path to block us; they are there to redirect us to something better, something more aligned with our true purpose. Each hardship and setback is part of a larger process of growth. Trusting that process, even when I couldn't see the bigger picture, became a source of strength.

When I accepted that everything happens for a reason, life became less daunting. I stopped resisting change and began to flow with it. I came to understand that God's plan is always greater than my own, and trusting in that plan brought me peace as I navigated life's uncertainties.

Stay Humble, Stay Grounded

Staying humble and grounded is essential for navigating life's difficulties. It reminds us that while we may achieve success and experience personal growth, it's important to recognize the contributions of others and the role of circumstances beyond our control. Humility allows us to appreciate our journey, and the lessons learned along the way, fostering gratitude for both the highs and lows. By remaining connected to our values and maintaining perspective, we cultivate resilience and an open heart. This grounded approach not only deepens our relationships but also keeps us anchored, empowering us to face challenges with grace and wisdom.

Let Go: We Are Never in Control; God Is

One of the most profound lessons Omer taught me was the importance of letting go. For so long, I believed I had to control every aspect of my life—every decision, every outcome, every detail. But in trying to control everything, I only created more stress, anxiety, and fear.

Letting go does not mean giving up on your dreams. It means releasing the need to control every aspect of life and trusting that God's plan is far more perfect than anything we could imagine. It means surrendering to life's flow, knowing that the Divine is guiding us toward the right path, even when that path is not clear.

This shift in perspective brought me a profound sense of peace. I still worked hard and made plans, but I no longer felt the need to control every outcome. I trusted that God would take care of the things I could not, and that trust allowed me to live with newfound freedom and joy.

You Are Where You Need to Be

When we put our trust in God, life has a way of unfolding exactly as it should. The right people enter our lives at the right time, the right opportunities present themselves, and we find ourselves exactly where we need to be—even when it does not always make sense. Omer's reappearance in my life was proof of this. His words came at a time when I needed them most, setting me on a path of spiritual growth and self-discovery.

As I embraced faith, I began to notice how life started aligning in my favor. The small moments I once overlooked became significant. I began to trust that every experience, no matter how difficult, had a purpose.

The Soul Always Remembers

No matter how far we stray from our faith or how disconnected we feel from the Divine, the soul never forgets its true home. Even in the years when I distanced myself from prayer and spirituality, my soul longed for that sacred connection. It yearned for the peace, love, and guidance that only comes from being in harmony with God.

It is easy to lose ourselves in the distractions of life, the pursuit of success, or the busyness of the world. But no matter how far I had wandered, I learned I could always find my way back through prayer, reflection, and surrender.

Our Purpose Transcends Survival

Life is more than just surviving; it is about truly living. And true living means connecting with something greater than ourselves. For years, I was in survival mode, simply trying to make it through each day. I had been so focused on external success that I lost sight of life's deeper meaning.

As I reconnected with my faith, I realized our purpose transcends mere survival. We are here to live fully, love deeply, and contribute meaningfully to the world. When we live in alignment with this purpose, we find fulfillment and peace.

Conclusion: The Journey to Inner Peace

Today, I can look back on my life with gratitude for the lessons I have learned and the strength I've gained. My journey has not been easy, but it has been deeply rewarding. Through prayer, faith, and surrender, I have found my way back to peace and purpose.

Our creator loves us unconditionally. It is our job to recognize that and believe in the Divine. All the obstacles that are given to us are meant for us, there to teach us something and to keep us humble and grateful. We need to reconnect our souls, return to Him with intention, and find our true purpose.

This book is my way of sharing that journey with you. I hope that through these stories and lessons, you, too, will find the strength to transform fear into faith, let go of the need for control, and embrace the fulfilling life that awaits you.

Shraddha Chandwadkar

Self Esteem & Mindfulness Coach

https://www.linkedin.com/in/shraddhachandwadkar/
https://www.facebook.com/share/HTvYdKtj5tMiEWyV/?mibextid=LQQJ4d
https://www.instagram.com/luminouslifelabs/
https://shraddhachandwadkar.com/

Shraddha Chandwadkar is a passionate Self-Esteem & Mindfulness coach who empowers and illuminates the lives of women and children. Her workshops, coaching sessions & mini-retreats focus on practical strategies to improve self-image, overcome self-doubt, and develop a positive mindset. They also include mindfulness techniques that help in stress management and self-care. When not coaching, Shraddha enjoys writing on topics related to self-esteem, mindfulness, teaching Reiki, and volunteering as an executive program director in a health and wellness non-profit. She recently received the silver 'President Volunteer Service Award' acknowledging her service towards bringing awareness in Mindfulness and Yoga practices. Shraddha is a mother of two teens and three cats. She is also a spiritual seeker who loves to spend quality time in meditative & contemplative practices. An Engineer by education, Shraddha has an MS, Computer Engineering, from NC State University USA and BE in Electronics Engineering from Pune, India.

Faith in Action: Transformative Power of Prayer

By Shraddha Chandwadkar

Prayer is a form of communication with Divine consciousness and is practiced across all faiths and cultures. I have an immense belief that prayers are answered when one prays with complete faith and surrenders to the Divine consciousness with no expectations. Acceptance of circumstances and being in the present helps make the prayer stronger. Prayers have been an integral part of my life since childhood. My grandmother sang prayers of praise for the Almighty every Thursday evening in her soulful voice, and her prayers aroused a sense of devotion and feelings of oneness within me early on. My mother, too, instilled the importance of prayer through her daily prayers for the family and community at large. Lighting an oil lamp and worshipping in silence or singing God's praise was a regular habit in our household. Gradually, the prayers invoked feelings of faith and devotion. Initially, the devotion was selfish. It was only meant to ask God to fulfill a desire or ordinary materialistic wish fulfillment. As I started experiencing life and came across enlightened spiritual masters, I started to dig deeper within. I slowly started realizing that there is a higher form of prayer—a prayer that summons God to eliminate all negative patterns and tendencies from the mind and to make it pure, loving, compassionate, and steadfast.

When we are faced with challenging situations in life, we tend to panic, worry, blame, and hurt. When we do this, we are harming our bodies on a deep cellular level. The thoughts and emotions of anger, pain, and worry cause deep-rooted patterns of anxiety, depression, stress, and resentment, which can further lead to psychosomatic diseases. Instead, if we choose to pray and surrender to the divine consciousness, miracles can happen.

Personal Stories of Miracles through Faith & Prayer

Prayers have helped me conquer every difficult challenge in my life and opened doors for higher wisdom and purpose. I would like to share seven different real-life examples of how prayer has helped in difficult situations I or a family member has encountered.

1. Prayer helps us understand God's Unconditional Love.

I was visiting my uncle and grandparents in Kalyan, Thane district, in the state of Maharashtra, India. After my vacation I had to go back home to my parents in Pune. My uncle bought me a first-class train ticket so that the compartment wouldn't be crowded, and it would ensure my safety. To my surprise, there was no one in the first-class compartment when I got in. After a few minutes, a man came in. He sat on the seat across from me. His behavior was very fishy. He started talking with me, asking some personal questions, and being overly nice. Also, he probably thought I was a young woman, while I was just a tall teenager in college. Luckily that day, I was carrying the book *Power of Positive Thinking* by Norman Vincent Peale, which was popular then. I started reading the book and ignoring the man. He still tried to talk to me. The compartment was empty. It was only me and him. I knew I had to be nice and, at the same time, protect myself. I kept reading the book and felt positive from within. My fear had turned into faith. I was very calm. I answered his questions. He asked me for my phone number. I decided to give him my number and also decided that I would never pick it up. After the journey was over, my father came to pick me up at the train station. The man got down one station before me. After I went home with Dad, I explained everything to my parents and told them that if the man called tell him that no such woman lives here. They supported me, of course, and did exactly what I asked them to do. After a few calls, he stopped calling. I firmly believe that the thought of carrying that book with me on the train was God's unconditional love towards me.

2. **Prayers provide solutions.**

   I was in 12th grade. My mother was very sick. She had swelling all over her body and was bedridden. She could hardly speak and was in severe pain. Also, her skin was itching throughout her body. The doctors could not diagnose what was happening. I prayed every day for my mother's well-being and asked my friends to pray for her too. After several weeks, one of the doctors changed her medicine, and it worked. She was back to normal life after a month.

3. **Prayers give us strength to avoid temptation in life.**

   My father was an alcoholic during my childhood years. He also smoked cigarettes. We have spent many nights in tears and sadness due to his alcoholism. However, my father also had a spiritual side to him. He believed in God and prayers. He also used to listen to enlightened spiritual master's discourses during his free time. He was a very compassionate and honest man and remains so today. One day, when I was in 10th grade, he suddenly had a moment of divine intervention where he had a deep desire to quit. I remember him praying and telling my mom that he had no desire to continue drinking anymore. After the sudden realization, he had friends and aquaintances in his life that helped him. They took him to Alcoholics Anonymous. My mother stood by his side through thick and thin. One day, my father brought the *'Serenity Prayer'* wall hanging with him that was given to him in an AA meeting. I am including this prayer below.

   God Grant Me The Serenity
   To Accept The Things
   I Cannot Change
   The Courage to Change the Things I Can
   And Wisdom to Know the Difference.

Reading the serenity prayer every day gave all of us a higher understanding of ourselves and a sense of comfort and reassurance that the good times were on their way. The darkness was wiped out, and wisdom prevailed. Within one year of deciding to quit, my father was out of alcohol and within 2 years free from smoking and remains so today at the age of 72. Several new and exciting opportunities came his way after quitting alcohol. He served as director and CEO of different companies for several years and continues to lead. He was given opportunities to travel to different countries for work during this renewed phase of life.

If you or a loved one is a slave of temptation, do consider praying every day to help bring about transformation.

4. **Prayers can work miracles.**

It was monsoon season in India. My maternal grandmother was visiting us in the city of Chinchwad in district Pune. After her visit, my father was supposed to drop her back to the city of Kalyan, district Thane, where she lived with my maternal uncle. I decided to accompany them as well. I was probably in middle or high school. I clearly remember it was Wednesday evening, and we were late to start. On our way to Kalyan Thane, there was a flash flood and traffic jam. My father then owned a tiny, red, used Maruti 800 car. It was our first car. I could see the water level rising through the window of our car. I was terrified! My grandmother took my palm in her hand and started praying. She told me everything would be fine. We were stuck in that position for quite some time. My heartbeat was racing, but I began to pray with my grandmother and also decided to stay calm. Suddenly, something happened. The traffic began to move. Everyone was asked to take a diversion. After some time, there was no water visible. We were out of the flooded area! If you are stuck in life today, believe that prayers can work miracles and help you get unstuck.

5. **Prayers can help us find lost objects.**

   My spiritual master Tejguru Sirshree mentioned in one of his discourses that when we pray to non-living objects, it is easy to find them. For example, when we lose a key or phone in the house and cannot locate it, I visualize the key or phone and pray and request that it be found. I have noticed that I find objects most of the time using this technique.

   Key points to remember:

   - Focus on the lost object: Pray and clearly state what you have lost and ask for help to find it specifically.
   - Visualize: Close your eyes. Bring the lost objects in your mind's eye. Clearly see them in your mind's eye.
   - Have Faith: Approach the prayer with genuine belief and be positive.
   - Search actively: Actively look around in places to find the item.

   This technique saves me from unnecessary worry and guilt.

6. **Prayers help us build courage and resilience.**

   A few years ago, I fell sick after eating bread and drinking milk during breakfast. I had a burning sensation in my stomach and abdomen, and it started to worsen by the end of the day. I decided to drink cooled-down cumin water, which eased the burning somewhat. However, I was unable to eat regular food for a few days. I decided to boil vegetables and eat those for a week. My appetite started to improve; however, my weight dropped drastically from 125 lbs to 90 lbs, and I am a 5 feet 5 inches tall woman. I decided to visit the doctor. Got all tests done, and nothing came out of the tests. The doctors weren't ready to listen to my story of eating bread and milk and blamed it on anxiety. Along with this, I started to have episodes of dizziness, burping, and body shaking suddenly for about

30 minutes after a few hours of a meal. If I was driving during such episodes I had to stop suddenly. This happened for about 2.5 years. Prayers were the only solution during this time. I prayed every day for a healthy body and mind, wrote affirmations, sent prayers of healing to my subtle body, and practiced meditation, a few yoga exercises, and walking. After about 2.5 to 3 years, the problem stopped. To regain the original weight, it took me 6 years. However, my energy and spirit did not go down as I decided to pray and practice gratitude and forgiveness. The prayers helped build resilience within me, and my mind remained calm and focused on the tasks at hand.

7. **Prayers give a higher direction in life.**

   I read the serenity prayer mentioned above every day while I was in middle and high school. Reading the prayer regularly helped me understand its hidden and deep meanings. I am a firm believer that the spiritual turns I have taken in my life and the thirst to know myself come from reading that prayer that was hung on our living room wall in my parents' apartment. It took me towards my higher purpose in spite of being in worldly desires of finding a job, having a family, and traveling. Spiritual masters and their teachings started appearing in front of me. The need to wipe out the patterns and tendencies within me, the urgency of helping the younger generations, knowing my true nature, and understanding the higher purpose of life have increased within me through prayer and conversations with the divine.

How to Pray?

1. **Create a ritual:** We can create a ritual like lighting a lamp or candle or burning an incense stick in front of the altar with the deities or God figures we want to worship. However a God figure or deity is not necessary. It is important to pray sincerely

and with best intentions. According to different faiths some have God figures in manifest form while others worship the formless God. In either case prayer helps invoke feelings of devotion, faith and surrender.

2. **Empty the mind:** While praying, it is important to empty the mind of all the clutter of thoughts. Close your eyes and observe the thoughts. Let them pass like a passing cloud without getting entangled in them.
3. **Start the prayer:** When your mind is quiet and you have no thoughts, start your prayer by inviting the Almighty to help you or others.
4. **Say what you need:** Be honest and say exactly what you need in the present tense.
5. **Praise the Almighty:** Praise the divine for the Grace.
6. **Ask:** For prayers of healing or guidance to take away all negative patterns and beliefs.
7. **Confess:** If you want to confess, be honest and ask for forgiveness.
8. **Visualize:** Visualize the prayer being fulfilled. Feel liberated, as if it's fulfilled at the very moment.
9. **Be grateful:** Express gratitude for the prayers being fulfilled.

Prayer As a Mindfulness & Self-Esteem Tool

Prayers have a profound effect on our body, mind, and spirit. They help us disconnect from worries, hatred, and anger and help us to center ourselves. They bring us to the present moment and connect us with divinity. They help us to manifest higher qualities. We elevate our vibration due to sincere prayers. They cleanse our mind and make it pure in thoughts and emotions. I consider prayers as an important tool in Mindfulness, Self-Esteem and in elevating our consciousness. Below are some of the ways I have used prayer as a mindfulness tool to increase confidence.

1. **Affirmations/Positive Self-Talk:**

   Prayers are nothing but thoughts. And if we can affirm these positive thoughts, they attract well-being into our lives. Affirmations like, "Day by Day in Every Way I Am Getting Better and Better," which I wrote on a board and hung in my room as a child, have helped instill confidence in me and improved my self-image in childhood. Louise Hay, the founder of Hay House Publishing, has written a beautiful book, *You Can Heal Your Life*, which shows us the power of affirmations and how it helped her heal from a severe illness such as cancer.

   By actively voicing affirmations about our worth, we can counter negative thoughts and replace them with a positive narrative.

2. **Chanting:**

   Chanting has been practiced in Hindu and Buddhist cultures since ancient times. Sanskrit chants like the "*Gayatri Mantra*" for higher wisdom and enlightenment, "*Mahamrityunjaya mantra*" for liberation from the cycle of birth and death or removal of sickness, or "*Om Chanting*" for praying for union of the individual soul with higher consciousness are effective forms of prayer. The vibrations from the chant help us relax and promote healing. When I was sick a few years ago, I listened to a Buddhist chant, known as the *Tara Mantra*. The mantra helped me heal from my sickness and develop a positive, serene state of mind.

3. **Kirtans or Devotionals:**

   Kirtans are similar to chants but more devotional in nature. Kirtan is a Sanskrit word that means narrating, reciting, telling, or describing. The ultimate purpose of kirtan is to facilitate the awakening of one's devotion to the Divine. Kirtans describe God or His/Her qualities and serve as a reminder to imbibe those qualities within us. If you listen to kirtans from India or modern-day kirtankars from the US, like the famous Krishna Das, you will know how powerful they can be. Similarly, church choir music raises our vibrations instantly, helps us alleviate sorrow, and brings happiness to our lives. I love listening to kirtans and choir on YouTube to uplift myself on a regular basis. With the repetition of chants and kirtans, it is easier to stay in the present.

4. Writing:

Writing positive affirmations or goals in the present tense is a form of prayer. It brings us back to the present and helps to focus on the positive and cultivate an optimistic mindset.

5. Visualization:

While praying, if we visualize the prayer being fulfilled, then it can help manifest it faster. I often visualize end results with a feeling that it is already manifested. The famous actor and comedian Jim Carrey mentioned in his interview with Oprah Winfrey that he visualized being successful and wrote a check to himself for acting services rendered when he was poor and not a star, which helped him in his journey to stardom and fame. It helped him defocus from poverty to feelings of contentment and prosperity, which helped them manifest in his life.

6. Gratitude as a Form of Prayer:

We all know the importance of gratitude. Being in a state of gratitude surrenders the ego and develops inner strength. Gratitude helps attract all positive things in life and eliminates sickness from the body. My personal favorite is to make a gratitude journal and write in it on a regular basis.

7. **Forgiveness as a Form of Prayer:**

   When we forgive others, we are not only helping others but helping ourselves by not creating unnecessary bonds. Every night before sleeping, asking for forgiveness from those whom we may have hurt knowingly or unknowingly can relieve us of unwanted baggage. On the other hand, forgiving those who hurt us clears our minds of mental stress and can also prevent psychosomatic diseases from lurking within our systems.

8. **Listening to Prayers or Chants While Cooking:**

   In Indian culture, it is believed that listening to chants or kirtans while cooking and praying before we eat enhances food vibrations, which in turn helps us improve our physical and emotional health. This also prevents us from unnecessarily dwelling on negative thoughts and emotions while cooking and eating and helps in cultivating mindfulness.

9. **Saying Prayers to the Water We Drink and Food We Eat:**

   It is beneficial to say positive thoughts and prayers to a glass of water. When we drink this water, it reaches every cell of the body. We were taught to pray to water by my reiki teacher, as well as my spiritual master and it was a common practice in India during ancient times as well. I say positive affirmations like, "Water, you are a healer. You enhance creativity and elevate consciousness. Thank you for healing and transforming me," and then drink it. Before eating food, I thank the food and the farmers and bless the food. This certainly helps to be in a mindful and grateful state while eating and drinking.

10. **Sending Prayers of Healing to our Subtle Body:**

    I have been practicing energy healing and I pray to the subtle body as taught by my spiritual master. The subtle body comprises the mind, ego, memories, conscious, unconscious, and supra-conscious and is a crucial part of our energetic makeup. It allows us to perceive energy and intuition. The concept of a subtle body appears in many ancient teachings in the Hindu (Sanatana dharma) scriptures like Rig Veda and Upanishads. From what I have read on the internet, it also appears in the Old Testament and many other religions like Buddhism and Jainism. It is believed that the disease first appears in the subtle body before it actually manifests in the gross body. Also, praying to the subtle body essentially helps in directing our focus to the energetic makeup within our physical body and is believed to help in accessing deeper spiritual consciousness, rather than praying to a deity like in traditional form. This also helps promote healing on physical, emotional, and mental levels.

11. Meditation:

Meditation is the ultimate form of prayer. Meditation provides spiritual clarity and develops a higher sense of awareness.

Example Prayers for Self-Esteem

1

Dear God/Higher Self/Consciousness,
Thank you for your creation.
Thank you for blessing me with unique qualities and abilities.
When I doubt myself, I am doubting your creation.
When I doubt, remind me of my worth and the highest potential you have given me.
Help me to accept myself, love myself, and have faith in myself.
Give me the courage to embrace my strengths and to accept challenges with Grace and resilience.
Thank You. Thank You. Thank You.

2

Dear God/Higher Self/Consciousness,
Thank you for everything you have given me.
Thank you for bestowing your grace and unconditional love upon me.
Thank you for filling me with gratitude and divine qualities.
Thank you for the courage, compassion, and love within me.
Thank you for physical, mental, emotional, financial, and spiritual stability.
Thank You. Thank You. Thank You.

Impersonal Prayers

We often pray for ourselves and our families. However, greater joy lies in praying for others. Praying for others can have many benefits.

1. **Empathy:** Praying for others helps us put ourselves in other's shoes and understand their worries and what they are going through.
2. **Comfort:** Praying for others can comfort them during their challenging times.
3. **Hope:** Praying for others can help cultivate feelings of hope in others.
4. **Compassion:** Praying for others helps us cultivate feelings of compassion and takes us closer to God.
5. **Faith in Action:** When we pray for others, we shift our focus from ourselves and put faith into action. When we lift others up in prayer, our faith multiplies.
6. **Humility:** Praying for others develops a quality of humility within us.
7. **Strength:** Praying for others cultivates strength within us.
8. **Elevating Consciousness:** Praying for mankind, animals, and plants helps them heal and elevates Consciousness on Earth.

Ultimately Impersonal prayers help us transcend from the feeling of 'I' or 'other' to 'We'- a feeling of Oneness.

Example of Impersonal Prayer

Dear God/Higher Self /Consciousness,
Thank you for providing all human beings with food, water, shelter, and wisdom.
Help us see divinity in one and all.
Fill us with unconditional love, compassion, kindness, and strength
So that we become your instruments in elevating consciousness on Earth.
Thank you for keeping us safe and happy.
Thank You. Thank You. Thank You.

Collective Prayers For All

Collective prayers in a group strengthen Faith in ourselves and God. It also instills a sense of belonging in the society. Collective prayers raise vibrations and help in healing. They are also instrumental in building unity and providing peace. Whenever possible pray collectively for a common impersonal cause like world peace, raising consciousness on Earth, praying for leaders of all nations, praying for a united world, praying for health for all living beings, praying for Earth and the universe.

Through this chapter, we have explored how prayer is a tool that instills faith, confidence, self-esteem, courage, contentment, healing, and resilience. By harnessing its transformative power, we can bring more harmony and bliss into our lives.

Wishing everyone a Happy, Healthy, Prosperous, and Conscious Life. Stay Blessed!

Shaniqua Gibbs

https://www.facebook.com/shaniqua.murphy
https://www.instagram.com/virtualhelperoffice/

Hello my name is Shaniqua Gibbs. I am a pretty easy-going person. My faith in God provides me with strength and direction. Family is central to my values, especially my wonderful husband and children, with whom I treasure every moment. I love meeting new women and am dedicated to creating meaningful connections and uplifting those around me. I am passionate about community building and actively giving back. My goal is to inspire, support, and share experiences with like-minded women, believing that each of us has something valuable to offer to help others through challenges. This chapter reflects how my faith, family, and community supported me during a challenging period in my life.

Faith in the Storm: A Mother's Journey of Strength, Loss, and Divine Reassurance

By Shaniqua Gibbs

My name is Shaniqua Gibbs, and I am a mother of three sons. Tragically, their father passed away due to a drunk driving accident. In our most challenging moments, we often discover our inner strength. One of my sons, who has autism, ADHD, and a mood disorder, struggled deeply after losing his father. Although my children received a settlement meant to secure their future, it became a source of heartache when someone we trusted manipulated my son and took his money. I vividly remember the day my son abruptly left home; it felt like the weight of the world came crashing down on me. The following weeks were filled with confusion and anger that seemed impossible to shake. I would lie awake at night, questioning how everything had gone wrong. Wondering if this is something I could have prevented. I felt completely overwhelmed by the weight of my worries and guilt for even allowing that person to take up space in me and my kids' lives. This hurt me and was deeply painful. Fear gripped me during those days. Every time I saw or heard that my son had struggles, the uncertainty of his future always came over me, and I felt completely powerless.

Alongside the anger that simmered within me was the injustice that I felt, along with a deep sadness that weighed heavily on my heart for all that was happening with my son. It felt like justice was slipping further from our grasp each day. While the authorities did begin an investigation into her actions and eventually froze the remaining funds she hadn't spent, my greatest concern wasn't about the money—it was my son's well-being. He was kept away from me and fed lies that prevented him from talking to me or sharing what was really happening. The thought of not being able to see or speak with him daily troubled me deeply.

Without the consistent support he was used to, countless distressing thoughts flooded my mind. This went on for a couple of years, my emotions constantly shifting like a rollercoaster.

Unfortunately, after a couple of years, they had to drop the case. They were not able to locate my son, because she was hiding him. The lack of resolution fueled my fear, anger, and frustration. I felt like the system had failed me and my son. I felt pain and wanted to get revenge for myself and my son. There was a constant battle with the temptation to take matters into my own hands, feeling every emotion magnified by the helplessness of our situation. Little did I know this journey would be one of stronger faith, prayer, and growth supported by the loving community around me.

I turned to God, seeking strength through prayer and quiet moments of reflection. I also reached out to my church community for support, and as they prayed for me, I began to feel less alone. Although it took a while over time, those quiet moments of reflection became my anchor. I prayed for my son's safety, for guidance, and for the strength to endure. The prayers started to offer me a sense of peace. Every morning, I have my quiet time with God, and I look at scriptures about faith. I came to Hebrews 11, and that chapter stuck out to me, especially verse 6 (NLT):

"And it is impossible to please God without faith. Anyone who wants to come to him must believe that God exists and that he rewards those who sincerely seek him."

This chapter, in my quiet time, brought me closer to God and increased my faith. I grew stronger, and I believe through my readings that God gifted me with an amazing sense of peace and calm. Although I couldn't really see my son as much as I wanted, I held on to the assurance that God was watching over him and protecting him. I moved from daily tears to a renewed sense of peace and purpose. It was through this transformation that I was able to truly connect with my loved ones and find strength in the community of prayer that surrounded me. Immersing in God's word, I discovered the strength to reengage in a new way with God, and with my loved ones and the supportive community around me.

Trusting in God's promises transformed my fear and panic into peace. As I released my burdens to him, this journey strengthened my faith, providing the courage to move forward with unwavering faith and trust in God.

Family & Community

My husband was an incredible source of support during these difficult times. The situation with his stepson weighed on him deeply as well, yet he remained steadfast by my side. His quiet strength, calm presence, and constant encouragement helped me hold onto my faith, even when I felt like giving up. Together, we faced each day, finding comfort in our shared hope and prayers. His unwavering support became a cornerstone of my journey, reminding me of the importance of a strong, loving partnership. My other children, along with my parents and siblings, were always by my side, offering their unwavering love and support. They were there to listen, provide comfort, and remind me that I wasn't alone in this journey. Together, as a family, we lifted up prayers and supported one another through the struggle. Their collective presence was a vital part of my journey, reinforcing the importance of having a strong, loving family.

During this challenging time, my prayer partner became a pivotal figure in my journey. She patiently listened as I poured out my heart, and her prayers soothed my soul, reminding me of the strength I held within. Our connection was powerful, and her faith reignited my own. Our friendship deepened, becoming a safe space, free of judgment and full of support. Though we had been close for years, she became my rock during those hard times. Every weekday morning, we would pray together on the phone for an hour or more, reading scripture and sharing our struggles. She listened to my tears and shared my pain, and I would do the same for her. We lifted each other up with unwavering support. Through our shared faith and daily connection, she helped me find the strength to keep moving forward.

My friends and community noticed my struggle and offered their support in ways I hadn't expected. They prayed with me, shared their own stories of perseverance, and reminded me I was not alone. God used my community to give me peace and comfort during this very difficult time. They went above and beyond helping me with resources, offering practical support for my other two children, and ensuring their safety. These acts of kindness helped me to realize that God was working through them, providing me calm and reassurance through their support. It was in these moments that I truly understood the power of collective faith. Knowing that I was not alone in this journey helped me to regain my strength in faith.

My Breakthroughs

In the midst of the chaos, I felt assured in my heart that God was in control. This divine reassurance whispered to me, it's going to be okay. After that, this newfound peace of faith became a foundation for my heart. It brought me a sense of calm and rest, allowing me to be vulnerable with my community. I began to notice what I call "God kisses", little signs and moments that I felt God orchestrated reassuring me that everything would be okay. These divine gestures, along with the support of people he placed around me, confirmed his presence and strengthened my faith like never before.

One of the most impactful "God kisses" came through my community. Just when I felt the lowest and did not want to be bothered. My friends, family, and community would reach out unexpectedly or send me different scriptures that were right on time. Even the rare calls or text messages that I would get from my son while he was in his wilderness felt like God's reassurance that my son was okay and that there was still hope for what God was going to do in my son's life through his journey as well as this situation.

Breakthrough moments occurred during conversations with my prayer partner, she never shied away from telling me hard truths, such as when she pointed out that I was operating out of fear or coming from a place of fear rather than faith. Her honest guidance made me realize that some actions I wanted to take could have made the situation worse. It was through these challenging, yet necessary dialogues that I began to see my own lessons in this journey. I understood that in my attempts to protect my son, I was interfering in God's plan (like he needed my help, smh). I had to learn to trust God's process and accept that I had no control over the situation. I couldn't control anything that was happening. I also had to come to terms with the fact that my son made the choice to listen to others, and I needed to trust that, in time, God would reveal the truth about people's character to him. This revelation shifted my perspective and strengthened my walk. This taught me how to be still and have faith. God showed me what it looks like to be still while he does the work.

Through the years I have had a lot of breakthroughs and kisses from God. They came through interactions with authorities that were working on my son's case. There were times when they uncovered critical information, like the moment when I managed to locate my son briefly, which brought a huge sense of relief. Moments of self-reflection, prompted by the insights and kindness of others, further reinforce my need to trust God and lean on the community. He provided all these experiences in my journey through fear, with faith and support from my community.

My journey and relationships, the breakthroughs and the discoveries, each moment, struggle, and triumph, built a foundation for my desire to create a safe space where other women can find strength in sisterhood, deepen their faith, their relationships, and experience their own breakthroughs. The presence of a community has touched my heart deeply, inspiring me to organize retreats focused on fostering relationships. These retreats are designed to equip you with essential skills to strengthen both your personal and professional relationships. They focus on sisterhood, communication, healthy relationships, and creating deep connections. Drawing inspiration from my faith, I offer a safe environment that fosters personal growth, and bonding. My retreats address various aspects of relationship building, including the internal, external, and psychological components that are vital for everyone to understand. Through a variety of sessions, we provide you with practical tools, tips, and strategies to help you build stronger connections and cultivate a resilient, supportive community. These retreats are a testament to how you can journey through life with a supportive community, free of judgment, embracing vulnerability, and filled with the love, joy, and encouragement that God has called us to share with one another. Below are a couple of scriptures that embody the support I received from my family and my community of friends.

These scriptures remind me that God never intended for us to walk through life alone.

Ecclesiastes 4:10 - "If one person falls, the other can reach out and help. But someone who falls alone is in real trouble."

Galatians 6:2 - "Share each other's burdens, and in this way obey the law of Christ."

I've witnessed firsthand how these scriptures came to life in my journey. The profound difference it makes to endure hardships alone versus having the support of others. Being able to walk through your journey with a community that you have resilient bonds with and friendships with is priceless and life-changing.

I am in awe of how God has truly watched over me and my family throughout this journey. My son and I are now talking daily, and the people who once negatively influenced him are no longer in his life. Though we are facing another challenge, I can clearly see that God has answered my prayers and is now working on my son through this situation. I have a sense of peace amidst this storm, and I'm reminded of James 1:2-4:

"2 Consider it pure joy, my brothers and sisters, whenever you face trials of many kinds, 3 because you know that the testing of your faith produces perseverance. 4 Let perseverance finish its work so that you may be mature and complete, not lacking anything."

I now view these trials differently, knowing that God is working on both me and my son, shaping us for the purpose He has for us. I can persevere through this, confident that I am not alone, and that God is watching over us and hearing my prayers. I continue to pray daily for my children and family, and God keeps showing me little signs of his presence.

My son is not back home yet, which isn't the outcome I would have hoped for, but I trust that God knows the plans he has for me and my son. We will work through this trial, and while I know my son has to face certain challenges that I can't protect him from, I find comfort in knowing that God is watching over him and keeping him safe. There is healing and self-reflection my son will need to go through, and that's work he has to do for himself. I believe God is working in his life and answering my prayers because I have faith and can envision a future where God uses this situation to help my son grow and maybe even support others who have faced similar struggles. This journey has brought a lot of self-reflection for me as well, preparing me for the trial we are facing now. I have faith that this, too, shall pass, and God is shaping and molding both of us for His greater purpose.

Kim Castrillon

Best-selling Author, Speaker

https://www.linkedin.com/in/dailypaymoney/
https://www.facebook.com/kimraycastrillon/
https://www.thesetfreelife.com/

Kim Castrillon is an inspiring author, speaker, and host of the upcoming podcast 'The Set Free Life.' Committed to helping women realize their God-given potential, Kim has penned the acclaimed book series 'The Set Free Life.' The series includes 'The Way,' 'The Truth,' 'The Life,' and the upcoming 'Purpose and Destiny.' Each volume helps readers on their paths to healing, understanding, empowerment, and discovering their divine purpose, affirming that everyone, regardless of their past, is made in the image of God and capable of achieving greatness.

Additionally, Kim has recently launched a new devotional for young adults, extending 'The Set Free Life' series into new realms of spiritual growth and personal discovery. In these works and through the forthcoming podcast, Kim offers practical wisdom and spiritual insights that inspire and equip individuals to be Healed, Restored, and Unstoppable—helping them overcome their past, embrace their present, and step confidently into their destiny.

With the launch of 'The Set Free Life' podcast on the horizon, Kim will engage listeners with solo talks, shared stories, and actionable steps to live a life of freedom and fulfillment. Off the mic, Kim enjoys exploring the outdoors—whether it's the air, land, or sea—further encouraging others and embodying the balance essential to a life well-lived."

From Fear to Faith: My Journey of Healing

By Kim Castrillon

Early Life and Diagnosis

I had epilepsy since the age of 3, and by the age of 25, my seizures had become so severe that I had to go on disability. I was experiencing 26 seizures a month, which left me feeling utterly desperate and without hope. The constant seizures disrupted every aspect of my life, making it impossible to hold a job or maintain any semblance of normalcy. Despite trying all available medications, nothing seemed to help. Each visit to the doctor felt like another step towards despair. My neurologist suggested brain surgery as a last resort, and in 1996, I underwent a partial left lobe lobotomy. The relief was temporary, and the seizures returned a couple of years later. Feeling desperate after doctors told me there was nothing more they could do, I turned to Jesus, the great physician, in prayer. This marked the beginning of my 10-year journey to complete healing.

Realization and Turning Point

The key turning moments in my journey included Jesus showing me that after being born again, I was still relying on others' faith and opinions instead of seeking Him directly. When I asked God for forgiveness for not seeking Him, everything changed. I realized that it had taken 10 years for me to experience healing because I was depending on others instead of seeking God for myself. During this time, I often reflected on my life and the choices I had made. I dedicated myself to learning my new identity in Christ and understanding God's love as described in the Bible. This revelation was like a light-bulb moment for me. I had been seeking validation and answers from people around me, thinking they had the keys to my healing. However, God revealed to me that it was His power and love that I needed to rely on. This powerful revelation confirmed His presence in my life and set me on a path to true healing.

Learning and Application

To deepen my faith and understanding, I asked God what was holding me back from His healing promises. He showed me that unforgiveness towards others, myself, and even Him was blocking my healing. This was a hard pill to swallow, but it was necessary. Unforgiveness is like drinking poison and expecting the other person to die. It holds us back and creates a barrier between us and God's blessings. I reflected on scriptures like Matthew 6:14-15 and Matthew 18:34-35, understanding that unforgiveness holds me hostage. These verses became my daily meditation. They taught me the importance of letting go and allowing God's love to flow through me.

Matthew 6:14-15 (AMP) says, "For if you forgive others their trespasses [their reckless and willful sins], your heavenly Father will also forgive you. But if you do not forgive others [nurturing your hurt and anger with the result that it interferes with your relationship with God], then your Father will not forgive your trespasses." This scripture highlighted the importance of forgiveness in receiving God's blessings.

Matthew 18:34-35 (AMP) says, "And in wrath his master turned him over to the torturers (jailers) until he paid all that he owed. My heavenly Father will also do the same to every one of you if each of you does not forgive his brother from your heart." This passage reminded me of the consequences of harboring unforgiveness and the freedom that comes with letting go.

I printed out scriptures about my identity in God and healing, speaking them out loud daily. This practice transformed my mindset. It was as if I was reprogramming my mind to align with God's truth. I also prayed for those I held unforgiveness against until it was no longer difficult, freeing me from torment and doubt.

Experiencing Healing

As I practiced forgiveness and spoke healing scriptures daily, I felt life, peace, joy, and love return to me. Within 90 days, I was healed. This was nothing short of a miracle. While watching a pastor on TV, I felt called to stand up and receive God's healing. I stood up, started sweating, and felt a powerful force going through me. It was an overwhelming experience that I can hardly put into words. I called a pastor friend to share what I had just experienced, and he said, "Kim, you've just experienced God's divine miracle over you." Since that day in 2006, I have been seizure-free and medication-free. This experience was the defining moment that solidified my walk by faith. It was proof that when we come to God in our weakness and persevere until we receive healing, it becomes a strength to help others and change the world.

Sharing My Journey

This experience impacted me so profoundly that I wrote four devotional books titled *The Set Free Life*, sharing my life's stories, challenges, and triumphs to help others experience the same transformation. Each book is a testament to God's power and love. They serve as guides for others to navigate their own journeys of faith and healing. I advise asking God where the fear is rooted and where it's coming from. Many people realize their fear is often based on a "bad father experience" in their life. This affects how they perceive God, feeling unworthy due to past experiences. Ask God what He wants to say to you during those trials. Often, you will hear reassuring and loving messages from God, such as, "I was with you in the midst of it... I wept with you... I've never left you, and I love you."

Daily Reflection and Forgiveness

Instead of asking, "Why me, God?" I now ask, "What is really going on here, God?" I reflect at the end of each day to ensure there is no bitterness building up in my heart towards others. This daily reflection is crucial. It helps me stay grounded and prevents any negative emotions from taking root. If there is bitterness, I bring it to God immediately. Forgiveness is essential, as stated in Matthew 18:22. If God has forgiven me, it is mandatory to forgive others. This practice has transformed my relationships and my life. It has taught me the true meaning of grace and mercy.

Matthew 18:22 (AMP) says, "Jesus answered him, 'I say to you, not up to seven times, but seventy times seven.'" This scripture emphasizes the importance of continual forgiveness, reflecting God's infinite grace towards us.

Scriptural Anchors

Proverbs 3:5-8 has been particularly meaningful to me. This passage keeps me focused and reflective. When feeling delayed or down, it prompts me to evaluate my heart in alignment with the scripture. I question if I am truly trusting the Lord with all my heart or leaning on my own understanding, and if I am fully submitting to His ways instead of my own. The amplified version of this scripture is also a favorite. It breaks down each part, making it clear and relatable. Knowing and applying the Word of God is essential for transformation. Fear is broken by love, which is why the Bible is called the Good News, showcasing God's love and redemption. Living in forgiveness leads to healing, restoration, and becoming unstoppable.

Proverbs 3:5-8 (AMP) says, "Trust in and rely confidently on the Lord with all your heart and do not rely on your own insight or understanding. In all your ways know and acknowledge and recognize

Him, and He will make your paths straight and smooth [removing obstacles that block your way]. Do not be wise in your own eyes; fear the Lord [with reverent awe and obedience] and turn entirely away from evil. It will be health to your body [your marrow, your nerves, your sinews, your muscles—all your inner parts] and refreshment (physical well-being) to your bones." This passage provides clear guidance on how to live a life of faith and trust in God.

Practical Application

When someone is unkind to me, I remind myself that I have no idea what they are going through. This perspective shift has been a game-changer. It allows me to respond with empathy rather than react with anger. Instead of reacting negatively, I check in with God and respond with love and grace. Once, after a difficult interaction, I approached the person, apologized, and offered to pray for them. This approach handled the situation immediately, preventing bitterness from taking root. Love wins every time. It diffuses tension and opens the door for healing and reconciliation.

Maintaining Faith

If I ever feel fear coming, I use Mark 5:36 and John 14:27. Anxiety, panic, and fear often indicate a low or empty faith tank. Just as we eat physical food for our body, we must fill our spirit with spiritual food, which is the Word of God. These scriptures are my go-to reminders of God's promises. They keep me anchored in faith and prevent fear from taking over.

Mark 5:36 (AMP) says, "Overhearing what was being said, Jesus said to the synagogue official, 'Do not be afraid; only keep on believing [in Me and my power].'" This simple yet profound message reminds us to trust in Jesus and not let fear take hold.

John 14:27 (AMP) says, "Peace I leave with you; My [perfect] peace I give to you; not as the world gives do I give to you. Do not let your heart be troubled, nor let it be afraid. [Let My perfect peace calm you in every circumstance and give you courage and strength for every challenge.]" This verse reassures us of the peace that Jesus provides, which surpasses all understanding and drives away fear.

Final Thoughts

My journey from fear to faith has been long and challenging, but it has also been incredibly rewarding. It has taught me the power of God's love and the importance of relying on Him completely. Through this journey, I have learned that faith is not just about believing in God's power, but also about applying His Word to our lives. It is about living in forgiveness, love, and grace every day.

Additional Reflections and Insights

As I continued to grow in my faith, I realized that each day was an opportunity to trust God more deeply. There were days when fear would try to creep back into my life, especially during moments of uncertainty. However, I learned to counter these fears by immersing myself in prayer and scripture. One of the most powerful practices I adopted was journaling my prayers and thoughts. Writing down my fears, prayers, and the promises of God helped me to see His faithfulness in action. Each time I looked back at my journal, I could trace His hand in my life, guiding me, protecting me, and healing me.

In addition to my personal practices, I also found immense strength and encouragement in my community. Surrounding myself with fellow believers who supported and prayed for me was crucial. We shared our struggles, victories, and lessons, creating a network of faith and support. This community reminded me that I was not alone in my journey. We lifted each other up, and their testimonies of God's goodness inspired me to keep pressing on.

Encouraging Others

Over the years, I have had the privilege of sharing my story with many people. Whether through speaking engagements, my devotional books, or one-on-one conversations, I have seen how my journey has touched others. I often tell people that their past does not define them and that with God, there is always hope for a better future. One of the most rewarding experiences is witnessing someone else find freedom and healing through their faith journey. It reinforces the truth that God can use our stories, no matter how painful or challenging, to bring hope and encouragement to others.

Expanding on Forgiveness

Forgiveness is a theme that I cannot emphasize enough. It is a powerful tool that not only frees us from the burden of anger and resentment but also opens the door to God's blessings. There were several instances in my life where forgiveness seemed impossible. For example, forgiving those who had deeply hurt me in the past was a significant challenge. However, each time I chose to forgive, I felt a weight lift off my shoulders. Forgiveness does not mean that what the other person did was right; it means that you are choosing to let go of the hurt and trusting God to handle the rest. This act of releasing bitterness and anger allowed me to experience God's peace and joy more fully.

Daily Walk in Faith

Living a life of faith is a daily commitment. It requires constant renewal of our minds and hearts. Every morning, I start my day with prayer and scripture reading. This sets the tone for the rest of the day, reminding me of God's presence and His promises. Throughout the day, I try to stay mindful of His guidance, whether in decision-making, interactions with others, or dealing with challenges. Staying connected to God through constant communication and reliance on His Word has been my anchor.

Impact on Family and Relationships

My journey of faith has also had a profound impact on my family and relationships. By living out my faith authentically, I have seen positive changes in those around me. My family has grown closer, and we have learned to support and encourage one another in our individual faith journeys. The principles of forgiveness, love, and grace that I strive to live by have also influenced how I interact with friends and acquaintances. It has taught me to be more compassionate, understanding, and patient.

Conclusion

In conclusion, my journey from fear to faith has been transformative. It has not been easy, but every step has been worth it. By trusting in God's promises, practicing forgiveness, and immersing myself in His Word, I have experienced true healing and freedom. My hope is that my story will inspire and encourage others to embark on their own journeys of faith. Remember, faith moves mountains while fear grows them. Choose faith, and you will see the incredible power of God's love in your life.

May your journey be filled with faith that overcomes all obstacles, and may you find the inner calm that comes from trusting in God's love and power.

Alison Levine

Ali Levine Design
Certified & Trauma Informed Breathwork Coach

https://www.linkedin.com/in/alilevinedesign
https://m.facebook.com/AliLevineDesign/?__n=K
https://www.instagram.com/alilevinedesign/
https://www.alilevine.com/
https://alilevine.myflodesk.com/gift

I'm a certified breathwork and somatics instructor with a deep trauma-informed approach, grounded in the power of God and the Holy Spirit. My mission is to help women, especially mothers, transform from merely surviving to truly thriving. Through faith-based coaching, nervous system regulation, and accelerated subconscious reprogramming, I guide women to reconnect with their divine purpose, unlocking their God-given gifts and restoring their sense of wholeness. By shifting from stress and anxiety to peace, clarity, and vibrant living, I empower women to step confidently into the life they were created for.

Breath as Prayer: Connecting to God's Life Force

By Alison Levine

Let's talk about the power of our breath, breathwork, and a little of my journey with it.

I am Ali (Alison) Levine. I am a certified breathwork and somatics instructor with a deep trauma-informed approach, grounded in the power of God and the Holy Spirit. My mission is to help women, especially mothers, transform from merely surviving to truly thriving. Through faith-based coaching, nervous system regulation, and accelerated subconscious reprogramming and rewiring, I guide women to reconnect with their divine purpose, unlocking their God-given gifts and restoring their sense of wholeness. By shifting from stress and anxiety to peace, clarity, and vibrant living, I empower women to step confidently into the life they were created for.

Now, let me share how I got here because I was not someone who ever knew how to take a conscious breath, let alone did I know what breathwork was. And to be honest, I wasn't close to God, either. I was actually really far from him. It makes me so sad to actually type that, but I want to be really real and raw with you and vulnerable so you can go back in time with me.

It was 2013 when my entire world fell apart. My grandmother left this earth physically, and my heart physically hurt losing her, my best friend, my person in so many ways. Maybe you've lost someone, and you know what I am talking about right now. I was a shell of a human.

I swore I wouldn't let myself feel that pain again, so I numbed myself out and threw myself into work. I became the best at my craft. By the way, at this time, I was a celebrity stylist living in Hollywood. I don't say that with an ego, I say that to explain who I was back then and where my priorities and focus were. I went 300% hell-bent on work. Checking off every box in my career, I checked off many. As I continued to check them off, I was feeling less and less fulfilled: my marriage was rockier than ever, my relationships were a mess, and my clients were becoming my #1 focus above my husband, my family, and anything else for that matter.

By 2016, my mind, body, and soul had had enough. I BURNT out! And I don't mean just a bit tired, I mean mental burnout on a level I had never experienced before. My nervous system was a wreck! That's putting it nicely; it was a train wreck. Fast forward, I had a lot of healing to do.

My spiritual journey began. I started crying out to God even though I hadn't in years, and he told me to walk away from the entertainment industry. Shortly after, I was pregnant with my first daughter and moving into a whole new chapter of life. I walked away from styling and I started focusing on content creation and documenting my pregnancy basically. I wanted to have a natural birth that led to a c-section after 42 hours, and that birth unearthed SO much trauma that was in my body. That's when the real work began. I had to feel EVERYTHING and start to HEAL. 2018–2019 was lonely, dark, and heavy, to put it honestly. Finding God on a deeper level, learning meditation, affirmations, a ton of mindset work, and cognitive therapy.

I finally started to love myself and heal. Thank God! Well, 2020 came, and it was like the rug came from underneath me. Trauma came back, and I realized I hadn't healed my nervous system. My body was still holding SO much. In 2020, it was a deeper surrender.

In 2020, it was where God showed me the breath and began to heal me deeper. My life forever changed from that minute. The breath, breathwork is heaven's frequency, the way we are meant to thrive and live. It is the homeostasis and the way we are meant to be. I went through many life-changing moments, from healing my nervous system to finding deeper faith in God and having a VBAC and peaceful birth in 2020. All thanks to my breath. Shortly after, I got certified as a coach, and now I coach hundreds of clients on how to breathe into their B.E.S.T. (Breathe, Embody, Surrender, and Transform).

Take a deep breath.

You are okay. You are more than okay.

I promise. Breathe with me.

I know life is heavy right now.

It's stressful. It's hard. It's dark.

It's a lot.

It feels like the world is collapsing on top of you.

Maybe you're looking at your bank account, and you have nothing left, or worse, you're in negative and in the red, and it feels like you can't get ahead and don't know what you're going to do. Where the next payment is coming from. What you're doing.

Bills are piling up, and it all feels like you can't catch your breath.

Or maybe you've lost a loved one, and you can't seem to get out of bed.

Whatever you are facing right now, I want you to stop what you're doing.

Take a few deep breaths with me.

Close your eyes.

Deep inhale, and long exhale.

Do that four times.

Once you are done, open your eyes.

Let's say a prayer Heavenly Father:

"Heavenly Father,

I come before You today, feeling completely lost, unsure, and overwhelmed. My heart is heavy, and my spirit feels burdened. The weight of this world is pressing down on me, and I find myself struggling to keep going.

Lord, I feel exhausted—physically, emotionally, and mentally. It seems as though every step forward is met with another obstacle, and the light ahead seems so dim. My hope is flickering, and I fear it may be fading.

But I know that You are the God of all comfort, and I trust that You see me in this moment. You know my heart, my struggles, and my pain. I surrender all that I am to You, asking for Your strength to carry me through. Help me to remember that You are always with me, even when I feel alone.

Lord, reignite my hope. Fill me with Your peace that surpasses all understanding. Remind me that Your love never fails and that You are always working on my behalf, even when I cannot see it.

Grant me the courage to keep going, one step at a time. Restore my soul, renew my mind, and give me the strength to rise again. Help me to trust in Your timing, knowing that You are faithful and You will never leave me.

I place all my worries and burdens at Your feet, Father, and I trust that You will carry them for me. Thank You for Your grace and mercy, and for being my refuge and my strength in every moment of need.

In Jesus' name,
Amen."

Now that you've said this prayer, take another four deep breaths with me.

Four long inhales, and four long exhales.

Surrender it all to him. Our God is bigger.

Our God is the miracle worker.

Our God tells us to give our cares and worries to him. He strengthens us.

A scripture I love to meditate on is:

"I can do all things through Christ who strengthens me."
— Philippians 4:13 (NKJV)

Now that we have taken some deep breaths and have started to regulate our nervous system, let's breathe into God's peace.

Breathe deep.

This is the way we are meant to feel and function.

This is homeostasis.

I like to say, come home to yourself through the breath.

Breathe in God's peace and Surrender and exhale out all that you are holding.

All that is weighing you down. Let it go.

As you continue to breathe, let's meditate on the scripture above.

Inhale deeply through your nose, filling your lungs with air.

Exhale slowly through your mouth, releasing any tension in your body.

Now, bring your awareness to the present moment and let go of any distractions, worries, or burdens.

With each breath, focus on the truth of Philippians 4:13—"I can do all things through Christ who strengthens me."

Inhale deeply as you say to yourself silently, "I can do all things…"

Exhale slowly, releasing any fear or doubt, and say, "…through Christ…"

Inhale again, drawing in strength, and think, "…who strengthens me."

Exhale fully, trusting that God is with you in this moment and that He provides the strength you need.

Continue breathing deeply and slowly, allowing each breath to fill you with peace and confidence.

As you breathe, feel Christ's strength rising within you. Imagine His presence surrounding you, filling every part of you with courage, peace, and endurance.

Let each breath be a reminder that you are not alone, that Christ is your strength and your help.

You can face today every challenge with His power in you.

Inhale His strength… Exhale your doubts.

Inhale His peace… Exhale your worries.

Take one more deep breath.

Inhale all that Christ has for you.

Exhale, letting go of anything that no longer serves you.

When you're ready, slowly open your eyes, knowing that with Christ, you can do all things.

Let this practice be a reminder that no matter what you're facing, God is always with you, and His strength will carry you through.

Our breath is prayer, and prayer is breath God breathed life into us.

John 20:22:
"And with that, he breathed on them and said, 'Receive the Holy Spirit.'"

Jesus breathes His Spirit into His disciples, showing the connection between breath and the Holy Spirit.

When we center, breathe, and allow the Holy Spirit, we can surrender and move into prayer, which is where the miracles happen.

We leave our busy and noisy minds and allow God's peace and calm to enter our lives. We can even shift our frequency to heaven's frequency through deep breathing and meditating on God's word.

I know this isn't our normal reaction when we are in a panicking situation, but when we can get back to God's breath, I like to call our sacred breath, we can release our worries and fears. We can return to homeostasis, listen, and be guided by the Holy Spirit on how to move forward and thrive.

This is our natural state.

This is the way we flow.

This is our home.

God dwells within us. Always.

I hope and pray you have received the power of your breath in reading this chapter and doing the mini breathwork with me. I hope this inspires you to use your breath as prayer.

Breath is not just a vital, physiological process—it is a powerful tool for connection, transformation, and spiritual awakening. Through the practice of conscious breathing, I have learned to slow down, tune in, and open myself to a deeper sense of presence and purpose. Breathwork has served as a bridge, uniting my body, mind, and spirit in ways that I never thought possible. It has shifted my perspective, giving me the space to release stress, embrace stillness, and experience profound healing.

By viewing breath as prayer, I have discovered that each inhale is an opportunity to invite peace and clarity into my life, and every exhale is a chance to let go of what no longer serves me. This practice has not only grounded me in the present moment but has also helped me reconnect with a greater sense of meaning and divine flow with God himself.

As I continue to explore the depth of breath, I am reminded that prayer need not be confined to words or rituals; it is in the simplicity of the breath that we can find our truest expression of connection, gratitude, and grace. Through breathwork, I have found a new way to pray, to heal, and to live with intention. May this chapter serve as an invitation for you to discover the transformative power of your own breath and experience the profound shift that it can bring to your life. I pray that you continue on, do not give up, keep praying, keep breathing, and keep believing God is shifting it for you, and when you can ground in your breath, you can quiet all the noise, all the chaos and return to peace and the way God made you thrive!

Dr. Josette Ga-an

Founder of Dr Sleep Solutions

https://www.facebook.com/josette.gaan
https://www.instagram.com/the_options_ph/
https://drsleepsolutions.com/
https://drgaan.carrd.co/

Dr. Josette Ga-an is a board-certified dentist specializing in Airway Dentistry, Myofunctional Orthodontics, and Dental Sleep Medicine. She holds a Bachelor's degree in Biology and is a U.S. Certified Sleep Science Coach. With a deep passion for bridging oral health and overall wellness, Dr. Ga-an is the founder of Dr. Sleep Solutions, where she empowers patients to achieve better sleep and health through comprehensive dental and sleep strategies. Known for her compassion and dedication, Dr. Ga-an believes true healing comes from addressing the body, mind, and spirit. Her personal journey has taught her the importance of balancing clinical expertise with faith, and she continues to inspire others with her unwavering trust in the power of prayer in the healing process.

Between Forceps and Faith

By Dr. Josette Ga-an

The air was thick with the scent of antiseptic, and the soft hum of the dental drill created a symphony of anxiety in my clinic. As I approached the dental chair, I could see the apprehension etched on my patient's face—dentists are often regarded as one of the scariest professions. Yet, in those early years of my practice, it was my own fears that would soon take center stage. Today, I was prepared to perform a simple extraction, or so I thought.

I positioned myself with the precision I had practiced countless times, the bright overhead light casting shadows across the patient's anxious face. With each gentle pressure of the forceps, I could feel the familiar resistance of the tooth, a sensation I had grown accustomed to in my training.

As I applied a little pressure, the tooth easily came out. Ahh, relief washed over me; I had extracted it smoothly, and my patient's anxious expression began to soften. Just as I began to relax, savoring the small victory, I felt a chill run down my spine. A few minutes later, as I prepared to close the extraction site, I glanced down and saw something horrifying—the gauze I had used to control the bleeding was soaked through, the crimson color spreading like an alarming warning sign.

Panic gripped me as I realized that the bleeding had not subsided. My heart raced, and I quickly repositioned myself to assess the situation. Despite my earlier confidence, the sight of blood pooling was a stark reminder of the stakes involved in this profession. I recalled my training: apply pressure, stay calm, and act decisively.

Determined not to let fear take hold, I reached for the surgical tools and began to troubleshoot. I needed to innovate quickly. In this moment, my mind raced with potential solutions: additional sutures, hemostatic agents, or even a referral to a specialist. Every second felt like an eternity as I fought against the tide of anxiety, focusing on the task at hand.

This wasn't just a test of my skills; it was a defining moment in my journey as a dentist, pushing me to scale my abilities and embrace the challenges that lay ahead.

My mind raced as I weighed my options. I needed to transfer my patient to the nearest hospital or clinic that could handle the situation, but as I picked up the phone, my heart sank. The first few clinics I called were either closed or unable to take on new patients. The realization hit me hard: I was alone in this crisis, and time was slipping away.

"Stay with me," I said to my patient, forcing a reassuring smile despite the growing concern in my chest. "We're going to take care of this." I turned to my assistant, who was watching anxiously from the corner of the room. "Can you grab some ice cubes? We need to pack the area well and slow the bleeding."

This was the moment when my training would be put to the ultimate test. With a calm voice, "Just a little longer," I murmured to my patient, my voice steady despite the storm of uncertainty raging within me.

While my assistant packed the area with ice, I focused on staying calm. I could feel the weight of responsibility pressing down on me, knowing that every decision I made could impact my patient's well-being. I closed my eyes for a brief moment, whispering a silent prayer for guidance.

I took a deep breath, reminding myself that when all options are exhausted, the true answer lies in surrendering to faith. In that moment of chaos, I knew it was time to trust in something greater than my own abilities. We would find a way, but not through my expertise alone—this time, it would be through prayer and unwavering belief.

At that point, I closed my eyes and silently prayed, asking for guidance and strength. It was a humbling moment, realizing that no matter how skilled I was, I was not in control. There was a higher power at work, and I had to trust in that. Miraculously, peace washed over me, and the situation began to shift in ways I couldn't explain.

"Even in the most precise of clinical moments, there comes a time when we must step back, breathe, and let prayer do what medicine cannot."

I was a young dentist then, and the weight of the situation felt even heavier without an older, more experienced colleague to rely on. The pressure was immense, and I could have easily panicked, unsure of how to proceed. But instead, I leaned into prayer. It was in those silent moments of prayer that I felt a sense of guidance, as if I wasn't navigating this alone. The chaos slowly began to transform into calm. For five long hours, I stayed by my patient's side, canceling my next appointments, applying every method I knew, and trusting that I was being guided. Eventually, the bleeding subsided, and as her comfort returned, I realized that faith had carried us through where medical expertise alone couldn't.

Since that pivotal day, I've made it a habit to whisper a prayer before every procedure. It's a simple, silent moment, but it grounds me like nothing else. In that quiet space, I find the calm and confidence that no amount of skill or training can provide. Each time I'm reminded that I'm not navigating the challenges alone—that my faithful Savior is guiding my every move. That experience taught me that when things spiral into chaos, prayer is my anchor.

Today, maybe you're a medical practitioner, facing challenges and feeling the weight of responsibility pressing down on you. Maybe you're the patient, in need of help and unsure where to turn. No matter where you find yourself in this story, I hope it gives you the confidence to know that you are not alone. Whether it's in the operating room or in your daily life, God hears every prayer. He answers at the exact moment when you need it most. It may not come right away, and it may not be the answer you expect, but trust that His timing is perfect, and His help is always reliable.

The truth is, we all face moments of fear and uncertainty—moments when it feels like everything is spiraling out of control. It's easy to let panic set in when things seem hopeless, to let anxiety dictate our next steps. But the key is to remember that we don't have to face these challenges alone. Whether it's the fear of making a medical mistake or the fear of an unknown future, the answer is the same: Pray, don't panic.

In my practice, I've seen how fear can affect not just the patient but also the practitioner. We are often expected to be the calm in the storm, but there are times when we, too, feel overwhelmed. In those moments, I turn to prayer. I find that by letting go and surrendering, I'm able to access a peace that is beyond understanding. It's not that the challenges disappear, but that I am reminded that I don't have to carry them alone.

If you're a practitioner, struggling with the pressure of decisions and outcomes, remember: It's okay to admit when you're overwhelmed. It's okay to lean into faith when the answers aren't clear. And if you're a patient, facing a difficult diagnosis or a moment of fear, know that you are not forgotten. God is with you, guiding you, and providing the strength to face each day.

Every day, I am reminded that in the most difficult moments of life, it's not about our own strength—it's about knowing when to lean into something greater. It's about trusting that the path forward may not always be clear, but that with prayer, we can navigate even the toughest of situations.

So, whether you're facing a moment of medical uncertainty, dealing with a difficult personal situation, or just trying to get through the day, take a deep breath. Remember that you're not alone in this journey. Pray, don't panic. Trust in the power that goes beyond what we can see or understand, and know that God's timing and His answers are always perfect, always reliable.

Angela Chademunhu

Hope of Life International Ministry
Pastor

https://www.linkedin.com/in/angela-chademunhu-114bb1332/

Angela Chademunhu Is a Pastor by calling and a professional life coach, she is also a graduate in IT. She is the founder of "Hope of life" and "Women on her knees" a women's prayer movement. She started her career 15 years ago, it was during her experiences in the struggles of emerging in her pastoral calling as a young female pastor in a looked down upon environment that writing books was inspired. With the dream of becoming an acclaimed author, she is currently absorbed in her debut work. She is also a Philanthropist in Zimbabwe Africa. As a coach she has helped women who feel defeated and broken by life challenges experience a breakthrough, regain control and confidence so they make a lasting impact on the world. Positive handling of life experiences in her brought out virtues needed to co-author pray, don't panic, which is a theme and life attitude needed to be successful against all odds.

Overcoming in the Midst of Challenges

By Angela Chademunhu

Life in itself is a mission, knowingly or unknowingly, you are on an assignment here on earth. God did not bring you here on earth just to exist and die but for you to accomplish a particular purpose. It is "beneficiary" to you and your generation to discover your mission and fulfil it. Failure to fulfil your mandate deprives your generation of what they are meant to benefit from you. Life is indeed full of challenges/troubles. Nobody passes through this world without having to engage in one challenge or the other. Challenges of life vary from one individual to the other. Challenges come in different packages and also times of occurrence, but know for certain that life is full of challenges. In the book of Job 14v1 "Man that is born of a woman is of few days, and full of trouble" rightly sums up life. It is how you manoeuvre through life that matters.

In your quest to fulfil your purpose/mandate, you will meet obstacles/hurdles/challenges that will test your "stamina". I do not know about others, but for me, prayer has been my entry and exit plan always. I have no other option. Christians' culture romanticizes prayer and waiting on the Lord for an answer as if it is easy. While results from prayer are beautiful, the waiting is very agonizing, it is not every prayer that receives instant results, some have to wait for weeks/months/years before the answer comes. This generation is an instant "gratification" generation they used to instant products on the market. We have instant porridge, instant pudding, instant noodles, instant internet, and instant marriages so the subject of waiting in this generation is not understood. We are to pray and wait upon the Lord for answers in faith, hope, and love and never to panic.

What is prayer? Prayer is engaging with God, thereby granting him permission to interfere in human affairs. Prayer is the antidote against worry and cares of this world. Prayer is when divinity touches humanity. Prayer gives you the power to pursue your dreams. What is the meaning of the word panic? Panic means fear and discouragement henceforth, when somebody panics, the first thing they think of is to exit. So when we say "pray, do not panic," it means continue to pray in faith even when the odds are against you. When fear grips your heart, whatever prayer you make is not prayer but noise before God. The Bible says let us come before the throne of grace with boldness and confidence; this is what is expected of us as children of God.

"Pray When It Does Not Make Sense"

I remember an experience I had four years ago with a close friend of mine who was born with a heart disease. Life was not easy for her, she was in and out of hospital as she grew up. She fought against the odds, graduated from "university", got married, and gave birth to a son. She was a fighter all her life. Her life is an example of resilience and strength. Have you ever seen someone in a hurtful position while you are worried about them, and you discover she is stronger than you are, and they begin to counsel you? She was a happy woman who loved to make a difference in other people's lives: She served in her local church assembly as a Sunday school teacher. She was sold out for Jesus and took her services in serving God to deeper heights. She loved teaching children. She fell sick and was rushed to the hospital. She had many tests done on her and was told she had kidney failure. While she was trying to live with the new reality of having weekly dialysis, another tragedy befell with her liver also collapsed. In the midst of pain and the reality of hope diminishing, she never, even once spoke negatively about her condition. She had faith, we had faith, we prayed, and we never allowed panic to arise, even in the midst of bad medical reports that came our way.

As days passed, her condition worsened as she continued to deteriorate. Daily we prayed for her, believing and asking God for a miracle. I believed she would pull through. One faithful day, during my visit to the hospital, she spoke at length, her soft voice uttered words that broke my heart, but I had to hold it strong for her. She had accepted her fate and was ready to go. She told me God had not answered my prayers for her according to his will, and since there was nothing more to be done medically, she was ready to meet her maker. She had made peace with herself and God. She gave us money that we took to church as a thanksgiving seed, thanking God for the 40 years that God gifted her to live despite her heart condition. She thanked everyone who had helped her with funds to cushion her medical bills while in hospital. God saw she was getting tired and in so much pain and decided to end the agony and took her away. With tearful eyes, we watched her fade away. Although we loved her dearly, we could not make her stay. Her story taught me that so many times, we expect God to answer us according to the way we want. We wanted my friend to be healed, we wanted God to perform a miracle on her so we could testify how good our God is, but God answered us according to His will. I did not see my friend panicking in the face of death, she was calm and at peace and continued to pray without ceasing. She left us with so much pain. May the good Lord know that we are not complaining, we are just hurt.

Conquering Sickness

Cancer is one of the most deadly diseases, there are many people who have died due to cancer. We have cancer survivors, and we have fallen heroes who braved the cancer but could not make it and met their demise in the end. Whatever disease comes your way, you do not have to be scared "or" panic, do not let it break your faith or break your mood. In times of sickness, never allow the devil to succeed in stealing your joy. My uncle, from a tender age, suffered from tonsillitis. He was in and out of hospital, but the problem did not go away. He grew up as an adult still challenged in his health. Time passed, he married and had his own kids, still being a victim of tonsillitis. One day, tragedy befell his throat and began to trouble him before we knew he was hospitalized and diagnosed with cancer of the throat. What started as something minor became a huge mountain that was almost impossible to climb. He was told to undergo surgery to remove the growth in his throat and go through chemotherapy. After completing his chemotherapy sessions, the doctor declared him cancerfree. We all celebrated him, not knowing our celebration was premature. Exactly two years later, he suffered another setback the same throat cancer had resurrected and attacked him once more. The doctor told him there was no hope for him this time around. My uncle left the hospital in pain, with tears streaming down his cheeks, seeing the reality of what was about to happen. He did not panic. Crying is not a sign of weakness. It just shows us the reality of pain in us as human beings. He got home and locked himself in his room to digest the news and realized that his case was different, only God could help him and not mortal men. As days went by, it became difficult for him to swallow any food or drink liquids as the growth grew bigger. One day, in the midst of pain, he asked to be taken to church. There was no service, but he wanted some personal time with the Lord in prayer. When he got to church, he found some people also praying individually.

In Matthew 14 v 28-29 When Peter asked Jesus, "Can I come, unto thee on the water" he said "Come". Peter was innocent when he said it and came out of the boat and walked on water, this is how my uncle stepped out in faith and went out for prayer. He began to pray, and the pain increased in the throat, little did he understand that his deliverance had come. As the pain increased in his throat, he asked to be taken to the car so he could rest while waiting to be taken home. Uncle was now behaving like Peter, who, after walking, started thinking about many things and became distracted and in the end, was drowning, but Jesus Christ reached out and pulled him "out" Thus when my uncle stood up, he screamed from the pain and fell down, started coughing uncontrollably, and chunks of flesh and clots of blood came out of his throat. Like Peter, who called on Jesus, my uncle was not going to drown, his breakthrough had come. When the coughing stopped, he found himself surrounded by people in the church who had come to pray. Someone gave him a bottle of water to drink and to rinse his mouth. To his amazement or greatest shock, the pain in the throat was "gone". He was carried to the hospital with those clots of blood having been placed in a small container to show the doctor. After several tests, the doctor confirmed he was "cancer free and that was how he got his miracle healing. The problem with most of us is looking at the size of our problem and panicking without realising our God is bigger than our challenges. It's 10 years since my uncle was healed of cancer, and he is strong and healthy, still testifying to the goodness of the lord. I challenge you no matter how big your mountain looks, pray do not panic, God will level it for you if you stay consistent in prayer.

Why Are You Sad?

I am a young woman in her early 40's, I have a career, I am a pastor pastoring an assembly, I am a life coach, I am a philanthropist, I do not have much money, I have never been married and "have" no children. Not because I don't want to have my own family. It has been a dream for me. I basically did all the things I was told would lead to the life I dreamed of since being a little girl, but it just never happened. Sometimes I feel like no one understands this grief. Even though I thought I was going to have all the things by now, it just has not happened, but it does not mean it will not happen in the future. As a pastor, I have prayed for so many young women who wanted to get married, and the results have come"; each week, I see couples committing their lives to each other in beautiful wedding ceremonies, and while I love my life, there are moments when I feel sad. I had a health challenge that almost took my life. While going through that health challenge, I prayed for many sick people, and they received their healing whilst I was in pain, but God was faithful, and I was healed eventually. I have grieved many seasons of my life when things didn't work out.

Despite the setbacks I have encountered in my life, I have no reason to be sad, to be crying, to murmur against God.

What is making you sad? No matter what you are going through in life, someone has gone through that situation before. If you are to listen to other people's stories, you will find out people have gone through so many traumatic experiences that have left them devastated or broken. We are that generation that will put makeup and smile hard for Instagram pictures over pain. We smile, yet underneath, there are tears. Life has taught me that maturity sometimes comes through pain, failure, rejection, disrespect, heartbreaks, health challenges, etc., and not through age. Recently, a close relative asked me a question, "Why is it that you pray and are more committed to the things of God than all of us but we don't see much result in your life" At first, I took offence but something came into my spirit, "Have you ever sowed seeds on the ground and waited for its germination, growth and harvest, yet you do not see any of the stages of the plant". Just because the devil is not bothering you does not mean he is not bothering me, he is still pressing me hard, and I am pressing him hard, too, in prayer, and I know I will overcome.

The problem with most people in this world is expecting God to do what you want at your specific time, and failing to do so, we find ourselves at the receiving end, crying, murmuring, panicking, and hopeless in our faith journey. God knew that in our journey, we would meet obstacles that would challenge our faith and make us almost give up, panic and scared, but one thing is certain, he promised he would never leave us nor forsake us. The Bible tells us that Jesus wept, Jesus the Redeemer of mankind was once weary and cried, so it is human to cry; crying is not a sign of weakness but a sign of strength.

I am not embarrassed to tell my story, I live in prayer, and I pray about everything in my life. The Bible has told us to pray without ceasing and to pray in all seasons. When you do not like your situation, pray about it, and God will give you direction. In the face of adversity, I always look at the good side of every situation. When life serves you lemons, turn them into lemonade, accept life as it is and work towards changing it. I have prayed and God gave me direction in my life. My resilience in all situations has been the spark that ignites triumph/victory in my life. It was in the night season that I discovered my purpose. I did not know I could write books, this book is one of the two anthologies I am working on this year, and I have a solo project I am also working on. I started writing books and did not have an idea that my books would one day be published through She Rises Studios, an international publishing house in America, when I was in Zimbabwe, Africa, thanks to a friend who referred me to this amazing community.

I am now a certified coach who helps women who feel defeated and broken by life challenges experience a breakthrough, regain control and confidence, and make a lasting impact on the world. My positive handling of life experiences brought out virtues needed to co-author *Pray, Don't Panic*, which is a theme and life attitude needed to be successful against all odds.

I am a philanthropist; my work largely deals with widowed women and poor women who can hardly feed or raise children. I focus on helping with clothing, food, and school fees for children who cannot afford to go to school but want to advance in their education. I give out financial assistance for feasible projects to these women so they become self-sufficient and able to raise their own children. I advocate for financial independence. I support general life skills for the sustenance of the poor and less privileged. As a pastor, I focus on the development of a balanced, healed person. A healed spirit internally results in a healed being who is ready to face life challenges, experience, and regain control and confidence so they make a lasting impact on the world.

It takes stamina to stand in prayer and not panic while believing and waiting for the results. The waiting season is not a good place to be, it is a realm where you ask God for strength to pass through. You must treasure the scars you acquired along the journey of life, they will be anchors for your victory in the future and give you a place in destiny. Your crown will come from your scars. I show my scars so that others may see and learn and, in turn, recover their own destinies. When the chips are down, pray. When you are overwhelmed, "pray; going through grief, pray; going through crisis, pray; when you are not feeling well, pray; facing betrayal, pray; when you are happy, pray; when you are celebrating, pray.

Loretta Lee

Loretta Lee Limited
Entrepreneur, Carer, Business & Life Coach

https://www.linkedin.com/in/loretta-lee-pjk-mba-86519464/
https://www.facebook.com/DreamBigBreakRulesLiveFree
https://instagram.com/dreambigbreakruleslivefree
https://loretta-lee.com

Women Entrepreneurs caring for children with special needs hire me to grow their business while maintaining family stability because most struggle with balancing business demands and caregiving responsibilities. So, I help them create effective business strategies, reduce stress and ensure their child receives the best care.

Bottom line, they have a thriving business that can function without full-time intervention. They align their caregiving and family responsibilities while maintaining leadership in their business and creating the impact that they desire.

Loretta founded, coached and grew 3 companies to over 7 figures, the first to obtain ISO 9001 accreditation. Loretta is a sought-after coach, trainer and speaker in Business, management, leadership, personal development, and franchise development. She holds an MBA (MsM).

She was featured in the Star, Malaysia; Leicester Mercury; BBC Sounds and Asian Business magazine. She was awarded a PJK, by the Sultan of Selangor, for her contribution to the community.

Challenges Propelled My Growth

By Loretta Lee

You either resign, or I sack you!

I will always remember that meeting with my boss.

In 1982, I returned home from London to Malaysia after finishing my professional education in the United Kingdom. I scoured the newspapers looking for vacancies and applying for as many jobs as possible. My classmate, who returned about a year earlier, commented that there were loads of vacancies when he returned. Little did I know that it was the start of the recession. I wrote 68 application letters, all handwritten, as there was no email then. And the reply rate was about 10%.

My first job in Malaysia was in a glass factory in Johor Bahru, which is a city near Singapore. It was a big factory employing about 200–300 people.

I was the assistant accountant. My responsibilities included costing, accounting, preparing reports, payroll, stock-taking, and other tasks performed by the accounts department. I loved my job, and there was a lot to learn.

I was one of the few ladies in management and sometimes got invited to go out for lunch with the guys. The factory was located in an industrial zone. They would drive to town, and on the journey, they would point out the landmarks and properties owned by the rich and famous.

One day, we passed by some rows of multi-storey shops. I commented, "This building is three storeys. Wouldn't it be nice if I owned a building like that, multi-storey, with my name splashed across it?"

One of my colleagues commented, "Oh, Loretta! You really are ambitious!"

Me: "Don't you have ambition?"

Another said, "Yes, you are very ambitious!"

Me: "Don't you all have dreams? It is normal to have dreams. We need to have a goal or something big."

Another said, "Well, I used to have big dreams when I first graduated. I dreamt of making it big and being successful. After working for three years or so, I felt that I could not achieve my dream. I realized that it was just a dream and unattainable. So, there is no point in dreaming. It doesn't really matter. We just go with the system." I was shocked by the response. This guy was a professionally qualified engineer.

"Don't dream so big. You will be disappointed. You are naïve," said another.

That evening, I realized that I had to leave that company. I did not want to be with negative work colleagues. I left about two years later because I did not want my employment history to look bad.

The next job was as a Personal Assistant to the CEO of a Diversified Holding company. The pay was 60% more than my previous salary. It had many subsidiaries: in manufacturing, property development, trading, insurance, and others. I held a variety of roles, including legal contracts, marketing, systems, processes, and audits, I even started a new bakery.

I was the first and only lady on the management executive committee. My boss was famous for working late. I had been warned that the Exco meeting would end in the evening and be followed by dinner. That was the company culture, and people worked late because the boss liked it.

I had many lady colleagues. One of the ladies' friends was opening a hair salon in the new shopping complex in town. So, one day I decided to visit the hairdresser. However, the owner was not there. I did my hair anyway. I found out they have a salon in Petaling Jaya, a suburb of Kuala Lumpur.

One day, while working late, I went to the ladies'. While washing my hands, I noticed a face in the window. A peeping tom!

I screamed and ran out shouting, and I told my secretary. She advised me to report it to senior management. The next day I reported it, and there was an investigation.

During the investigation, I could not positively identify the peeping tom, and I decided not to pursue it. When my boss found out, he was livid! He accused me of wasting company time. The company was not doing well, and the investigation was a waste of time and resources. He accused me of making things up.

The next day, he called me to his office and told me that I should resign or he would sack me. I told my boss, "OK, I will resign if you can give me 3 good reasons why I should resign, based on my professionalism or lack of it." He could not even give me one. So, I stayed put. He sat me next to the photocopier. He did not give me any work. I did not budge. I suspected he instructed the rest of the staff to ignore me.

I continued to act like everything was normal. This went on for a few weeks. I felt so angry and frustrated; the world was so unfair. I felt ashamed. I felt even more frustrated when the boss sent a colleague to persuade me to leave, trying to convince me to give myself less headache. I said, "NO."

How dare he! I am the one who was wronged. I felt like the world was against me! No one deserves this! And I am now potentially jobless!

I have no one to turn to. I lived 725 km/450 miles from my family and did not have close friends. The feeling of being oppressed, wronged, and ridiculed, motivated me to fight this.

I went to the Labour office to get advice. I was told that as a management staff, I did not have any protection under the Labour law, except under The Industrial relations Act, 1967, Constructive Dismissal. I was advised to record everything that happened so that I would have ammunition should I want to take action against the company.

After a couple of weeks, The General Manager of the group came down from Kuala Lumpur to settle this matter. I told him that the boss did not want me here, and I did not want to work in a place where I was not wanted. I reminded him that for me to just leave would be so unfair. I asked for some extra payment to see me through until I could get another job.

We settled, I got a bit more money to live on, and I moved to Kuala Lumpur.

The pain of being unfairly dismissed never left me. It took me many years for the pain to go away. At that time, it consumed my everyday thoughts. It was the darkest period of my life. The memory kept running in my head, I cursed it, replayed it, and sometimes, nursed it. I have always been a positive person. I started reading self-development books when I was in my late teens. My faith in my own ability and myself kept me going; however, I was in a state of hell.

I joined a Singapore company that organized conferences and seminars. As a conference producer, I closed many speakers and events in the given time frame. Once, I closed eight speakers in a week, and like all things, it took me another two weeks to close another two speakers.

From being an accountant to a conference producer was like stepping into a different world! From dealing with figures and making rational decisions to copywriting! I loved the job as it gave me time to be out of the office for research and time in the office to be creative.

One day, I decided to visit the salon owner in Petaling Jaya. He did my hair. We had a good chat, and he introduced me to Buddhism. I had been looking for a religion or a philosophy that I could lean on in troubled times. I tried that while I was in Johor Bahru. I visited a few Buddhist centers. None of their philosophies resonated with me. I even tried vegetarian food, but I ended up with rashes.

He introduced me to Nam-myoho-renge-kyo[1] and showed me how to chant to the Gohonzon,[2] the object of worship. The Gohonzon was placed inside a box known as a Butsudan.[3]

Then, he lit the candle and incense, and I chanted Nam-myoho-renge-kyo.

He gave me some articles to read. It resonated with me. He invited me to a meeting held at the back of the salon. I found it quite fascinating. People came together to learn about Buddhism and were very open and friendly. They shared their life experiences. And I was hooked! I read more about this Buddhism, and it all made sense. I decided to start chanting. As I chanted, I noticed my life changed. People were more friendly to me. Even taxi drivers, many of whom I encountered were rude, are now friendly! The irritating rashes that I frequently had, and the perpetual feeling of 'under the weather' all disappeared! I knew this worked due to the actual proof that I experienced.

It was during this time that I faced another traumatic event. I had yet to get over the pain of the previous termination.

Again, due to the recession, the company had to downsize and they told me to leave by saying that I was not good at my job, I was not good at closing speakers, and all that.

I was offended as that was an insult to my professionalism. Anyway, I did not have a choice as they gave me my termination letter there and then.

Since this was not the first time, I did not panic. I decided to sue them for constructive dismissal. I got the best lawyer (attorney) who specialized in Labour Law (for the employee). This was due to my research when I worked as a conference producer.

The case took 18 months. The lawyer was in remission from cancer. My case was one of the last submissions before he passed. I won the case!

I have always wanted to have a business of my own since I was 14 years old. At that time, my life was controlled by others, which caused me pain. I want to be in charge of my own destiny. Whether I succeed or fail, it is up to me and I have no one to blame.

During this difficult period, I chanted and read a lot about Nichiren Buddhism. I chanted for wisdom, protection, and courage to do the right thing. Part of our practice is to add value to whatever we do. I took an active part in our Buddhist activities, initially learning as much as I could and, later on, supporting fellow young women. I was appointed a group leader.

I felt that I had to get out of the invisible shell that was holding me back. I decided that when I have my own business or company, I shall treat my employees with respect and dignity, follow the law, and make the company a great place to work.

I started as a sole proprietor. I rented a place in a shared office cramped with tables in a large commercial complex right in the heart of Kuala Lumpur. The office address was prestigious enough to mask my lone ranger pursuit.

I marketed my courses by direct mail. I remember typing a lot of business addresses on a donated old typewriter. I photocopied the addresses and cut and pasted them on the envelopes and stuff in the brochures. Then, I took them to the post office to post them in bulk.

My first few attempts at posting the brochures were difficult. I had to park in front of the bulk mailing section, which was congested and busy. I had to take the boxes to the counter, count them, pay for the mailing, and then leave. It was quite a hassle.

In Malaysia, there are a lot of public holidays. It was one of those forthcoming holidays that I decided to thank the guys who worked in that section. So, I brought them a card and a cake, to be shared by all of them. I thought nothing about it then.

In the following posting, I noticed that the guys were a bit more friendly. Some of the guys were talking about me. And I sussed out that they were pointing out to their colleagues that I was the one who gave them the cake!

The result was they treated me better by being more polite to me. After a while, my list got bigger and the mailing got bigger, too. I was allowed to drive into the compound to unload my mail, which made things much easier. The more times I gave them food (that was my way of saying thanks), the better I was treated. Later on, I was able to get sub-contractors to do the mailing for me.

The moral of the story is to treat people kindly and express your kindness. Sincerity opens hearts.

I remember receiving the first registration for my seminar. I felt like I was walking on air! I was so happy!! It was from a bank. My first seminar! I only had about 10 registrants. It went smoothly. It was still the recession, and I was pleased with it.

I met a business partner, and we formed a company. I was to do all the running while he held a senior corporate position. With a small capital, I started the new company with a part-time staff. I started with one programme a month, then two, then three.

I worked very hard. Some months I did not even pay myself. I know it sounds stupid. The motto now is to pay yourself first. However, I was not in a position to do that. Money was very tight. I remember my partner saying that I should be paid. But then, where to get the money to pay me? There was just not enough to do that, sometimes.

Building a company and a team takes time, dedication, and effort. Cash flow and uncertainty are the norm in business. It was very stressful.

When I traveled for business or holidays, upon return, my heart would pound when the plane circled the airport to descend. Coming home to the business was really stressful. I thought I was the only one that felt that way. When I checked with my Singapore business associates, they felt the same way, too. Running a business is not for the faint hearted.

Each time I faced a problem, I would chant and put effort into my Buddhist practice and my business as well. Chanting helps me to attain a higher life state and this assists me in making wise decisions. By taking part in Buddhist activities, and working on the business, there was always a way, a solution. I do not know what would become of me and the business if I had not taken faith in Buddhism.

I grew the company from a 1-person business to having 3 businesses and employing close to 30 people. My first company was Consembition Jaya Sdn Bhd. We produced conferences, seminars, and training programmes. It was a woman-led, women-managed company, the first company in Malaysia to get accredited to ISO 9001 certification in the training industry. We beat all the large companies and training subsidiaries of large companies like Shell, Esso, Petronas, Maybank, and publicly listed companies. We were registered with the then Human Resource Development Council, which meant that the training cost was claimable by the employers. I became a corporate trainer, too.

My second company Peplow-Warren Sdn Bhd was a Quality Management Consultancy that helped companies get accredited to ISO 9000. We served the production, engineering, services, food, manufacturing and other industries.

And the third one, Techno Regional Training Sdn Bhd, offered certification courses, and we were the first to bring the British Standards Institute Auditor Training course to Malaysia.

I grew the business to seven figures.

I would like to share this quotation:

> *"The real struggle in life is with ourselves. The true secret of success is the refusal to give up, the refusal to fail; it lies in the struggle to win the battle against one's own weaknesses."* —Daisaku Ikeda[4]

I remember the time when I had already paid the deposit for my office building. Some of my staff were not able or willing to travel to the new office, and a few of them informed me that they would not be moving with me. I accepted that it was not for everyone.

Later, I sensed that something was not right with the team. I had built a brilliant team—effective, open, working like clockwork, everybody was having fun, work was done, and projects were implemented quickly. Now, the production of the conferences and seminars was delayed. I could sense a reluctance to get things done in some of them.

One day, I decided to check some of their desks. I found evidence of a few of them planning to start a business—the same business as me! They were using company time to contact and deal with the speakers and do all the work. There were minutes of their meetings, the seminars that they were planning, the copywriting, and even the advertisements they planned to do. There were invitations to a celebratory BYO party for the occasion. All this while still getting paid by me!

I had no choice but to confiscate the documents. The manager and three producers were involved. I trusted her as she was a very professional person. Unfortunately, greed took over her.

This was big! I did not know what to do! They left and claimed unfair dismissal, and I had to go to the Labour office to settle the cases.

I did not fight the cases in the Labour office. My sister, who was my assistant, was surprised as she knew me as a fighter. I told her I had a bigger fish to fry, which was my In-Vitro Fertilization treatment.

They were not able to claim as much as they wanted due to my past experience in unfair dismissal. I did not break the law. In fact, I withheld their salary and leave pay as bargaining tools. There were four cases. The Conference Manager and one Conference Producer settled the matter with the assistance of the Labour Office without me losing any money, I only paid them what was due. I even gave the Conference Manager her insurance policy that was bought as a retirement plan/golden handshake.

Another Conference Producer decided to sue me in the small claims court. Her case was dismissed. She faked a lawyer's (attorney) letter of demand.

The third Conference Producer sued the company, which has not been resolved until today. She has yet to get her case heard.

Prior to this saga, one of the administrators decided to resign. She gave the resignation letter and then decided not to turn up for work without any reason or informing the company. She then demanded that she be paid her salary, payment in lieu of notice, and a bonus. The bonus was not contractual. I stood firm. She sued the company.

After many court appearances, she could only claim the money due to her for the notice period. In my lawyer's opinion, she was trying to get as much money as she could because she knew the company was doing well.

I learned that one should not just take things lying down. One must actively fight for one's reputation and justice. If false information is not checked or rebutted, it will become the truth.

Did any of my former staff win? I don't think so. I used their brochure copy and advertised my programmes, using their ad copy so that they could not use that in their business.

The goal of owning my own office building was always at the back of my mind; I did not write it down. The purchase of the building was also fraught with delays. We moved to the new premises in 1995. It was also the year we got our ISO 9001 accreditation. It was a long eventful journey, and finally, my own four and a half-storey building with my company name splashed over it!

Dream Achieved!

I learned the importance of moving one step at a time. It's challenging to keep up the long fight to realize all our dreams and goals.

I would like to share this quotation:

Be diligent in developing your faith until the last moment of your life. Otherwise, you will have regrets. For example, the journey from Kamakura to Kyoto takes twelve days. If you travel for eleven but stop with only one day remaining, how can you admire the moon over the capital?
—"Letter to Niike," The Writings of Nichiren Daishonin[5], *vol. 1, p. 1027*

I am grateful for this practice, which has allowed me to grow and be the best person that I can be.

Note:

All the experiences and views in this story are entirely mine and do not represent SGI or its members.

Foot Note:

1. Nam-myoho-renge-kyo

    The fundamental Law that pervades the entire universe and all life. Myoho-renge-kyo is the full title of the Lotus Sutra in Japanese and literally translates as 'The Lotus Sutra of the Wonderful (Mystic)

Law'. We believe that chanting this phrase (also known as Daimoku) enables us to bring the qualities of the Buddha to our lives.

Nam - meaning 'to dedicate one's life

Myoho - the Mystic Law

Renge - the lotus flower and

Kyo - meaning Sutra, or writings.

2. Gohonzon

    Members of SGI carry out their daily practice of chanting to a scroll which is a visual representation of the life-state of Buddhahood inscribed by Nichiren Daishonin.

3. Butsudan

    A Butsudan is a protective enclosure in which the Gohonzon is enshrined in Nichiren Buddhism.

4. Daisaku Ikeda (1928–2023)

    was a <u>Buddhist philosopher</u>, <u>peacebuilder</u>, <u>educator</u>, <u>author and poet</u> who dedicated his life to fostering a lasting culture of peace through dialogue. As the third president of the Soka Gakkai Buddhist organization, founding president of the Soka Gakkai International (SGI), and founder of several international institutions promoting <u>peace, culture, and education</u>, he championed the power of dialogue as a central means to addressing global challenges.

5. Nichiren Daishonin (1222–1282) - Nichiren Daishonin was born in a small village in Japan, and he and his family earned their livelihood from fishing. At the age of 12, he began his schooling at a nearby temple. During this period, he made a vow to become the wisest person in Japan. He later traveled to the main centers of Buddhist learning, and his studies led him to confirm that the Lotus

Sutra is the foremost among all the Buddhist sutras and that the Law of Nam-myoho-renge-kyo is the essence of the sutra and provides the means for transforming the suffering of individual people and society as a whole. We consider Nichiren Daishonin to be the Buddha for our age.

Dr. Elizabeth Pritchard

Co-Founder of WALT Institute Pty Ltd
Authentic Leadership Coach

https://www.linkedin.com/in/dr-elizabeth-pritchard/
https://www.facebook.com/DrElizabethP
https://www.waltinstitute.com/

Dr. Elizabeth Pritchard, is a distinguished international keynote speaker, researcher, authors and Authentic Leadership coach from Aotearoa, New Zealand, currently based in Melbourne, Australia. She is a trailblazer in cultivating Authentic Leadership among women executives and leaders, globally. As Co-founder and Director of the WALT Institute (Women Authentic Leadership Training Institute), Elizabeth's three-decade career spans neuroscience, leadership, and research.

Her journey, marked by overcoming self-doubt, childhood adversity and extensive health struggles, serves as a testament to resilience and transformation that is possible, for anyone. Through dedicated growth and learning, in the academic and personal development spaces, she has honed her expertise in Authentic Leadership, navigating challenges, and empowering others to do the same. Elizabeth serves as an inspiration for women across the world, to discover their influential voice and lead themselves and others towards self-fulfillment and true success.

From Shadows to Light: Transforming Fear into Freedom

By Dr. Elizabeth Pritchard

The Brick Wall

In 2002 I hit an emotional, physical and mental brick wall. It was HUGE. It was all-encompassing and totally stopped me in my tracks, lasting for several months. I was a health professional, a mum, a wife, a master's student, a daughter-in-law, and a friend, yet I was unable to summon the momentum to function. I was unable to get out of bed. Unable to fulfil any of my roles in life, unable to look after my family (two girls aged 15 and 12) or myself. I needed to totally rely on others for every single aspect of life, from personal hygiene to nutrition, to any decision needing to be made.

The only thing I could do was feel despair, panic and grief. It was an incredibly dark place and one where I could not even imagine living beyond the fog. A place filled with unknowns, medication, fear, sadness, guilt and deep pain. A place of loneliness, being alone, being misunderstood, locked in a darkness so overpowering, that I constantly thought about how to end the pain I was inflicting on my family each day.

The only glimmer of hope I had in the depths of this darkness, was that this *must* get better. That this pain couldn't last forever, could it? There *must* be something I could do, to take even a shuffling step forward and stumble through the fog, to find some degree of solace. Finally, after many, many weeks, I was able to see a glint of hope beyond the gloom as I reached out to a skilled professional and slowly – oh so slowly, began to rebuild my mind, body and emotional strength. It took all of my skill, willpower, grit and determination, to begin this long arduous journey.

Recovery Is a Must We Can Choose

Recovery from this acute and traumatic setback has taken me many years. It was almost a decade before I could say I am strong and KNOW I will never go back there again. The doctors told me I would always "suffer from bouts of depression", that I would "always need medication because of the extent of the episode". Even though the diagnosis of severe depression was real and true, I decided I would not accept their prognosis. I decided that I would be the one who determined my future level of mental and emotional health, and I would not live with the fear of this limiting prognosis. I decided I would not resolve myself to a life that was dictated or pre-destined by pain, panic attacks, depression, medication and hurt. I would choose to be the director of my life and rise up to create the destiny that I wanted to experience. And so, I did.

This episode of burnout, which was diagnosed as severe clinical depression, occurred because of the levels of stress I had in my life, my ineffective ways of recognising stress and my inability to do something about it. It occurred because of my default patterns of thinking, believing and acting that were unconscious to me, and ones that I had never looked at with curiosity or inquiry.

This is not to attribute blame, this is simply to determine the reality and truth of the situation with honesty and clarity. I did not know how to effectively recognise or manage stress, how to regulate my emotions, choose my mindset, prevent the spiral, or shift towards living a happy and fulfilled life. I thought I was powerless. I believed that the current situations and past experiences controlled me, and that was "just the way it was". I believed that I had no control over my life, that it was predetermined, and would play out the way it was ordained, and that I had nothing to do with the direction of it. Oh, what a set of false beliefs this is, which created a life based on fear, lack and anxiety.

Fear in the Driver's Seat

The youngest of nine children brought up in a very strict, conservative Christian family, I lived my life in fear. Fear of being seen, fear of speaking up, fear of doing things wrong, fear of being punished for thinking or doing wrong, and fear of being rejected. I made sense of the world by thinking my opinions didn't matter. I learned to toe the line, not ask questions and not rock the boat. I learned to accept the adage of "children should be seen and not heard", and get on with being part of a noisy, conservative and, at times, fun family. This all led me to develop the beliefs and patterns that I built my life on, "I am not enough", "I am not allowed a voice". Don't get me wrong, my parents loved each of us dearly, sacrificed absolutely everything they had for their family and only wanted the very best for each of us, yet despite their best intentions and a strong religious faith, my parents could not always keep me safe.

I was driven by the fear of not fitting in, the fear of not being accepted and the void of thinking I was unworthy. I believed I had to be all things to all other people first, before even slightly contemplating what I wanted for myself. Be the high achiever, be the super-mum, the amazing work colleague, the best music director, the most caring and supportive wife and daughter-in-law. Yet despite all my "achievements", I constantly felt I was not good enough, that I was failing and did not meet my own, or other people's expectations, no matter how hard I pushed myself or what I was involved in – it was not enough.

I believed that **I** was not enough.

I allowed fear to take up residence in the driver's seat (Elizabeth Gilbert) and dictate every step of my life. I had not yet learned that "other people's opinion of me is none of my business" (Lisa Nicholls). I had not yet learned that I did not need other people's approval. I had not yet learned to give myself approval, validation and the belief that *I AM ENOUGH.* I had not yet learned that I did not have to Be or Do anything different to experience this level of enough-ness. I have since learned that by the simple fact of being, living and breathing on this planet (apparently a one in over four trillion chance), **I am enough** and always will be and that enough-ness has absolutely nothing to do with what I *do* or what I *have*!

The Toughest Stuff

As with all our lives, our past experiences shape what we think and do, if we let them! When I was 8 years old, I was sexually abused by a person who was our surrogate grandad. A situation that I did not know how to respond to, or even talk about until many years later. A situation where I unconsciously withdrew from my parents because, as I worked out decades later, I believed my mum didn't love me enough to even notice such a catastrophic event had happened to me. I knew that I felt different and that my behaviour was different, but being that young, I didn't have the words, understanding, or method to share this with anyone. So, I shoved it down inside of me into that deep shameful void that fed the monster of fear. As an adult looking back, I realise that my mum kept me safe from there onwards, and I was never, ever alone with that person again.

This event deeply affected and shaped me, as would be expected, however, as I look at the event through my eyes now, as a 61-year-old strong, vivacious and dynamic woman, I am grateful for all that I have learned from that event. I have learnt that "my past does not define me". I am not my past, nor do I need to cling to the suffering of my past. I have learnt that I get to attribute any meaning I choose to a situation, and that includes ANY situation that comes across my path today or that I have already experienced. As ugly and life-changing as sexual abuse was for me and is for anyone who has experienced this, as an adult, **I get to choose** how I think about this event. I get to choose how I think about the perpetrator, and whether or not I choose to stay sitting in the pain. I get to choose if I stay tethered to the fear and suffering of holding onto the emotions around that event experienced as an 8-year-old, or see it as an event in the past to which I am strong and courageous enough to release my grip off it, and recognise it as simply a part of the rich tapestry of my life.

If I stay sitting in the hate, blame or even shame of the situation and events that followed, then I am tying myself to 'his' actions. His darkness, his disgusting behaviour, his abuse of power. Yet, when I attribute the meaning of neutrality and lightness to the event, I am releasing myself from the spiral of hurt, anxiety and despair. I am not letting him off the hook for what he did – hell no! I am choosing my response to the situation. I am looking after myself, I am preserving my mental health, I am disconnecting and severing the cord of hate, fear and panic that was once connected to the event that I held tightly for so many years. And in releasing my grip, I am able to rise above the ugliness of the situation and feel a sense of freedom and lightness.

I choose the path of liberation and freedom. Freedom from the negative emotions that I attributed to the event. Freedom from the self-blame that I put upon myself for "allowing it to happen". We all know that this is simply the mind of an 8-year-old who has ABSOLUTELY no fault or part to play in being abused by a perpetrator who obliterated the trust of a child, as someone they believed would protect them. We know the fault is 100% squarely and totally on his shoulders, and there is never any blame or shame to be placed on a child's innocence and beauty, in this situation.

But to move through this experience and be able to bounce FORWARD with resilience (not just back to the same place I was in before), I must choose a different narrative and response. One that serves ME. One that releases ME. One that sets me up to be free from the evil act that occurred.

FEAR – False Evidence Appearing Real

What if FEAR is just False Evidence Appearing Real? Notice the emphasis on FALSE – the meaning I have attributed to the situation or experience is simply a meaning I have chosen in that moment – I have created it as my own reality. I have chosen the meaning, the words, the narrative, the story that I have given to a specific situation, and this becomes my reality. What if I choose a different reality? What if I choose a different narrative about my mum: "My mum DID love me dearly and, from that moment on, protected me from ever being at that person's place alone again". What if I choose the meaning of a diagnosis of severe clinical depression to be: "I was given the diagnosis of clinical depression, which was the beautiful catalyst for me to begin questioning my beliefs and rigid thoughts that held me trapped, and allowed me to begin the journey of becoming whole and move towards finding a life of fulfilment and joy".

You Get to Choose!

What if I choose to believe that every single event in my life (*all* of them!) has forged the strong, capable woman I am today and that without these experiences, I would not be able to experience the height, depth, colour and richness of who I AM, and therefore I would have been sentenced to a life of beige, mediocrity and unhappiness.

This is how I view myself now. I accept every situation that has occurred, as a precious gift for me to learn more about myself and who I get to BE every day.

You also get to choose. Within every moment of every day, you get to choose your response. Recognising this choice does not excuse what other people do or say, but what it does is stop the cords that shackle you to them, to their hate, to their deeds, to their anger, to their words, or to their unkindness. Whatever the situation, you get to make the powerful choice, to put YOU first, and sever the emotional ties of that situation from you, forever! This allows YOU to walk free. To rise up from the pain and hurt. To set your sights on here and now, and the pathway forward, rather than always looking back to the pain and ugliness of events that once were.

From Shadows into Light

I chose to step out of the shadows and into the light. Two things that helped me move from the shadows into the light were learning the art of reflection (noticing my thoughts and responses, without blame, shame, guilt or judgement) and the practice of meditation. To me, this is my way of praying. This is my way of connecting with the universe, the source that is bigger than me and always has my back. This is my way of finding fulfilment in my life and living a life that is full of greatness, gratitude, abundance, love and goodness. Meditation is a place that shifts my focus from the external things where people control and pressure me, to internal things where I create calm and strength. Where I find the space that allows me to breathe, rest and be still, amidst whatever is happening in my day.

One specific method of meditation that has helped me sever the tenuous strands of fear from my past experiences and step into the light is cord-cutting meditation. Many people use this imagery in meditation to bring relief, freedom and release from the energy of past events, and I share my version with you in the hope that you, too, can use this to cut the cords of those situations and people you feel are holding you back. Download your free version, here: https://bit.ly/waltinstitute_cordcutting

Transformation Is Possible

Transforming fear into freedom is the ultimate gift I give myself, every day. It happens in the moment when I realise I am overthinking something, when I am beginning to focus on lack instead of abundance, or when I am beginning to head down the spiral of negativity and self-blame again. When I feel myself getting defensive because I have judged myself or another person. When I have set expectations of myself or others at a height that is impossible to reach, and therefore, have set myself up to feel the fear of failure or regret.

When I set myself up each day through meditation and set my intention to be free and flow through the day with grace and ease, whatever happens, this is exactly what occurs. This stuff works. It is not a pie in the sky, positive thinking BS. This is about what I choose to focus on, the meaning I choose to attribute to things, and the thoughts I choose to have. All of these choices then release the positive 'happy' chemicals in my body (dopamine, oxytocin, serotonin, endorphins) that I interpret as emotions, which fill up my cup and allow me to choose what actions I do next.

Unleash This Strategy Yourself!

Never again, will I stay stuck in the emotions of past events, or keep bouncing back to the same horrible place as before. I get to release the hold of past events every day, embrace the future and keep growing and changing, one tiny tweak at a time! I choose to step into the light.

You can also use these strategies! It does not mean that you won't go through the tough stuff. It does not mean that life will be all roses and unicorns. What it does mean, is that you will know that you get to choose the meaning you give to any situation. You get to choose the narrative you put to the events. You get to choose to find a way through the situation and bounce FORWARD with resilience and personal power! You get to choose to become the director of your life! I hope you choose this path from shadows to light too!

When you believe 'I AM ENOUGH' and shine *your* light bright (regardless of the situation you have had the gift of experiencing), you show the path for those behind you who are still confused or lost. You 'get to' then walk in front or alongside them and help them embrace their truth that "I am enough". You get to lead the way and show them how you reclaimed YOUR power and walked from the shadows into the light, triumphant!

Anastasia Mouzina

Founder of Goddess World, LLC

https://www.linkedin.com/in/anastasia-mouzina/
https://www.facebook.com/anastasia.mouzina.37
https://www.instagram.com/anastasiamouzina/
https://anastasiamouzina.com/

Anastasia, originally from Greece and now based in Florida, is a seasoned expert in advanced transformational techniques with a focus on integrating mind, body, and spirit. She is the founder of the Neurospiritual™ Framework, a unique approach that combines neuroscience and spirituality to help individuals overcome barriers and achieve their highest potential.

With a Master's in Metaphysical Psychology and certifications as a Mental Health Counselor, NLP and Hypnosis practitioner, Reiki Master, and Kundalini Yoga teacher, Anastasia offers a holistic approach to personal and professional growth. Her expertise also extends to business coaching and project management, where she helps entrepreneurs and high achievers translate their visions into reality.

Anastasia is dedicated to empowering others through her workshops, retreats, public speaking engagements, and upcoming book and podcasts.

Faith, Fear, and the Call to Lead

By Anastasia Mouzina

My Journey to Divine Connection

"Faith is daring the soul to go beyond what the eyes can see."
—William Newton Clark

To write this chapter, I had to travel back in time to remember who I was and the transformation over the last few years. It brings tears to my eyes, and I am in awe of how I did all this. I cannot believe it!

But let's start from the beginning.

I still remember the day I decided to apply for the Green Card lottery.

The Green Card lottery isn't something that many people around me in Greece were even aware of at the time. For most, it sounded like a far-fetched dream akin to chasing the stars. But for me, it was a calling.

Since I was young, I have dreamed of coming to and living in the USA. I didn't know exactly why; it was just there.

When I was nineteen, I told my mother I wanted to leave, but my dreams were not met with much encouragement.

Quite the opposite. And don't take me wrong. I am not the kind of person you can stop if I want to do something. However, Greece was different then, and family bonds were very strong. I felt guilty about pursuing my dream, but I never forgot it…

Or it wasn't yet the time.

After two marriages, two divorces, three kids, and my third marriage, it seemed like I was ready. Lol! The day I decided to apply for the Green Card lottery was the day I chose to bet on the unseen. This wasn't anymore a personal dream; it was about my family—my three boys and my husband. Together, we had built a life in Greece filled with love, laughter, and stability.

But something deep inside me knew there was more out there, something waiting for us beyond the borders we knew. It wasn't about dissatisfaction but a yearning for expansion, for growth. The moment I hit "submit" on the application, it felt like I was sending a message to the universe on behalf of my entire family: *We are ready for more.*

This decision was not taken lightly. It was a quiet yet powerful moment of surrender—an act of faith in which I placed my (our) future in the hands of something greater than myself.

My boys, full of life and curiosity, deserved every opportunity in the world. My husband, my rock, stood beside me, supportive and optimistic, but we both knew the path ahead would be filled with unknowns. We just never imagined how quickly those unknowns would start unfolding.

The Moment of Surrender

> *"Miracles are not in opposition to nature but only in opposition to what we know about nature."* —St. Augustine.

Four years have passed since my application was submitted again every year. I applied for ten years to play in the lottery.

For years, I felt like I had one foot firmly planted in Greece while the other was already stepping onto foreign soil, yearning for a new life in the United States.

There were moments during those four years when I wanted it so badly that it caused me physical pain. The idea that I might never win, that I might have to give up on this dream, gnawed at me daily. The desire wasn't just in my heart but in my bones. I was ready to move forward, but every year that passed without winning felt like a door slowly closing.

One night, lying in bed, exhausted by the internal tug-of-war, I decided to let it go. But before I could completely release the dream, I turned to the only Source I knew. I spoke to my higher self and God, asking for guidance. I said, "Please, if it is for the good of my family and me, let me win. I will forget the whole thing if it's not meant to be."

And then, I added something more. I asked for a sign. Not just any sign—a sign so clear that I couldn't possibly miss it. I needed undeniable confirmation from the universe that this dream was meant to manifest, or else I was ready to let it go and move on with my life in Greece.

The Universe Responds

> *"When you want something, all the universe conspires in helping you to achieve it." —Paulo Coelho.*

The very next day, I was with my middle son at a travel agency to book tickets for a trip that had been planned months earlier. We were preparing to travel to San Francisco to explore business opportunities. We had set everything in motion, and it felt like the logical next step. Little did I know that life had something else in store for me.

My phone rang as I stood at the counter, arranging our travel plans. I didn't think much of it at first, but when I answered, everything changed. A voice on the other end asked for my name, and then, in what felt like the most surreal moment of my life, they told me I had won the Green Card lottery.

I couldn't believe it. My body reacted before my mind could process what was happening. I screamed, tears pouring down my face, and in an instant, I dropped to my knees, overwhelmed by the magnitude of the moment. Every fear and doubt seemed to dissolve as I whispered, "I received the message. Thank you!" It was the sign I had asked for—the impossible-to-miss confirmation that this dream was meant to be.

At that moment, I knew, without a shadow of a doubt, that we were on the right path. The doors had been opened for me and my family, and all that was left was to step through them.

Takeaway: Life offers you gifts when you least expect them, but they come wrapped in the challenge of the unknown.

The Weight of the Miracle

> *"You must find the place inside yourself where nothing is impossible." —Deepak Chopra*

With this miracle came a profound sense of responsibility. I knew that winning the Green Card was not just a stroke of luck—it was an invitation, a directive. The universe had given us a path, but now it was up to us to walk it. My husband, my three boys, and I prepared ourselves for the biggest leap of our lives.

But wait... Life had some more challenges!

Just days after discovering that I had won the Green Card lottery—a moment that felt like divine confirmation of the future I had dreamed of—I received news that would challenge everything: my mother had been diagnosed with stage 4 cancer. Our relationship had been complicated, marked by distance and closeness, yet we have started to bridge that gap in the last few years. Now, with her diagnosis, I faced a choice that tore at my heart: to step into the life I had prayed for in the U.S. or to stay by her side as she confronted the hardest chapter of her life. I wrestled with the decision in silence, my heart torn between my family's future or staying by her side through the final, most difficult chapter of her life.

I ultimately decided to move to the U.S. (because the sign from the Source was clear), carrying hope and a deep sense of loss. Yet, nine months later, I returned to Greece to be with her through her final two months, a time that allowed us to connect in ways we never had before. I stayed by her side up to her very last breath, and in those quiet, profound moments, I felt the presence of a love that transcended all of our past struggles. Her passing was a profound loss for me, and now grief has added to the overall challenge.

Saying goodbye to family and friends was heart-wrenching, and I'll never forget my mother's tear-filled eyes as we hugged one last time at the door.

She then took a bucket of water and spilled it behind us. Spilling water for luck is an old custom tradition. We spill water behind the person who goes on a journey for good luck, and everything goes smoothly, like the flow of the water. It hurts. Yet, there was a fire in me that burned brighter than the fear. I had to believe this move was for the best—for my children, husband, and me.

Leaving Greece was like closing a beloved book halfway through. Every goodbye to family and friends felt like tearing away a piece of myself. I was leaving behind the identity I had built, the comfort and familiarity of home, and the support of those who knew me best. The ache in my heart was deep, but I knew I couldn't let it hold me back. We were meant to live this life, and every ounce of pain was simply the price we paid for growth.

As we boarded the plane, my heart raced with a mix of excitement, fear, and loss. We were stepping into a new world, a blank slate, a chance to start over.

We were about to change in ways we couldn't fully comprehend, and leaving wasn't easy. Greece was more than just a country to us—it was the land that shaped our family, traditions, and values.

I remember the last few weeks in Greece being a whirlwind of emotions. Along with the excitement came the fear—fear of the unknown, fear of failure, fear of leaving behind the life we had built. We were stepping into uncharted territory with no guarantees of success. But if there was one thing I had learned through this process, it was that faith requires you to leap before you see the landing.

I often found myself asking: *Can I do this?* Can we uproot our entire family and begin again? But every time doubt crept in, the voice of faith was louder. We were meant to take this step. The journey wasn't about surviving; it was about thriving and creating a new life for our family filled with endless possibilities.

The First Steps Toward a New Life

The first days in the U.S. were far from the dream I had imagined. The streets were unfamiliar, the language barriers real, and the system often seemed like a maze with no clear exits. Loneliness creeps in quickly when everything around you feels foreign—when every task, even something as simple as grocery shopping, requires twice the effort.

The day we landed in Florida, everything felt surreal. The sun was shining, and the warmth of the air welcomed us. But there was no time to bask in the glow of our arrival. Life was waiting for us to build from scratch.

We lived in a hotel room for two weeks, trying to find a house to rent. We had no credit history or score. When finally an Italian homeowner decided to rent us the house asked for five rents ahead.

There was no other choice. We paid five rents, which greatly limited our startup money!

Our apartment was bare. We had a sofa and a bed but little else. It was a new world—new systems to navigate, a new culture to adapt to, and a new way of living that felt exciting and terrifying. But I was determined to make it work.

In my moments of doubt, I realized that vulnerability is not a weakness but a portal to growth. Every challenge forced me to stretch beyond my limitations, to unearth resources within myself that I didn't even know existed. I began to trust that the same force that had delivered the Green Card into my hands would guide me through the turbulence of starting over.

The journey taught me that resilience isn't about holding your breath until the storm passes—it's about learning to breathe in the storm.

> *"Vulnerability is not winning or losing; it's having the courage to show up and be seen when we have no control over the outcome."*
> —Brené Brown

Hurricane Irma: A Baptism of Resilience

Then, just 20 days after we arrived, Hurricane Irma hit.

I had never heard of a hurricane before. Back in Greece, natural disasters of this magnitude were stories you heard from afar, not something you lived through. But here we were, fresh in a new country, barely settled, and suddenly facing a storm that sent the entire state into panic mode.

The storm ripped through Florida with a force I wasn't prepared for. We had no idea how to protect ourselves. We had just a sofa and a bed; in the aftermath, we were left without power for ten days. Ten days of heat, uncertainty, and darkness. I remember lying awake at night, wondering if this was a sign that we had made a terrible mistake. My boys, scared but resilient, looked to me for strength, and I knew I couldn't show fear.

But those days without power did something extraordinary—they stripped away every illusion of control. The hurricane humbled me and brought me to my knees in a way I hadn't expected. When the future seemed uncertain in those moments of darkness, I learned to let go of the ego's need for safety and certainty. I learned to surrender.

We were stripped down to the basics—no electricity, no luxuries, just our family, huddled together, finding strength in each other. During those ten days, I understood something profound: the miracle of our journey wasn't just about winning the Green Card. It was about learning to trust that even in the storm, we would be okay.

I closed my eyes, took a deep breath, and began to pray. But this time, it was different. This wasn't a prayer for answers or solutions but for calm, peace, and the strength to trust that we would be okay whatever happened. I let the words flow without holding back, speaking from the most vulnerable parts of myself.

"Please, show me how to find strength. Help me see beyond this fear. Guide me back to the peace I know is within me, somewhere."

As I whispered these words, something inside me shifted. It was subtle, like a gentle exhale, but the panic began to lose its grip. My heartbeat steadied, and a warmth filled me, a sense that I was not alone in this journey. It was as though, in that quiet surrender, I had tapped into a well of resilience that had always been there but had been clouded by fear.

In that moment, I realized that prayer wasn't just about asking for what I wanted; it was about creating space to let go, trust, and reconnect with a strength greater than my own.

> *"The function of prayer is not to influence God, but rather to change the nature of the one who prays."*
> —Søren Kierkegaard

Humility in Work: Smashing the Ego

Even after the hurricane passed, the challenges didn't end. I quickly realized that building a life here would take more than just a stroke of luck. We needed jobs, money, and stability—and none of that was guaranteed.

The practicalities of building a life in the U.S. were far more challenging than I had anticipated. Back in Greece, I had built a career, an identity, a level of respect. But here, in this new world, none of that mattered. There were bills to pay and mouths to feed, and I quickly realized that starting over meant swallowing my pride. I had to take whatever work I could find, and that's how I ended up working as a bartender.

At first, it felt like a blow to my ego. Here I was, a woman with a wealth of experience and knowledge, serving drinks to people who didn't know my story, didn't know what I had sacrificed to be here. There were moments when I felt small and invisible, as if all my accomplishments were meaningless in this new context. But as the days went by, I came to understand that this job was teaching me something invaluable: resilience.

The work was hard, the hours long, but it gave me time to think, reflect, and appreciate the value of humility. This wasn't the glamorous life I had envisioned when I won the Green Card lottery, but it was necessary. Every shift behind that bar became a lesson in letting go of ego, in learning that no work is beneath you when you are building a new life from the ground up.

> "Adversity introduces a man to himself." —Albert Einstein

Building a New Life

Slowly, I began to carve out a space in this new world. It was a combination of persistence, faith, and sheer willpower. I found people who saw me, understood the immigrant journey, and reminded me that I wasn't alone. I built a community of friends, ideas, and shared dreams.

> "The only way to make sense out of change is to plunge into it, move with it, and join the dance." —Alan Watts.

This was a physical journey across continents and a transformation from the inside out. I had to become the person who could handle the blessing I had received.

Takeaway: The life you dream of requires you to grow into a person who can live it fully.

The Identity Shift

One of the most profound shifts came when I stopped seeing myself as an outsider and started embracing my new identity as a global citizen. I realized that I was no longer just a Greek woman living in the U.S. I was a bridge between worlds—between cultures, between who I was and who I was becoming. My spiritual practice deepened as I began to embrace the concept of surrender, trusting that the universe was guiding me every step of the way.

My struggles in this new country were not signs that I had made the wrong decision; they were lessons, teaching me that every door closed is a doorway to a higher understanding of myself.

It was the beginning of an internal revolution. It taught me that life is a series of initiations, each asking, "Are you willing to step into the next level of yourself?"

Today, I help others answer that question for themselves. Whether through coaching, transformational programs, or speaking, I have become the guide I once sought. My story is about surviving as an immigrant and thriving as a creator of my destiny.

> *"A human being always acts and feels and performs in accordance with what he imagines to be true about himself and his environment." —Maxwell Maltz*

Today: From Panic to Purpose

Today, I look at my family with immense pride. We have come so far from those early days of uncertainty and fear. My boys are thriving—each carving out their path, full of confidence and potential. They are a testament to the power of resilience, to the fact that no matter how turbulent the storm is, you can always find your footing on the other side.

My husband and I have built a life here that I could only have dreamed of back in Greece. We've overcome so many obstacles, both external and internal. And though I've let go of the need to control every outcome, I've embraced the journey with an open heart. My work now, helping others transform their lives, reflects my transformation.

Winning the Green Card was indeed a miracle, but the real miracle has been the journey—learning that we can stand strong, united, and full of faith even in the face of literal and metaphorical hurricanes.

> *"Out of difficulties grow miracles."* —Jean de La Bruyère

Building Meant to Lead

Meant to Lead™ was born from this journey—from my experience of facing what I call "cosmic abandonment" and discovering that we are often closest to divine connection in the moments of greatest isolation. Through prayer, reflection, and inner work, I learned that cosmic abandonment is not the end of the story; it is the beginning of a deeper relationship with ourselves and the universe.

In *Meant to Lead*™, I guide others to connect with their higher self, that part of them that remains unshaken even in times of crisis. I show them how to transform panic and fear into faith, trust in a purpose even when it feels elusive, and lead themselves through the storms of life. This program is more than a set of teachings; it is a blueprint for transformation, a pathway from isolation to empowerment.

One of the core teachings in *Meant to Lead*™ is that true leadership comes from within. It's about learning to trust the unknown and seeing it not as something to fear but as something to embrace. In the program, I guide others to use spiritual practices and science to transform adversity into the highest leadership.

Instead of letting life "just happen," learn to create it with intention. Whether it's about personal transformation, business, or a path to true self-confidence, I built this program to help anyone step forward and become the one you know you're meant to be.

The Framework I teach in *Meant to Lead*™ is the bridge between fear and faith, between being lost and unfulfilled, and between Success and purpose. It is a reconnection.

We are meant to rise, to find our connection to the Divine, and to lead ourselves even when the path is unclear.

It is about emotional state control, mastery of the self, connection, success, abundance, love, and everything you can dream of because you were **MEANT TO LEAD**.

If you're reading this and wondering if your dreams are worth pursuing, let me tell you: they are. The road may be long, and the challenges may seem insurmountable, but I promise you, the rewards are beyond anything you can imagine.

> *"Prayer is not asking. It is a longing of the soul."*
> *—Mahatma Gandhi*

Antonette Jeske

FLOURISH In Your Life
Christian Health Practitioner

https://www.facebook.com/groups/unlockgodsgreatness
https://www.instagram.com/antonettejeske
https://ajeske.qrkit.es/main

Antonette Jeske is a physician assistant, Christian Health Practitioner and founder of the "Flourishing Formula", a wholistic approach to health and wellness integrating faith, science, and the blueprints from Creation. After being told she couldn't have children, Antonette's journey of faith that the Lord would open her womb deeply shaped her views of the profound connection between the soul (will, thoughts and emotions), spirit, and physical healing. Passionate about the divine design of the human body, Antonette encourages women to be the best versions of themselves by embracing their God-given potential, living empowered by the Holy Spirit, and pursuing optimal health so to fulfill their life purpose glorifying their Creator. Through her work, women learn to honor their bodies as sacred vessels, capable of healing and flourishing. In her chapter, Antonette shares her story of faith, resilience, and divine intervention. Discover more about her transformative journey in Pray Don't Panic.

Flourishing by Design:
Finding Healing in God's Original Blueprint

By Antonette Jeske

Your first period...do you remember that fated day? Like most women, I do, as if it were yesterday. I was actually 27 years old when I had my first period. So technically, it was about 2 decades ago. I was in graduate school, and it was a Sunday morning. I woke up thinking that I wet the bed. And to my dismay, I discovered my first bleed...and that I had absolutely no feminine pads or tampons. Why would I if I had spent all those years never needing them? But there I was, looking at that huge red spot, and remembering that my friends were going to be headed to my little studio to carpool to church. So with a quickness, I had to scramble and throw my bedding into the laundry and run to the closest store to get the necessities.

It just so happens that I also remember my younger sister's first period. I was in the bathroom that school morning—likely re-enforcing my 3-inch tall bangs with White Rain hairspray and the trusty blow dryer when she woke up. And instead of shock, she was horrified. I peeked out of the bathroom to investigate the yells from my sister and the laughter from my mom. "You're a woman now," my mom exclaimed. I had an early AP chemistry class and didn't have the time or interest to contemplate...until later.

My mom and sister cycled together, like clockwork. Every month, I knew what was going on. But I didn't think too much about not having started my period until my freshman year in college. A friend, with good intentions but as naive as myself, thought that I must have cancer. So when I returned home, I begged my mom to make an appointment for me to finally get checked out by the doctors.

I thought for sure that all the tests would tell us what was wrong with me. Instead, the bloodwork and ultrasound all came back normal. The doctor couldn't give me a reason why I wasn't menstruating yet. But that wasn't what I really wanted to know. As a pre-med student at that time, I knew what a period signified for a female and what not having a period meant.

What I really wanted to know was, *would I be able to have kids?*

This doctor dismissed my concerns, stating that I shouldn't worry about having kids since I was in college. And so—more because I was a driven, goal-oriented individual—I didn't worry about it. To be perfectly honest, I didn't worry at all about the amenorrhea (or not having a period). Even after my first period, I only had 2–3 bleeds per year. And I actually appreciated that. Let's be real—only bleeding two or three times a year is a good deal, right? But what I did worry about was never being able to bear children of my own.

I had no reason at all to think that. But in my young mind, I had already resigned to the idea that I would have to adopt if I wanted to be a mother—because I just wouldn't be able to have kids. Matter of fact, as a kid, even before I understood menstruation or periods, I had a premonition that I would not be able to conceive. It was one of my biggest fears as a kid. That I was dealing with a generational curse. (Both my paternal grandparents were involved in witchcraft in the Philippines.) Could this thinking, from so early in life, have been the cause of my abnormal bleeding? Was it a self-fulfilling prophecy? There were no signs or indications that I would actually be able to conceive or even carry a child.

I knew my body was betraying me. It wasn't working the way it was supposed to. A woman of childbearing age is supposed to have periods. I had a successful career as a physician assistant. Bought a new townhouse and recently paid off my medical school bills and car payments. I had accomplished, essentially, the American dream. But I faced never being able to have my dream of being a mom.

Weeks after getting married, I visited a second doctor who didn't believe that I would be able to get pregnant. She told me that even though all my labs were normal, my body wasn't acting it. And if I even conceived, I would most likely miscarry. Defeated by that prognosis, I dropped the dream of being a mother and focused wholly on being a newlywed wife.

Entering into marriage is like building the foundation of a house. I wanted the life my husband and I were building to stand upon the Rock. I wanted that foundation to be whole, unshaken, and ready to support whatever came next. We had had premarital counseling. And I read tons of books about relationships and how to be a holy wife. One Scripture that I really circled back to over and over was Psalm 127:1.

Psalm 127:1
Unless the LORD builds a house, its builders labor over it in vain; unless the LORD watches over a city, the watchman stays alert in vain.

But it was the rest of the psalm that planted seeds of hope that God was already working things out.

Psalm 127:3-5
Children are a gift from the LORD; they are a reward from Him. Children born to a young man are like arrows in a warrior's hands. How joyful is the man whose quiver is full of them!

The house symbolizes the foundation of a marriage, whereas the city symbolizes the enduring impact of that foundation across generations. Just as a city grows and flourishes from strong, guiding values, so does a family shape the future, expanding outward and touching the lives to come.

With this in mind, I knew I had to rely on God to be the builder of our home. Build up my marriage so our family would take root, spring up, and grow. If I allowed Him to guide our steps and direct our paths, His way would lead us precisely to the inheritance He had promised. It had to be entirely His work, His timing, His plan. So, my husband and I focused on our marriage to ensure that we were building a strong, faithful foundation—one that would be ready to support the children we trusted God would eventually bless us with. I resolved to walk in faith, trusting that wherever He led, the journey would end with me bearing my own children.

One evening in March 2013, my husband and I attended a worship concert in San Francisco. We had just celebrated our first-year anniversary. We were still figuring out how to construct our life as husband and wife, so we weren't really thinking of "trying to get pregnant." Honestly, I was also struggling deeply with doubts that I would be able to conceive. In the middle of that crowd, I stood with my eyes closed. The worship leader was preaching and asked that whatever was keeping us from getting closer to God would be revealed to us. As my arms were stretched out, another voice began to speak: "You need to pray that I will open your womb." I immediately knew that it was the Lord. I felt a surge of emotion pulse through my body. And in my mind's eye, I saw light flowing to my uterus.

Though I had already been praying about getting pregnant, I realized that my doubt was preventing Him from answering. God began to show me that my thoughts of Him were not the same as what I professed. I sang that He was a strong and merciful God, mighty to save. I knew all of the stories and of the miracles, familiar with all of the things God was famous for. Yet I did not really believe it all. I did not truly believe that—though the Bible told me so—He healed the sick and lame, restored sight to the blind, and opened the ears of the deaf. More than that, I did not believe that He would do any of that for me.

But the Holy Spirit settled within me and changed that. From then on, my prayers were not just asking for a miracle. I prayed that I would be ready for it.

I had become so certain that God would open my womb that I determined not to use conventional medicine for my infertility. I didn't want modern advice. I wanted Jesus' promise of having an abundant life (John 10:10).

Knowing how God created our bodies with a divine design empowered me to allow my body to do what God intended in His time and in His will. Surrendering control and giving up my own power or self-sufficiency was the first step toward truly having faith that God was going to do it.

Conventional medicine had no explanations for me. No answers to my questions about *why*. Rather, conventional medicine bypassed all of my concerns and simply recommended manipulating my body with different medications or doing treatments. I have always seen this approach as slapping duct tape over the check engine light, hoping that the weird noise the car is making will eventually go away. Though I understood how certain medications could potentially help me get pregnant, they weren't going to correct the underlying, unrelenting issues. I recognized, after having practiced medicine for several years, that we often do not give our bodies the time or necessary resources they need to heal. All too often, we feel the answer is found in a daily pill or the edge of the scalpel.

I was accustomed to patients wanting that magical pill or treatment to instantaneously fix everything. I never could grasp why people didn't want to fix the problem causing their issues and would instead rely on prescriptions or surgeries. I felt that there was this unconscious belief that doctors and Western medicine have outsmarted the Creator. But He is the One who really knows what's going on. The One who sees the end as well as the beginning and middle at the same time. The One who wove us and knows us, nearer to us than even the skin on our bones. So, I decided that since I was His masterpiece, my plan of attack needed to intentionally and strategically be the Master's plan.

I referred to Genesis, looking at God's original blueprints for creation. In chapter 2, verse 18, God decided to make Adam a helper for the specific purpose of partnering with him in an endearing and productive relationship. Adam and Eve were to journey together, their union was essential for the success of their mission, which was to live a fruitful life. Through marriage, God established companionship rooted in love and in mission—a reflection of His own relationship with us. In His creation of the first family, I saw a model of unity, fruitfulness, and shared purpose. This blueprint reassured me that my longing for marriage, overall health, and family was not just a personal desire but part of God's original intention for all of us.

My study of God's original blueprints didn't end there. I was deeply aware of the complexities of His creation. In college, I majored in cellular biology and minored in chemistry and philosophy, which gave me an understanding of the intricate workings of the body. During an internship with the American Heart Association, I isolated RNA and sequenced it to obtain the genetic code. I learned how genes and cells interact to keep organs functioning properly, in turn allowing the body to stay healthy. I recognized that to understand how to physically flourish in life the way God intended, I needed to return to the basics—to the essentials that were buried beneath layers of science, medicine, and technology. The key lies in understanding God's design of humans was always within the context of all of creation.

I could not believe that all life started from random, fortuitous joining and combinations of quarks to atoms, molecules, DNA/RNA, proteins, tissues, organs, and then organisms. If obtaining the genetic code of lab rats was extremely meticulous and precise, there is no way

God would be haphazard in creating the universe. Hence why, the first act of creation was bringing order to chaos. God was intentional. Everything He spoke forth had a specific purpose and function. Everything brought stability and coherence.

Once all things were precisely as they needed to be to sustain mankind, amongst the trees and the plants, God dug His hands into the dirt and molded man. Next, He breathed the breath of life into Adam's nostrils before setting him in the garden. God sets us within a living, interconnected world. Just as plants need soil, sunlight, and water to thrive, we are designed to flourish when we live in harmony with the natural rhythms and resources God provided. Our bodies weren't created in isolation but as part of a wonderfully interconnected system—where every living organism and function is harmonized with the rhythms of nature.

Creation is intended not only to sustain us physically but to enrich us spiritually. It isn't merely functional but also awe-inspiring, prompting wonder and reverence. It is an expression of God's beauty and power, drawing people closer to God (Psalm 19:1-4).

Healing was not just about addressing symptoms; it was about returning to the foundation of how we were created, respecting the connections God intended between us and each other, us and the natural world, and, moreover, us and Him. These connections are what guide us toward true wholeness. Health and wellness come from aligning ourselves with God's design, not just biologically, but in how we interact with and live within His creation. Moreover, I saw healing as a beautiful part of God's redemptive plan. Just as He redeems our souls, I believed He could redeem my health. By committing to heal and prepare my body, I was participating in the redemption He offered, allowing Him to restore every part of me. I trusted that this process would make me whole—mind, body, and spirit.

Surrendering my health to God was more than just an act of faith; it was an act of sacred trust in His promise to restore what is broken. I believed that the same God who longs to restore all creation could bring healing to my body as part of that grand design. He would allow me to get pregnant in His timing, His way...and according to my faith. I knew this was the kind of God He was. I saw healing as a beautiful part of God's redemptive plan. Just as He redeems our souls, I believed He could redeem my health.

So, I prepared my body. I literally wanted my body to be good soil in which God could plant and spring forth fruit from my womb. I changed my diet. I cut out all of the artificial ingredients and preservatives. We ate only nutrient-dense, organic, and non-GMO foods. I began to workout again, preparing for the marathon of labor. I got more natural light, getting outside more often. I also invested more time in building relationships, sleep, and rest.

I prayed that He would bless me and my husband the only way He could. I prayed that I would accept whatever that would be, that I would be aligned with any and every thing that He gives. As long as it glorified God, I would be glad to have it. Come July 2013, without having bled since that night in San Francisco, I had a positive pregnancy test. And in February of the following year, we home birthed our first of three children.

Looking back, I see how God led me on a journey not just toward motherhood, but into a deeper understanding of His design for wholeness. Healing, I've learned, isn't just about addressing physical issues; it's about aligning every part of ourselves—body, mind, and spirit—with God's blueprint. True health comes when we recognize that we're part of a larger, interconnected creation, intentionally crafted by a loving Creator. For anyone facing their own struggles, I offer this encouragement: God designed you with care, and His plan is for you to flourish. Trusting His timing and surrendering to His wisdom opens us to receive the blessings He's prepared, in ways we may never expect.

Healing requires both surrender and strength—a willingness to let go and let God work through us in His own way and time. When I surrendered control, I made space for Him to show up and show off. My story is just one example of how God brings redemption and wholeness to all of creation, one life at a time. To those seeking hope, I want you to know that your life is also a part of His grand design for restoration. With faith, a heart open to His guidance, and a desire to live in harmony with His creation, we can find true healing, abundant peace, and a life that bears fruit.

It's my prayer that my story gives you hope, whether you're on your own journey to healing, navigating uncertainty, or simply longing for more. Healing begins with faith, and faith comes from hearing the Good News (Romans 10:17). Commit to aligning yourself with God's wisdom, His care, and the rhythms He wove into creation. Find strength and encouragement to seek His guidance in every step, believing that He has made you for wholeness, purpose, and blessing. When you allow God to be your builder, the foundation of your life becomes strong, resilient, and ready to flourish as He intended. Remember this: Flourishing begins when you trust the Creator's blueprint for your life. You were made to thrive in His design, and through Him, your life can become a testimony of His love, redemption, and power.

Virginia Walters

Author

https://www.facebook.com/virginiawaltersisblessed
https://www.facebook.com/profile.php?id=61559259616939&mibextid=LQQJ4d

At 52, Virginia Walters, a resilient Sydney woman, has transformed her life through immense challenges. A survivor of domestic violence and cancer, she raises her son, who lives with profound cerebral palsy, alongside her three other children. Through education and self-discovery, she conquered her fears and became a passionate advocate for her son, embodying strength and compassion.

Her artistic talents have earned her several awards, reflecting her creative spirit and dedication. Achieving homeownership and building her own home testify to her determination and hard work. Her journey has instilled strong ethics, morals, and character, shaping her into an unstoppable force. She shares her powerful message of choosing faith over fear, inspiring others to embrace their strength and rise above adversity. She uplifts those around her with unwavering resolve, proving that resilience and love can create a brighter future.

The Unseen Strength: From Sanctuary to Advocacy

By Virginia Walters

In 1996, I escaped from a violent marriage. I hid for nine months in a convent turned women refugee. It was a place of sanctuary for women fleeing domestic violence. It was named St Michael Women's Refuge after the archangel Michael.

The nun who lived at the refuge helped me navigate the legal system, obtaining restraining orders against my husband, a Christian Orthodox Priest. I still remember the day we went to court, and the magistrate asked me the last words exchanged with my estranged husband; as I thought to remember the words, translating them into English, speaking them aloud, I began to realise just how bad my situation had become. Earlier that week, he asked me whether I would try to escape that day. It wasn't that day, but later that week, I saw an opportunity, seized it, and at 24 years of age, fled the eight-year relationship with my two children, who were four years and eight months old.

It was during the court proceedings that followed that the court-appointed psychiatrist diagnosed me as having 'battered woman syndrome' and my ex-husband as having "cluster B personality disorder"; I wondered how life had led me to this point and how I would overcome such a thing.

I experienced nightmares. I would wake up and then calm myself by praying. The prayer went something like this: "God, I know what has done cannot be changed, but I ask that you take my heart back to a place where it can be innocent, where it is free to love with all of my heart and to be able to trust again with the knowledge that I would never be hurt or harmed in that way again." It seemed like an impossible request as if such a thing were possible. I know that life could be otherwise. I feared hell, of being eternally damned for leaving. However, my love and desire for the safety of my children felt more significant than any duty I felt towards my marriage.

It was several years later and in a different relationship that I discovered I was pregnant. It was an unplanned pregnancy. The irony was that earlier that day, a letter had arrived confirming an appointment for my then-partner to have a vasectomy. As I chuckled, I decided it would be okay; I'd love this child, my very last biological child. I reasoned that it was only the first 12 months that a babe remained in arms until they got up and became more independent. It would be okay, I had this.

I must say he was born a healthy, robust 10 LB. He came out completely encased in the caul. The midwife marvelled at how it was a sign of luck and how we no longer see these things.

I decided to name my baby Michael after Saint Michael to remind myself, like in my previous life experience, that even the things we don't plan for in life can ultimately lead to blessings.

Michael was an adorable, peaceful baby; all he wanted was to be held or nursed, and I enjoyed him. It was around five months of age that Michael developed tremors in his arms; wondering what it was, I took him to the doctor, who referred us to a paediatrician. It was at this appointment, at eight months of age, that the paediatrician diagnosed Michael with having microcephaly and cerebral palsy. An MRI at 15 months of age confirmed that he had brain damage, suggesting that he suffered an ischemic injury during his birth. Other testing revealed that Michael had cataracts and underdeveloped optic nerves, which rendered him legally blind. He had some vision but not enough to function as a typical person would. From there, the paediatrician referred him to the neurological team, which began trying to unravel what had happened. These various conditions suggested the likelihood of a metabolic disorder rather than a birth injury.

From there, the neurologist referred him to the metabolic specialist; however, no genetic testing, tissue sampling, or examination could determine what was happening. Several neurologists, including a retired one, were brought out to see Michael, and even with his 70-plus years of experience and what he'd learned from the patients and doctors before him, he'd never seen such a combination that didn't show up in the regular tests that detect such diseases and conditions. What we were dealing with was a one-off, so there was no way that the specialists involved could predict an outcome.

I began to research, and as Michael grew, we realised he wasn't sitting, babbling, or crawling. The best he could do was roll. I enrolled him in early intervention, and we attended physical therapy and other therapies four days a week. Michael would participate with other children with my support. Eagerly, I learned how to support Michael through physical, occupational, speech, and vision therapy instruction. Over the next few years, Michael's personality emerged over these sessions. To my delight, he was highly animated, social, and engaging, with a well-developed sense of humour.

After the children had gone to bed, I'd do some research at night. I would use Yahoo message boards to talk to parents and caregivers from overseas to see if anybody had anything like my boy. I spent several years researching. It was tormenting not to know what had happened to him and whether this would be progressive. When he was about 3, I just put the topic to bed and decided to enjoy him. That something would always come along and potentially steal your joy if you allowed it to. His story would unfold daily, and indeed, the God that had created him knew what they were doing; all I had to do was love this child, navigating his life the best I could.

My focus began to change. It was not what had happened to my child. What was wrong with my child? Instead, how could I give this child life and the best shot at life, and how could I continue to keep this child in my life when we needed wheelchairs and hoists and medical beds along with further aids and appliances? We needed a purpose-built home and all the things that come along with caring for a person with a physical disability. After a chance meeting with another special needs parent, I learned about a not-for-profit organisation building homes in partnership with people in challenging circumstances. I applied and was willing to do whatever it took to keep my family together, to keep all my children under the same roof.

I remember the day we went for the interview, feeling a strange sense that whatever is meant to be will be. I got into the car and instinctively drove the three suburbs away through the Rabbit Warren of suburbia and found an empty plot of land surrounded by other dwellings. I thought, "I would not be surprised if this is it". To my delight, it was, and several months later, we began building a partnership with the organisation. We would have an interest-free mortgage, with the catch being that we had to be part of the house build, putting in 500 hours of sweat equity. I remember the first day of the build was scorching, the temperature quickly rising to 40 degrees Celsius. As I dug that foundation by hand with a shovel and pickaxe, I wondered how I would build this house within a year. However, I was determined to see the project through to completion.

I needed not to worry, as during the following months, swarms of volunteers came along, which made the goal more achievable. The goodwill that existed through corporate sponsorship, employee programmes, community groups, and general well-wishers from the community was terrific. Everyone came to help. I remember the students from Sydney University coming out and marvelling; a boy was wearing a kippah, working alongside another boy wearing a cross, and working with a boy named Mohammad, installing the ceiling frame. The trio worked fabulously together. It didn't matter that they came from different worlds; their shared goal of supporting our build for Michaels's disability united them towards a common cause.

The beautiful thing about Michael and others like him is that he brings many people together. I began to see a different side of humanity, a kinder, softer side that wished to serve the greater good. The therapists I met along the way studied for entire degrees and dedicated many years to working with children like Michael, often because their hearts call them to a higher purpose. It was a humbling experience, and as I felt my heart swell with love and trust build back into my life, I began to understand that Michael was not damaged but rather a type of healing presence in this world, inviting others to act in ways that align with their values, ethics, and moral code. His presence offers an opportunity to step into a better, more selfless version of us and put these beliefs into practice. I will forever be grateful for the people who gathered to make so many things possible that would have otherwise been impossible to achieve on my own.

Moving into my very own home was a long-held dream come true. The kids loved it. With nearby bushland, parks, and a busy neighbourhood, they quickly made friends and fell into community life. There was just one problem: How or where would Michael attend school? I started exploring options; there were two local schools available to us. One specialised in autism; many of the children, although mobile, were nonverbal with co-mobilities, including behavioural challenges. The ratio between adult to child was around 1:8 or 1:10, depending on the age groups. I wouldn't say I liked the thought of him being defenceless in that environment. To change his diaper from an occupational workplace safety perspective was 2:1.

The closest appropriate school was 52 km away. It would mean justifying the need to travel on government-funded transport, the 104 km round trip, along with a travel aid and driver. Feeling overwhelmed as I read through the criteria, I put together an application addressing each point. I was both surprised and delighted when Michael received the placement at a school for deaf and blind children. He would receive the required support there, including access to therapists, teachers, specialists, volunteers from sporting, corporate, and educational industries and the community.

The school had a well-developed culture focused on achieving one's full potential. After consulting with the head speech pathologist involved in putting together the language programme, it was through her encouragement that Michael, legally blind and non-verbal, would be taught sign language and learn this alongside the culturally and linguistically diverse CALD community. Michael thrived in this community, where the emphasis was on being culturally and linguistically diverse rather than disabled. Yes, everybody had their challenges and differences; however, each school community member was celebrated for what they could do and could achieve rather than trying to fix what couldn't be fixed.

During these years, I began to understand that Michael was born the person he was meant to be and had his unique destiny. He was, after all, a creation of the Almighty, made in His image. Indeed, God's source that resides within me also exists within you. Are we not united in our humanity? Therefore, let me see God in all his forms, like the different faces on each flower. Is there not room for variety within the garden of humanity?

As Michael's care needs grew more extensive and I had three other children to care for, I needed to bring in help in the form of community caregivers. I'd have a community caregiver come in each morning and afternoon for an hour to assist with showering and feeding.

I noticed a theme in the people coming through the house: women much like myself who had left difficult circumstances and challenging relationships as part of their healing journey felt drawn to champion the underdog. I would see them start quite defensive and, over the months, witness the unfurl of their hearts, singing and dancing along with

Michael to his favourite TV shows. I remember one caregiver, after many years of working with us, confessing the shame that she carried and what her father had done during his role as a Hitler youth during the holocaust. She wanted to leave a better legacy for her children. "When we know better, we do better" was her attitude. She genuinely loved Michael. I am 6 generations Australian, and Michael would be seven on my side; however, it's interesting that my grandmother is a descendant of the Ashkenazi Jewish community that found their way to Australia. My great-grandfathers on my father's side were some of the first kosher butchers in Australia. My grandmother's father broke this family profession by joining the Navy and serving in Europe throughout the Second World War. The remainder of my family is of Celtic origin, and I was raised as a practising catholic. It's amazing when I stop and think of it: with the world and its way, everybody has their pain, suffering, and insecurities. However, it is through the most defenceless and the most vulnerable that an opportunity is given for humanity to shine its brightest.

At around seven years of age, Michael began to struggle with eating and swallowing. I had successfully breastfed him until he was 5, and soon after weaning and having some medical procedures, he developed silent aspiration, and a feeding tube was surgically placed. It was an extensive surgery, and the stress on his body from the surgery caused Michael to develop grand mal seizures.

I realised during this time that this would be a journey I would take with Michael alone. Through the experience with Michael's father, I came to believe that some people are brought together so that certain souls go into this life, which is as far as they travel together. I felt that having Michael, being Michael's mother, allowed me to live what I believed to be, morally and ethically, the testing of my humanness. I have read that just as the blacksmith places the gold and silver into the fire until it is purified, so does life trial us through the symbolic fire or hardships, which are what define us, challenge us to withstand the heat of life and transform us into a more refined version of ourselves. I didn't know how I was going to do it, only that I was going to for as long as I was able, that I was going to give Michael a safe and happy childhood, and that I would expose him to all the opportunities and activities that would nurture and develop him.

Michael was legally blind. His optic nerves had never developed. He had a similar thing with his teeth where the enamel failed to create. It seemed that the theme of hyperplasia was what had affected him. He was like a perfectly formed oil painting that had, while still wet, a streak drawn down the middle, almost like somebody came along and ran their finger through the damp painting, consequently rendering him Michael. I want to think that God's finger did this. It was as if God had made a masterpiece and then contemplated upon it and thought, "Now, how can I make this perfect?" and added the extra touch, rendering every system of Michael's body affected. In cerebral palsy terms, he is a level 5 in the Gross Motor Function Classification System (GMFCS). In terms of the Care and Needs Scale (CANS), Michael is a level 7, rendering him more disabled than 97% of the population. However, he is the happiest child, is highly animated, has an infectious giggle, and is engaging. He loves life with his adventurous, determined spirit; it was by no mistake that he was this happy as he'd had input from so many people.

The term, it takes a village to raise a child, is aptly fitted for the experience of having somebody like Michael. Of course, advocacy played a role, forcing me into positions I would normally have shied away from. I began to advocate and push forward. In the years before the national disability insurance system, life for people with disabilities was pretty rough. Funding was scarce and limited, so parents and people with disability had to become strong at advocating and, where needed, fundraising. During this time, I wrote to several ministers, I met with local members, disability members, and even two former prime ministers. I attended many workshops and advocacy sessions, and my submissions were selected to be included with the Senate Standing Committee on Community Affairs Inquiry into the National Disability Insurance Scheme Bill 2012. Additionally, I gave a testimony at the Royal Commission when it was required for Michael's voice to be heard amongst the many other people who had encountered abuse in the system.

I decided to return to school as I had never completed my schooling and educate myself as an adult, obtaining marks to attend university. With a grateful heart, I enrolled in a Bachelor of Law and Social Sciences. My goal at that point was to become a human rights advocate. I represented myself in obtaining an annulment from my first husband due to his bigamy and a divorce from my second. I'd advocated the legal system many times for Michael. I wanted to be that voice for the underdog and stand up for people who wouldn't otherwise be able to fend for themselves. I loved studying the social sciences, learning about societal structures, and reading case law; everybody has a story leading them to where they find themselves. But most of all, I like discussing historical cases with my grandfather. Living in East Balmain, he knew of the Robertson v Balmain Ferry Co (1905) case and felt the ruling unjustly. My grandfather and his brothers took on advocacy roles in their working lives and fought to bring unions for the working man. His brother made it higher within the unions, and eventually, a street was named after the family. I feel enormous pride whenever I pass by that street and know I come from a family of advocates. This is what we do; we fight the good fight. What I loved about laws was hearing the story behind the case. Similarly, what I love about mediumship is bringing a message about the afterlife and learning its story, message, and significance to the person being read. I also enjoy case management: learning the story and setting a practical plan to assist the person.

Michael became very sick following his surgery for the feeding tube placement. His body seemed to shut down; the commercial formula that the treating specialist routinely prescribed him was killing him, as the sugar content was too high. He had developed a variety of associated health issues, and his body refused to digest it. I would open the tube to feed him, only for the previous feed to come out; his body just was unable to process it. I remember going to the specialist. He had dropped down to 17 kilos, and at eight years old, we were waiting for him to drop down to 14 kilos to admit him to the hospital for end-of-life. It wasn't something that I could accept. I didn't know what to do. I only knew I should try anything, so I started to juice. I bought a commercial blender and began blending whole fruits and vegetables, which worked. It was like his body snatched it up, and over the following two years, Michels health took a big turnaround. I remember the wheelchair Rep marvelling at how he had never seen a child outgrow a wheelchair so quickly. He seemed to thrive on this new formula. Life began to turn around for him. He went from 17 kg to 20 to 40 quite quickly.

During this time, my life began to take a different turn. The years of stress were catching up. I developed fibromyalgia and migraines, and chronic fatigue set in. I developed ovarian tumours, which had grown to 3 litres in size, causing serious borderline tumours, the first stage leading to ovarian cancer; I then developed endometrial cancer. Thankfully, both were treated surgically. I would require monitoring for five years, which turned into seven until I would be given the all-clear.

A few years earlier, I had stepped into the world of mysticism, looking for answers, and I decided to explore spiritualism more. I found meditation calming, helpful, and valuable. I meditated for up to several hours a day. I found that it helped me manage the pain and anxiety of my situation.

It wasn't long before phenomena began to occur, and to my delight, I found that I had a natural gift for the sight. This family trait spans several generations and is widespread in my family tree. It seemed to be the thing that worked well with the care that Michael required, and so I stepped into it when I had time. I wondered if life, for me, was about working towards a future serving the majority. Or doing what I could for the ones before me in the now? The thought that came to me was who does for the least of me does unto all of me. I felt that my soul called me out of any situation that led me away from caring for Michael or being available to support my children and now grandchildren; it was with a heavy heart that I resigned from the course and decided to put my studies on hold until I was clear from cancer. I needed to live as stress-free and low-pressure as possible until life levelled out and time became more my own.

Here we are 22 years later, and my boy continues to thrive. He loves music, animals, people, and high-fives. I was given the all-clear from cancer in February of 2020; however, I have extensive osteoarthritis through my neck and spine with mild rheumatoid arthritis. Michael spends time in hospice from time to time as his condition is life-limiting, and he requires around-the-clock care. Our life is simple, but it is blessed. If I could share some life wisdom with anybody about being an unstoppable woman who chooses faith over fear, it would be to know your truths and to be true to yourself and your why. What makes you return and recommit when life gets tough? There will always be something that will potentially steal your life and your joy, so choose your battles and walk away from situations and people that are not ethically or morally in alignment with your own, and that loneliness is often a byproduct of this. Know that happiness is a decision followed by often hard and painful work, but is it worth it? Yes, indeed, it is worth it.

Gabrielle Burton

Licensed Marriage and Family Therapist, Speaker, Author

https://www.linkedin.com/in/gabrielle-burton-3a616812a/
https://www.instagram.com/gabriellemburtontherapy/
https://www.gabriellemburton.com

Gabrielle is a Licensed Marriage and Family Therapist, and speaker. She is a creative at heart and uses various art mediums with her clients from music, drawing to movement. Gabrielle refers to herself as a "Gold Digger" as she believes everyone has wealth and value and won't stop until her clients discover the hidden treasures they possess within. Gabrielle has a book entitled The Ultimate Guide to Becoming a Gold Digger where she combines mental health and biblical principles.

A Love Tap

By Gabrielle Burton

One day after a hard workout, I was craving my favorite salad from Chick-fil-A. I head on over, and as I was waiting in the drive-through line, someone hits me. I was caught off guard and thought, "Surely, this person was distracted!" I got out of my car and took a look at the bumper and the person behind me was still in the car. Which confirmed my suspicion. DISTRACTED and unaware. I start examining my bumper, and two minutes later, the driver finally gets out of the car and says, "Oh my goodness, did I hit you?" I thought this must be a joke. How did she not feel it? So, I politely reply, "Yes, you hit me." Because my car was a little dirty, I couldn't tell if there was any damage to the bumper, and it was dark outside. As I'm trying to assess the damage, I'm licking my finger and then wiping the car to see if I'm able to see any scratches.

The employees in the drive-through said, "We are so sorry, but can we ask you to take this outside of the Chick-Fil-A line?"

"Of Course!" I replied.

After I get my food, I pull out of the line and into a parking space, waiting for the other driver to meet me. She eventually makes her way over to my car and gets out of hers, saying, "Oh my gosh, I'm so sorry. I've never done this before." She is so sweet, and I just see a young 20-something just trying to figure things out. I soften and say, "It's okay."

She continues, "Listen, I'll give you whatever you need. Do you need my license? My insurance? I don't know how this works!"

I go back to trying to clean my bumper, and I'm not able to see if there's any damage, so I tell her, "I'll tell you what. I'll take a picture of your information, and I'll take your phone number. If I need anything, I'll let you know, but I have a feeling it's really not that serious!"

She hands over her information, looking terribly remorseful, and then pleads, "And if you need cash, we can do that too. Really, anything you need!" I hand her back her things and say, "I'm pretty sure it's nothing serious, but if I find anything wrong after I wash my car, I'll reach out to you first!"

We both get back into our cars, and I start eating my salad because I am starving! A few bites in, I look over and see that she is bawling in her car. I get out of my car and knock on her window. As she rolls it down, I ask, "Can I pray for you?" "Oh my gosh, I will never deny it!" she says.

I start praying for God to let her know that she is loved, comfort her, and let her know she's forgiven. After I prayed, I noticed that she had a bunch of food in her front seat.

"Who is waiting on food?" I ask.

"My family." She says in between sniffles.

"Girl! Go home, I'm pretty sure it's going to be fine. When I wash my car, I'll reach out to you and let you know if I need anything, but I'm pretty sure it's nothing." "Okay." She said as she wiped her tears. She thanked me and then headed home.

A couple of weeks went by, and I texted her, "Hey girl! I haven't washed my car yet, but just wanted to reach out and see how you're doing."

She replied, "Oh my goodness, I still think about it every day. Please let me know if you need anything."

I said, "I'm sure it's fine, just wanted to make sure you are doing alright." She expressed that she appreciated that and assured me that things were going well in her life. Another week goes by, and I text her again, "Hey girl! I finally washed my car, and it's fine! But you do owe me. I was wondering if you would be interested in going to church with me sometime."

"Oh my goodness, I would love to!"

The moral of the story is what comes out of you when people bump into you. Is it criticism, judgment, anger, or will it be prayer? The funniest part about this whole story is the shirt I was wearing that day after I showered at the gym said "Faith" on it. Could you imagine if I would've been nasty to her? I didn't even realize I had that shirt on until I got home and brushed my teeth and saw it in the mirror. The truth is, that we, as Christians, are always representing Christ. Whether we have a faith shirt on, a cross necklace or not. It's important that we are safe people and display the fruit of the spirit. To be honest, she bumped into me on the right day. I had been prayed up, had been spending some quality time with the Father, and had a lot of grace to extend. But the truth is, we are all human and have our moments of weakness.

It's important that we tap into the wealth of heaven by spending time in prayer with God. Each morning I pray, "God, help me be aware of your presence today. And use me as your vessel." We are to be conduits of his presence, and the only way we can do that is by spending time with him. There was a season where I dealt with significant church hurt and didn't want to be around other believers. I almost felt more loved by unbelievers because at least they weren't judgmental. But the truth is, it is our responsibility to heal and resolve our pain. God took me on a serious journey that required a lot of forgiveness.

As believers, we carry a beautiful and weighty responsibility: to love deeply and to shine as examples of grace. My wisest counsel? Dive into His presence and seek His guidance. I'll never forget the day that girl bumped into me; through our encounter, she discovered Jesus. It's humbling to realize that His love and kindness far exceed even my best moments without Him.

Carmen Maendel

Nate's Property Maintenance LLC
Co-Owner & Business Office Manager

https://www.linkedin.com/in/carmen-maendel-17510944/
https://www.facebook.com/ncmaendel
https://www.instagram.com/maendelcarmen/
https://natespropertymaintenance.com/
https://www.facebook.com/profile.php?id=100093303554586

Who is Carmen K. Maendel? I am a child of God, a wife, and a mother. I have owned and operated 4 businesses (Genoa Denim & Leather Apparel, Carmen Maendel Photography, and Maendel Fitness Gym & Spa) in the last 12 years and currently am Co-Owner/Business Office Manager for Nate's Property Maintenance LLC. We are a husband wife team! I handle all the business stuff on the home front, and my husband, Nate Maendel coordinates everything on the job sites with our clients and crew. Nate has over 30 years experience with removing and trimming trees of any size and shape! Nate is also five star approved through Home Advisor/Angi. With over 30 years of expertise, we specialize in tree removal, trimming, and total property transformations. Year-round tree work, free estimates, and a passion for serving our community make us your go-to for a beautiful, safe outdoor space.

Moments of Impact

By Carmen Maendel

Introduction: My Identity in Christ

I am Carmen Maendel, and I am a child of God. God has blessed me with an incredible husband and son to travel through life with. Heaven is our true home, and we are just passing through. Everything belongs to God, always has, and always will. I want to preface that any accomplishments or accolades that have happened to me came from God, not me. Everything I do, I do for the glory of God. "I can do all things in Christ that strengthens me," Philippians 4:13.

I graduated from several colleges and universities with degrees that have helped me honor God in a variety of different ways over the years. I am sharing these details so that as you progress through my narrative, you can see how God used all these life experiences I had to His Glory. My first and only love is Jesus, and everything else stems from there. I am incredibly thankful to have the husband and son I do today. I feel very well grounded in my identity in Christ and have a handful of very close friends I do life with. We have an incredible and supportive church family as well. I married into an amazing God-fearing family and inherited many wonderful relatives in the process. My mother and stepmother have also always been there to help guide me along the way. My father and father-in-law passed away in 2009 and 2021, however, prior to that, they both have also been an incredible beacon in my life.

Formative Years: Glass Shatters & God Shows Up

My story begins with being born and raised in a very influential family. Through God's grace, I discover that my family inheritance pales insurmountably to the inheritance I have waiting for me in Heaven. As I have gotten older, God has revealed to me that money is simply a vehicle used to bless others and for our immediate needs; it is not a means to an end. Family memories are much more precious and valuable than money ever was. I grew up with two siblings older than me, my brother and sister. I remember racing my sister to our dad's lap after dinner while my brother watched and grinned. Lots of competition in our home, some healthy and some not so much. I remember being asked a number of times, "Why can't you be more like your sister?" Today, I am confident in the woman God has created me to be, flaws and all. My mother has been a tremendous influence in my life in a number of different ways. She reminded me about a specific childhood incident that will become a repetitive analogy to the narrative I share with you in the pages to come.

Our family was in the process of adding several additions to our home, and there was a large storm glass window that was propped up against our home. I was playing, and somehow that large window fell over the top of my head, causing shards of glass to poke into me on all sides. My mother screamed, "Don't move!" and miraculously, I walked away from that without a single scratch. So back to my analogy of my life and this large glass window. Just the same way as the window slammed to the ground and shattered into many pieces, there are moments when life could have fallen and shattered. I look at the moments of impact in my life and how God has used them to completely transform the situation and me to His glory. This has happened a number of times, and God has always faithfully shown up and orchestrated the mini miracles in my life. My life verse is Proverbs 3:5-6, "Trust in the Lord with all your heart and lean not on your own understanding. Acknowledge Him in all ways and He will direct your path."

Our family verse today is Isaiah 40:31, "They that wait upon the Lord shall renew their strength, they shall mount up with wings as eagles." These two verses have been extremely prevalent in my life, and I have called upon them to solidify my faith in Jesus over and over again.

Middle Stages of Adolescence: Overcoming Parents' Divorce & Salvation

It was during eighth grade that my parents decided that they were no longer compatible with one another, and they got divorced. I always thought my parents would be together forever. I remember how painful this portion of my life was, and how lost I felt as one parent would switch out weekends of being at our home with the other. There were different sets of rules for each parent and massive confusion with consistency and stability at that time of my life. God was present and with me before I even understood who He was. At some of those lowest times in my life, I felt a calming peace about the situation and knew everything was going to be alright. I remember going to this FCA Fellowship of Christian Athletes retreat and I received salvation in Jesus Christ for the first time in my life. I felt an overwhelming sense of peace all over my body upon salvation, and this brought me to tears. I call them my happy and relieved tears. A huge weight was removed and replaced by a tranquil sense of peace and serenity. The window had come down and shattered, and yet God picked up the pieces and helped me get through that time of extreme sadness and confusion. Through deep prayer and writing poetry, God helped me work through the pervasive feelings of sadness and loneliness at that time in my life. Things slowly seemed to get better, and I learned to start drawing upon God's strength and not my own.

College Years: Two Major Events God Used to Shape My Life

I had always thought I would get married directly out of high school, however, once again, God had a different plan for my life. Sometimes, unanswered prayers can be blessings in disguise as it was in my case. I went directly to college after high school, and there I remained for several years and earned degrees in various areas of study. I worked a variety of different jobs, from a jewelry store, retail store, RA in my apartment complex, and an oriental rug boutique, to an assistant director at an art gallery. I worked three full-time jobs while carrying a full load of classes for my Speech and Language Pathology undergraduate program at UW-Madison. As I reflect back on that time in my life, I was clearly operating on God's strength and not my own.

I feel it is important to share two major events that happened while I was still at Cornell College studying art and business. Once again, that glass window came crashing down, and God was in the middle of my healing and growing my faith. I remember sitting by her bedside with her mother and praying fervently in prayer for her recovery that summer. I remember the call with the bad news like it was yesterday; the trip I almost went with them on. My best friend had fallen asleep at the wheel and crossed the centerline while coming in direct contact with a truck head-on. Her little brother and his fiancée were killed instantly, and she would miraculously come out of her coma with a head injury. I remember very clearly how God worked in our lives that summer of 1992. We would visit her each day, hoping to hear about some improvement in her condition. One day we were even told to prepare ourselves for the worst; however, God had another plan for her life. She did come out of her coma at the end of the summer, and I will always remember how God orchestrated all those events in only a way He could.

The other very impactful event that happened while I was still in college was that my father was fighting his upward battle with cancer. He would share his PSA count until it became apparent that the cancer had metastasized to the bone level. The analogy was that of someone throwing many seeds into a field, and the seeds just began growing exponentially. Broken pieces of glass once again, and God was preparing my heart for my dad to pass away. I was devastated when my father went unresponsive, and it was clear he was near the end. I prayed for my dad's salvation as he got closer to the end of his life. I also prayed that he would finally be at peace without all the pain cancer had caused him for several years now. I remember making a pledge to myself that I would get in the very best physical shape that I could and remain there. Cancer ran on my dad's side, and strokes and diabetes on my mom's, so I figured I better get in top physical shape in case something ever happened to me. Thus, the idea for Maendel Fitness was conceived, and God brought it to fruition in the next eight years. I am very passionate about health and fitness and delighted to share everything I learned in these areas with my clients. I formed very tight relationships with them and helped them break through barriers they did not even know they had, using God's strength and not their own.

I do not want to get ahead of myself, though. I continued to work in various positions while I was still in school and even after I finished my program at UW-Madison in Speech and Language Pathology. I saw God show up repetitively in my life, a number of times when I knew I was not making wise decisions about my life. I had a failed first marriage and made foolish decisions about relationships thereafter. Even then, I felt God prompting me away from my poor lifestyle choices toward his safe haven. He always gave me an out in every situation possible, and usually, I was obedient to take it. I know He was putting a hedge of protection over me and had His hand on my life, even before I understood what it means to have a personal relationship with Jesus Christ to the depth that I do today.

Working in Corporate America: Heading Toward Wealth & Rededication to Jesus Christ

So this brings me to the period of life when I worked as a Special Education Teacher down South while I was still married to my first husband. I loved teaching and felt very privileged to make a difference in these children's lives. I taught middle school for a couple of years and then made the switch to high school upon our move out West. I continued to get one-year teaching contracts and would be forced to move to another position the following year as I was one of the youngest teachers aboard, and the others already had tenure at that time. When enrollment dropped, so would my contract. Once again, shattered broken glass. However, God showed up loud and clear. I prayed about the continuation of teaching Special Education or branching out to something new. God brought an answer to that prayer through one of the parents of my high school students. One of the parents of the young man I taught math to was the Executive Director of the Edward D. Jones investment firm. She asked me if I had ever considered becoming a stockbroker and financial advisor. I taught English and Math, so it seemed to be a pretty sensible progression toward that field. After several panel interviews, passing the Series 7 StockBroker exam, and acceptance to the company, I was well on my way to the top. I was starting new after my divorce with a new career, a new place to live, and a new car, my JAG. My father was an orthopedic surgeon and became very wealthy by age forty and I was heading in that same direction myself. The focus was more accounts and more money resulting in the higher I moved up on that corporate ladder. Instead of shards of glass coming this time, my husband offered knowledge that would help me grow closer to God. God was using my husband as a conduit to help pull me away from the love of money and materialism and closer to Him. I remember when he would come and frequent the bank I worked at on a regular basis. We had an incredible friendship that eventually grew into love and marriage down the road. Both of us had been in failed marriages the first time, and we wanted to move slowly and trod carefully. My husband was instrumental in leading me to Christ as a full-grown woman. There were also two other close friends at the time who helped with that process as well, Mariana and Shari. On November 4, 2006, I rededicated my life to Jesus Christ while Mariana held my hands and prayed with me. I once again felt the heaviness lifted away from me that was replaced with warmth and peace. It was a cold evening that night. I remember feeling like a warm blanket was enveloping my body.

Married Life Years: Drawing Closer to My Savior, Jesus Christ

My husband would lure me away from the nightclubs by standing in the doorway while I was on the dance floor. I saw something in my husband that was so pure and beautiful, and I wanted that for myself. The very attractive quality that I saw permeate my husband's whole being was Jesus Christ in him. The bar had less of a pull on me, as my appetite was growing for this new attractive quality about my husband that I had never experienced before. It was the opposite of confusion and chaos, and it was a feeling of purity and overwhelming peace that drew me in. He also changed the automatic music settings in my JAG to Christian music. I began to like the Christian music and the feeling I got when I listened to it in my car. We began to attend church and Bible study outside of church together. I remember a turning point in my life where I was confronted with a decision: 1) go downtown and party with my colleagues from working at the bank or 2) go to church to meet up with my future husband that night. I obviously chose the latter of the two choices, and my life progressively began to improve on all levels. I left my position at the bank and spent more time with my future husband and his friends. Later, I found out that my husband's friends had been praying that I would come into his life without even knowing who I was at that time.

My husband and I had a sweet friendship and were the best of friends for an entire year prior to any romantic involvement with one another. God shielded us both from focusing on a physical attraction to one another and instead helped us form a lifelong bond of emotional attraction. Today, we still comment on how happy we are that we did not rush into things and took that year to get to know one another. He asked my dad and stepmom for their blessing for my hand in marriage. He planted daffodils in the shape of a heart with them on the day he asked for my hand in marriage. We were engaged in March of 2007 and married that July with a very short length of engagement. A couple of years later, our son was born. Glass came flying at us once again, as he was an emergency c-section birth with the cord wrapped very tightly around his neck. God showed up and gave us the strength, "Trust in the Lord with all your heart and lean not on your own understanding. Acknowledge Him in all ways and He will direct your path," Proverbs 3: 5-6, we all needed to get through this complicated birth. Our family verse, Isaiah 40:31, was painted on the nursery of his room and also showed up in the chapel of the hospital where he was born. Coincidence or not? I think not. This was all God! We later had the same artist create a mobile replica of the same eagle painting with Isaiah 40:31 verse on a painting we have hanging in our living room today. Also, when we had him dedicated and gave him a plaque, the same dedication verse Joshua 1:9, "Have I not commanded you? Be strong and courageous. Do not be afraid; do not be discouraged, for the Lord your God will be with you wherever you go," was found on the wall of the room he was dedicated to. Confirmation!

Several times we started to make a move back to where I grew up, and God intervened. The home we almost purchased in my hometown was flooded a year later. The same thing happened when we tried to move to a home in the area where we live now. Scattered glass and God was putting it back together. Both times, the sales fell through at the last minute, and it was a blessing in disguise. We almost moved to the cities, and after our near encounter with a drug lord, we decided that was not where we wanted to raise our family. God revealed the plan to us to have us live in the home we have now, with five acres, to accommodate our company we have today.

Married Life Years: What You Will Never Be Prepared to Have Happen in Life

We need to revert back to our lives after our son was born and see possibly the greatest area God has impacted my life at a deeply emotional time of sorrow. We had gotten the news that we were pregnant again. A few short weeks earlier, I remember a trip to the state fair with close friends, Traci and Heather. They did not understand why I was eating everything under the sun at the fair, and neither did I at that time. Shortly after that trip to the fair, we received the incredible news that we were pregnant with twins. We celebrated and were absolutely elated when we found out it was twins! Two heartbeats, not one. I remember hitting my knees and calling out to God, "Thank you so much for this incredible blessing of twins in our life." Twins run on my husband's side of the family and no one had twins yet in the family. His mom was a twin. We were super excited and started to mentally, spiritually, and physically plan for the arrival of these two precious bundles of joy in our lives. We began to plan for more space in our home and made the necessary accommodations for their arrival. Broken glass hurled at us at an exorbitant speed, hitting us with the news that our doctor could no longer detect any heartbeat inside me. We were absolutely crushed, and it would require God's healing hand to help me emerge from my deep pit of despair and instant depression. I fell to my knees once again, "God, why would you give these two beautiful children to us only to have them snatched from our hands?" This started the lifelong process of healing my heart, mourning broken dreams, and just getting my head above water again. A little over a year later, we lost another baby at the exact same time, six weeks and two days into the pregnancy. Healing and encouraging scriptures in the Bible in Psalms were particularly comforting then and continue to be so today. At one point, I made the decision that I could either be sad about losing our babies, or glad for the gift of our son we already had. I could become bitter about this scenario in life, or I could become better and let God heal me over the course of time. I opted for the latter on both accounts.

Married Life Years: Exploring An Alternative to Expand Our Family

Adoption was something we would start to explore over the next few years. My husband and I got certified and ready to accept a child or even a children group into our family. We were preparing our hearts and letting God do the rest. We read books and watched hours of videos about adopting young children into our home. Our son was super excited as well as he had always wished for a sibling or siblings to join our family. We were ready to start the process of fostering to adopt. Broken glass showed up again in our lives during the process of attempting to adopt children into our family. "They that wait upon the Lord shall renew their strength, they shall mount up with wings as eagles," Isaiah 40:31. Timing seemed to be our biggest hurdle, as the adoption agency only had children for us at inopportune times in our lives. We tried one other time later as well, and broken glass guided us back to the struggles our son was having at that time. After heavy prayer, we decided it may not be the best time to introduce more children into our family equation.

Married Life Years: Traveling the World & New Business Dreams

Over the next few years my husband and I did a lot of traveling abroad. We went to Mexico several times, once with our son even, and to Italy, to celebrate ten years of marriage together. We enjoyed the freedom of not having young children in our home and occasionally offered to watch our friend's children to help fill that deep void inside. Broken glass shattered, in the form of adoption, was soon to be replaced with other dreams God had for us. God was saying no to one dream and was about to introduce us to a whole other set of dreams for us and our family. As our son was in school, I began to pray about ways I could invest my time wisely during the day. This is how the idea came about to start a company, Genoa Denim and Leather Apparel, with a close friend of mine, Traci Galles. We bought designer jeans and purses wholesale and sold them at retail. We traveled around the state and set up trade shows to introduce our merchandise to the community. At the end of the year, we sold the company for a profit.

I have always had a passion for photography, and enjoy taking pictures of a variety of different topics and subjects. After heavy prayer, I felt led to launch Carmen Maendel Photography that following year. I was able to capture photographs and sell them of families, birthday parties, graduations, and of course, wildlife. I started placing my photographs on various social platforms to see how they would perform with other fellow photographers around the world. The piece that has received the most attention with worldwide contests and has placed in the top ten percent of the world is called, "A Little Loony." This piece was taken when we were out on our boat, and a family of loons was close to us on the water. The father and mother loon did not dive down deep because their baby could not dive, and remained on the surface of the water. They did the same, and as we crept closer to them, the father loon put his wings out and leaned toward me and my camera. The light was perfect to pick up the vivid reflection on the water. God blessed me with the perfect timing of that shot!

New Business Dreams: Overcoming Fear in My Life Through Jesus Christ

Reflecting back on my father's passing, God led me to start a ministry with health and fitness which eventually became Maendel Fitness. When we first moved to this home, I decided to set up a mini gym in the basement. I felt selfish just using it myself, so I started inviting my friends to come work out with me in the gym. I realized how much of a blessing it could be for many ladies at once, and I started a health and fitness ministry in my church. For four years about five to six ladies came consistently to work out in the gym with me. We even had an area designated for their small children directly connected to the gym. I loved it so much that I decided to pursue my Certified Fitness Trainer license and opened Maendel Fitness officially in 2016. I later added my Master's in Nutrition and Precision Nutrition, followed by DNA Testing and Analysis. There were many lessons learned, and I overcame a variety of different fears embarking on this adventure from 2016 to 2023. My biggest fear was the fear of live video. I came to the realization that I did not have to be perfect. I could be "perfectly imperfect" or even "flawsome"! I could be full of flaws and awesome at the same time. I am created in God's image, and I am beautiful in His sight as a perfect image bearer of Christ. Jesus is the only one who is perfect, so I learned that I should not fear being less than perfect on live video. This was very freeing and allowed me to be authentically me in front of the camera now. I have learned to improvise and work with ad-lib situations, and half the time, I realize that I am the only one who would view something as a mistake on camera. Others may not even detect that mistake at all.

This realization has allowed me to go way outside my comfort zone and crush different fears and obstacles that used to stand in my way! God blessed me with a YouTube channel with workout videos and health and fitness information that I created. I created this with God's strength, not my own. I worked with two mentors and coaches who helped me break through barriers and accomplish business goals, James Allen and Mercile Martinsen. I am very thankful for their wisdom and guidance. They both helped me push through some of my own fears that would have prevented me from helping my clients crush their own fears, limitations, or suppositions. One of the ways God showed me to help my clients overcome their fears is by having them pick a Bible verse that they can stand on and identify with as their life verse. He also showed me how to help them identify and record "I Can" statements on paper to increase their level of confidence in themselves. One final way God led me to help them is by using my Confidence Boost System:

"MFC: Getting Rid of Insecurities, Negative Thoughts, and Negative Beliefs"

1. Learn to Shift Your Negative Thoughts
2. Push Your Negative Thought Out
3. Question the Belief
4. Create a Negative Association with this Old Belief
5. Create a Positive Association with the New Belief

My clients used this system when they were trying to get rid of negative beliefs and thought patterns about themselves. This system did just that.

God also guided me in creating and implementing the MFC Muscle Menu into my business, which taught and allowed my clients to pick and choose various exercises they would perform. This was set up similarly to a menu you would find at a restaurant. I divided the body into various subheadings with individual exercises targeting those muscle groups. For example, if one of my clients wanted to work the upper body in their biceps, triceps, and pecs, then they could pick from that menu to create three to four exercises working those muscles and muscle groups. Along with this, God also showed me, through prayer, how to put together a Gym List of the top ten items you would need at the gym. My clients appreciated these additional resources to help them work out independently.

Another tool God helped me create, after heavy prayer, and implement with my clients was my MFC Guru Grocery List. I created a list of foods using the Divine Nine food groups and categorized each under every vitamin and mineral. A person could use this in conjunction with my DNA Testing & Analysis and supplement the areas of vitamins and minerals that they may be deficient in. They would simply need to search for the foods listed on my sheet to help them boost up a particular vitamin or mineral. This was very helpful for my clients in guiding and directing them toward healthy eating patterns, and shopping for food at the grocery store for their families. In addition to the MFC Guru Grocery List, God also guided me toward the production of an MFC Tasty & Savory Cookbook with several recipes that were healthy and kept my clients on the right track.

Another fear I faced was the fear of being an imposter. The closer I drew to God and realized my identity in Christ, the less fear I had in this area of my life. It was easier to be the person God created me to be, and more of my authentic self than it was to pretend to be someone that I was not for several years. I did several sports and fitness modeling shoots when I first started my company. I thought I had to portray a "perfect image" in order to sell my company. In retrospect, a lot of my clients liked the fact that I was real and not like a Barbie doll. I also came to the conclusion that it was not my company, it belonged to God, not me. I needed to honor God in all I did, including treating my body as a temple of the Holy Spirit. I was convicted in this area of my life and stopped doing the sports and fitness modeling shoots altogether.

One final fear I addressed while I owned Maendel Fitness was the fear of the unknown. I learned amazing lessons about trusting God and holding on loosely to everything in my life. None of it belongs to me; it all belongs to God. We had to remodel our gym twice due to storm damage, and in the end did an expensive full waterproofing project just to save our gym and my company. I learned to trust God and have faith in Him. Thus, I had faith in myself. Faith is where there is no evidence or proof, an unshakable faith in God. "Therefore, since we have been justified through faith, we have peace with God through our Lord Jesus Christ, through whom we have gained access by faith into this grace in which we now stand. And we boast in the hope of the glory of God," Romans 5:1-2. I had peace and trusted the fact that God wanted me to close everything down in the business when my husband was offered a position out of town, and we were forced to put our home on the market for sale. I was obedient and closed everything including the online program as well, Rock Hard Body. I did not understand at that time that He was going to ask me to work side by side with my husband in our company today, Nate's Property Maintenance LLC.

New Business Dreams: Husband & Wife Team Owning/Operating Nate's Property Maintenance LLC

Glass shards shooting toward me once again and calling out to God, "Why?" Why did God bless me with a complete gym with all the extra amenities, only to have me shut it all down? This is biblical faith in God. He knows better than I do, and He knows my needs and desires better than I do. I see now that we were not supposed to sell our home with five acres on it, because we now use this home and acreage to run our business today. I needed to close one business in order to help run the next one. It makes sense to me now, and God has blessed our current company exponentially since last year on many different levels. God has shown us the most tremendous growth in the last year and a half through our profits, expanding our business inventory, and adding a team of workers to our company.

We are a husband and wife team. I handle all business on the homefront, and my husband works with our clients and his team of workers on our job sites. One of the strategies God showed me, through prayer, was to use our existing SEO for Maendel Fitness to help raise the SEO for Nate's Property Maintenance LLC quickly by advertising on the same strong social media platforms. I gradually adapted all of them to our new business. It is all about the algorithms when it comes to Google and SEO. After praying with my husband about branding our company, I decided to post before and after pictures regularly to FB, IG, LinkedIn, Angi, and Alignable, and we have begun to rise toward the top of the

Google list. We get the majority of our client leads for our company through referrals of existing clients and organic marketing off the internet. We do very little in paid advertisements, with the exception of our website and marketing through First Hit LLC, for our company at this time. I know God has prepared me for all my business financial responsibilities in our company's partnership through the past degrees, career positions, and life experiences God has blessed me with. Each day God shows me how we can be a blessing to those around us, and I am paying close attention. We are blessed in our current company so that we can bless others. I know I can trust God with everything in my life. "For I know the plans I have for you," declares the LORD, "plans to prosper you and not to harm you, plans to give you hope and a future," Jeremiah 29:11. I will continue to trust God and be obedient in the areas that He has asked me to serve, and I will not lean on my own understanding in my business and personal life.

The Ultimate Life Lesson: It's Not About Me & It's All About Jesus

The biggest lesson I have learned through the summation of all my life experiences is the following: It is not about me, it is everything about Christ! Whatever I do in life, Christ needs to be at the center, and He gets all the credit, accolades, and glory, not me. A Godly friend of mine pointed me toward these incredibly encouraging verses. I would like to share them with you now, in hopes that they will touch your heart as they have mine: Philippians 3: 7-14.

"But whatever were gains to me I now consider loss for the sake of Christ. What is more, I consider everything a loss because of the surpassing worth of knowing Christ Jesus my Lord, for whose sake I have lost all things. I consider them garbage, that I may gain Christ and be found in him, not having a righteousness of my own that comes from the law, but that which is through faith in Christ—the righteousness that comes from God on the basis of faith. I want to know Christ—yes, to know the power of his resurrection and participation in his sufferings, becoming like him in his death, and so, somehow, attaining to the resurrection from the dead. Not that I have already obtained all this, or have already arrived at my goal, but I press on to take hold of that for which Christ Jesus took hold of me. Brothers and sisters, I do not consider myself yet to have taken hold of it. But one thing I do: Forgetting what is behind and straining toward what is ahead, I press on toward the goal to win the prize for which God has called me heavenward in Christ Jesus."

The Gospel: The Good News

"For those of you who don't know the joy of serving the Lord Jesus Christ or the peace that comes from His forgiveness, I'd like to introduce you to my Savior..."

The word Gospel means "good news". It's pretty important to understand that. The Bible is not a book that tells us what we have to do to earn salvation, it is a book that tells us what God did to earn our salvation. What He did was send Jesus. Jesus did for us what we could never do for ourselves, and He paid for what we had done in His body on the cross. God created human beings and intended for them to be ruling creatures. We were supposed to be under God but over everything else. We were supposed to rule over creation under the guidance and authority of God's Word and to function as conduits for all the blessings of heaven. That's how it was supposed to be, but unfortunately, the Bible tells the story of how our first parents, Adam and Eve, fell into sin by choosing to rebel against God's Word by being tricked by Satan into eating from the Tree of Knowledge of Good and Evil. From that point on, humanity has been on a downward spiral, moving further and further away from God and our original design and glory. The heart of the Gospel is the Good News that Jesus has come as

God in the flesh and has obeyed God perfectly and has therefore obtained the right to all the blessings God originally intended to give to men and women. Furthermore, through His sacrificial death on the cross, He has paid the debt that we owed to God for disobeying his commands. There is, therefore, no need anymore for us to hide from God. In Jesus, we can come home and we can be restored through His forgiveness and repentance of our sins. We not only get the gift of Eternal Life, but we also get the honor and privilege of having a personal relationship with Jesus after accepting Him into our hearts. We praise Him, worship Him, and come to Him in prayer daily. We were created with the sole purpose of honoring and glorifying God through all of our thoughts, actions, and verbal utterances. The climax of the Gospel is the great news that He rose from the dead and ascended into heaven, where He now intercedes on our behalf. He gives the Holy Spirit to all His people, and He slowly but surely changes our hearts, reforms our desires, and teaches us how to be the children of God we were always intended to be. For now, Jesus remains in heaven, changing the world one person at a time, but one day He will return and judge the world in righteousness. He will remove from this world all sin and all causes of sin, and He will restore all to a state of peace, prosperity, and flourishing, and all those who have received Him as their Lord and Savior will participate in His rule and enjoy His goodness forever.

Please refer to John in the Bible for further explanation of the Gospel.

Debra Hillard

DK Hillard Art, LLC
Artist/Designer/Author Founder

https://www.linkedin.com/in/debra-hillard-93526913/
https://www.facebook.com/dkhillardart/
https://www.instagram.com/dkhillard/
https://www.dkhillard.com
https://www.dkhillardart.com
https://www.wraptures.net
https://www.threads-of-time.net

Debra is a creator. It is how she lives and what she does in her work. Her art has been a consistent thread throughout her life, whether it be painting, writing or working with others. It is based in her spiritual journey, her Shamanic practice and her connection to nature.

For 20 years she was a life coach and personal trainer, a career that evolved out of her experience transforming her life through bodybuilding. During that time she developed a 12 week program using the body as a vehicle for transforming your entire life.

She transforms her paintings into sensual, luxurious fabrics-clothing, blankets and pillows called "Wraptures", bringing the energy of her artwork into forms you can touch. They are filled with the love that she puts into everything she creates. She works with individuals and small groups using many of the interactive processes she developed while teaching her program.

The Wisdom Tree

By Debra Hillard

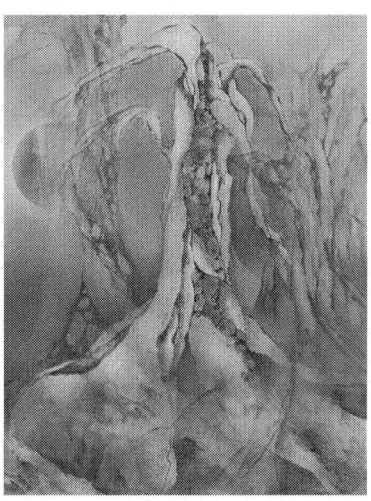

Ripening

A ripe peach is soft and must be handled with care
Housed beneath its tender skin lies the most glorious sweetness imaginable
As it ripens, its skin loosens for the meat within to ooze its juice

When a peach is ready to be picked, it makes its way into the world
To be sold, traded, and its worth judged
Those that look fresh and new bring the highest price
The skin must be taut, firm, and free of blemishes to be viewed as worthy
Of a front-row seat on the grocer's shelf

The sign says "tree-ripened" and the price is high
But a peach cannot fully ripen on a tree
It must have time on its own to mature, to develop its own luscious taste
This is the beginning of a process that will one day yield precious sap

A woman's ripening is much like that of a peach
It begins once she has been "picked"
First, she is new and fresh, firm and solid
Her flesh is tight, holding her juices at bay
The world views her as worthy of placement on the top shelf
Media ads cater to her, movies are made about her
and fashion is geared her way

The sign says "ripe", but she is not
A woman cannot ripen in youth
It takes life, wisdom, and experience for her precious nectar to mature
And yield its heavenly aroma

It is at the point when she is considered past her prime for the marketplace
That she begins to fully ripen
With her bumps and bruises in view
Her flesh softens, allowing her juices to flow freely

The softer she becomes, the less the world looks her way
She is dismissed as old and used, valued as less
Then, left alone to determine the significance of her life's gifts
Without the attention of the outside world
She can experience the magnificent sweetness flowing through her body
Her eyes become less crucial, and her soul leads the way
She is no longer for sale
Not someone else's commodity to barter and trade

With the world ceasing to look her way
Measuring her against others also newly picked from the trees
Her blemishes and bruises
Skin lacking its youthful luster

And her body, softened and molded by time
She is left behind with the freedom of invisibility to live as she chooses
Her juice flows, gifting others with the taste of sweet nectar that appears
Only with full ripening

It is the nectar, not the flesh, that is priceless
A mystifying nectar that enriches the soul
Those who partake of it frivolously pronounce it "A gift from the Gods"
Little do they know
It is

* * *

I wrote the poem above, inspired by the fear of being left "on the shelf", alone and abandoned, my attempt at shifting my perspective to one that would serve me, rather than create more anxiety.

Fear has been a constant in my life since birth. I believe I bathed in it in my mother's womb. They call it an anxiety disorder, but I know it as terror in my gut. My personal brand of this focused on fear of unworthiness. I was continually told that I had nothing of value to offer, and for a very long time, I believed it. It caused nightmares, both asleep and waking, throughout my younger years and well into adulthood, so much so that I was willing to run myself into the ground in an attempt to prove my worth. I damaged my health and forfeited years that I could have been living and pursuing my dreams.

When I found myself aging, fear struck hard. It reminded me that age is not valued in our society, and I, as an older woman, was at risk of losing whatever value I had. It was the fear of completely disappearing, becoming invisible, that haunted me. Aging is inevitable. I was going to have to find my value elsewhere. That led me to a miraculous shift in my perception and a reclamation of what I know to be my true value. Now, in my 70s, with old age upon me, I am no longer living in fear, but beginning a new life with enthusiasm and hope. My dreams of long ago are becoming a reality.

The reality is that aging continues to be a challenge for many of us, especially as women. We watch as our bodies change without our consent, and our once-taut skin loses its hold on our bones. To a large extent, we are out of control of this process. It cannot be stopped. The years, especially those at the turn of a new decade, mark the passing of our lives and the shortening of the years still ahead to fulfill our dreams.

As I get older, I find myself more vulnerable to the effects of "too much". I can't juggle all the balls I used to and be OK anymore. My shoulders don't want to carry as big a load either. Aging has brought with it a certain humility, and for that, I'm very grateful, because I no longer see my strength in the same way. It is not how much I can carry that shows me my value. It is my ability to listen to the cues as they present themselves. It is my willingness to be honest and true to what is necessary for my well-being and to say "no" to what I would have shouldered in the past. I don't measure my strength in the pounds of iron I can lift as much as the courage I have to let go of the extra weight that I no longer need to burden myself with. To say "no" to more. To say, "I've had enough," before I crash to the ground. I do wish I had learned this at a younger age. Perhaps aging would have been a bit easier and gentler.

I believe that we are all here to serve the planet in some way, each of us using our unique gifts to contribute to others, to the earth, to animals, and to raise awareness. The piece that I wasn't aware of until now is that we don't have to do anything special in order to serve. We just have to be ourselves and let our light shine. We have to be willing to step out of hiding what we consider to be our shortcomings, out of trying to be perfect before showing our faces, and out of our limited beliefs about what service is. Serving is nothing other than offering ourselves, our love, our attention, our wisdom, our gifts. It doesn't have to be on the level of

Bill Gates to make a difference. And being older, no matter the physical effects that accompany it, actually gives us an advantage in this area. We have more to share and less to lose in doing so.

If you were raised anywhere in the Western Hemisphere, you probably grew up with the belief that we become less valuable and more invisible with age, which easily leads to feelings of isolation. Stepping out of the shadows, warts and all, takes courage. The willingness to be seen, especially when we don't fit our society's standards of youthful beauty, is a way to overcome the fear that our age means we have less to offer. It is actually a way to serve.

We share our humanity and make it OK for others to show that they, too, might be experiencing something similar. We create connection, which is a powerful gift to offer anyone since so many of us go through life feeling terribly alone. There is no shame in not being able to juggle ten balls at once anymore. And there is no shame in growing old. It's a privilege that not all of us are afforded.

With all of this said, I have still found myself grieving the loss of my youth in a way I hadn't before reaching my seventh decade. There is something about 70 that feels final to me. A marker that I can no longer fool myself into thinking I'm young or going to reclaim my youth in some way. It is more than the loss of physical attractiveness that strikes a bit of fear in me. It is the concern that I will not have enough time left to realize my dreams or the physical wherewithal to carry them out if I do. This isn't something most of us verbalize, even to ourselves, let alone share with others. Even admitting that we're at this stage of life can trigger anxiety in some of us.

I was sharing my feelings with a trusted friend, and she asked me what the vibration of 70 felt like. To some, this might sound odd, but it made perfect sense to me. Words, thoughts, and emotions have a frequency to them, a rhythm and vibration that can be felt. This one felt ancient and deep, like the beating of a tribal drum. Then, I had a vision which I began to describe to her. It was of an old, majestic tree in the forest. This tree had lived for what appeared to be hundreds, if not thousands, of years. With gnarly bark and twisted limbs, it stood alone in the middle of the forest, its heart beating the beat of that ancient drum, deep and resonant, vibrating through the silence. Her roots ran deep beneath the earth, and her heart felt heavy and sad. She carried the weight of the world, of so many years of surviving whatever nature threw her way. This was a weight that could not be shaken off.

I felt a kinship with this tree. She was the embodiment of all that I was feeling about myself. Through this vision of her I saw my own grief, but I also saw all that I had been through to be as majestic as I was standing there. All of the wisdom I had gained and the abilities I had honed, the gems I had discovered on my travels within and the beauty of my soul.

My friend reminded me that trees speak to one another. They give each other nourishment through their roots, and when one of them is struggling, they intertwine their roots as a way of building a network between them, a community of sorts. Trees seem so much wiser than we are, don't they? Without the stigma attached to their age, they simply live, present at whatever stage of life they are in. Their trunks take on the imprint of the seasons they've weathered, revealing the richness lying beneath. Flowing through their veins is the river of wisdom gained, the courage to stand through every storm, and the essence of life renewing itself with each turn of the sun. Her beauty is majestic, strong, and regal. Her energy runs deep. "Aging" is not a term she fears because it signifies the power of her resilience.

I thought again of myself. I had felt so alone and filled with shame most of my life and am now experiencing the first threads of connection to something larger than myself. By extending my roots and sharing who I am from my heart, others have been responding and my loneliness is disappearing. Shame has also dissipated along with isolation.

I'm sensing that there is a network of other "roots" out there to share nourishment with. I'm finding that my own resilience and strength are valued, and my fears of being less are unfounded. Others see the light in my eyes, not the wrinkles on my face. They respond to my life force, stronger now that I have the years behind me to surrender all that was.

What I saw as I was speaking with my friend was the image of this majestic tree in the dense forest, reaching deeper into the earth with her roots, spreading them wider and further until she had received enough nourishment for her branches to grow and expand up beyond the forest ceiling. Up higher than she had ever been, where there was a world outside her secluded forest home, she turned her newly extended branches to the sun, and leaves sprouted from each one. It had taken all of those hundreds of turns of the wheel for her to be strong enough and solid enough in her roots, to be able to break through the forest out into the light. This was not the job of a sapling. It required an ancient, solid, jewel-filled tree.

"Old" didn't look undesirable on her. It was a mark of honor, respect, and even adoration for all that she was, all that she carried, and all that it had taken of her life to be the tree she was now. I didn't look at her and think she would have been better off as a young sapling with smooth bark. I looked at her in wonder at every knot on her trunk, every scar accumulated by weathering storms, and every twist of her branches, revealing all of the changes she had been through along her path. I was in awe of her majesty.

The tree is a symbol of who I am in my seventh decade. Old, with scars, and twisted branches, I stand with greater strength in my roots than ever. They have reached deeper and spread wider than ever before. I am finding a community that recognizes who I am and is feeding me what I need to reach beyond the forest ceiling. Within me lies thousands of years of jewels I have found on my journeys, giving me strength. There is a different beauty about me now, not one of youth, but of wisdom and truth that I never had when my skin was taught and firm. Would I trade who I am now for a younger version of myself? Never. Am I grieving a loss? Absolutely.

There is something in being young, with all possibilities ahead of me, that I will never have again. But like that tree, I will not waste the time I have left worrying about when it will all be over, or if I'll have enough years to enjoy the fruits of my work. My mind tells me that turning 70 means something that is worth grieving, but my soul is telling me that this is the time to live on *my* terms—to embrace being such a majestic tree that I *can* reach beyond the forest ceiling and spread my branches for miles. To celebrate that I have the roots that I do, so strong and deep that nothing can uproot me. And to realize that I am big enough to hold all of it, the grief, the years, the loneliness, the joy and celebration, along with a deeper knowing than I have ever had. Being in my 70s means having the freedom to pursue what I want without the restraint I practiced when I was younger. There is little to lose and no time to waste.

I realize now that had I lived more this way, my dreams might have already come to pass, and I might have moved on to even greater visions than I ever allowed myself to imagine. But there is no sense in thinking "what if". All is as it was meant to be, and this is just another lesson learned. If it took seven decades to free myself to live without the shackles I imposed upon myself, then so be it. Maybe that's a gift I have to offer others in sharing my story now. No experience is wasted when it's shared.

I have come to the conclusion that the saying "less is more" is true, at least for myself. Being older, which means letting go of striving to recapture my youth, is actually being *more* in my view because *fully being myself,* whatever that happens to be, is more than enough for me.

It is not about trying to be more than I am, as if who I am is not adequate. It is *being all that I am at every age,* that makes even the simple act of being, more than enough. Now if only I can say that I have finally learned and integrated this one, I'll be light years ahead of where I was yesterday. I know only too well that this one is so challenging to the patterns of a lifetime, that I will have to relearn it again, possibly in the not-too-distant future. Being older doesn't necessarily negate the need to learn. It simply gives us the advantage of learning more quickly. As I said, there is less to lose and more freedom to gain as we let go. At some point in our lives, we have to graduate from "school" and take what we've learned out into the world to create and contribute. If we allow our fear of being old and less worthwhile as a result of our age to stop us, then we are standing in the way of our own unique beauty and power, our wisdom gained, and our gifts fully realized. We are depriving others of our contribution. Owning the true power of our years is not hubris. It is self-esteem. It is self-respect. And that is a beautiful thing to behold.

Back to the tree in my vision—what do I imagine she is feeling as she enters her final years? What I know without doubt is that she does not mourn the loss of being a sapling. She stands wearing the crown that she has earned with eons of living and surviving every storm. The tree holds the wisdom of the universe in her knotty trunk, the riches of the earth, and a world of new possibility in each seed she sprinkles on that forest floor. Now, isn't that an example to live by?

Hiedi Emily

Warrior Princess Enterprises
Founder, Author, and Coach

https://www.linkedin.com/in/hiedi-doyon-a2094811/
https://www.facebook.com/hiedi.doyon/
https://hiediemily-leaderinspirercreat.godaddysites.com/

Hiedi Emily is a gifted author, speaker, teacher, and coach. She thrives on helping others know the Lord better. Her life's mission is to nurture believers in discovering their destiny and gaining insights to live victorious godly lives.

She grew up in a non-Christian home. While attending St. Joseph's school she first learned about God, and later accepted Jesus as her Saviour a week before her 13th birthday.

Hiedi has weathered many difficult storms which taught her to love like her Father with a compassionate heart, strategies for retaining joy, and the importance of sharing how to move past pain, and walk in victory.

She has two great children, and a brilliant grandson.

She is the co-author of 7 Women 7 Words, and author of Warrior DNA.

Hiedi's hobbies include quilting, cooking, and dancing. She loves to serve at her church and is excited to see God's future for her.

Praise and Gratitude:
The Most Powerful and Effective Tag Team

By Hiedi Emily

We live in a time of polar opposites. Some of the diametrically opposed schools of thought today include Cancel Culture and Manifesting Abundance through positivity. Additionally, we have folks that as soon as things go wrong they want to know who to blame instead of looking for solutions. Also, many talk about gratitude, whether or not they are truly grateful. When times are filled with such opposites and faux images along with the serious problems facing our world, how are we to discern what is right and how to approach life's problems? How do we stay free of panic and anxiety in our souls? Philippians 4 in God's Word shows us the way.

"Don't worry about anything; instead, pray about everything. Tell God what you need, and thank him for all he has done. Then you will experience God's peace, which exceeds anything we can understand. His peace will guard your hearts and minds as you live in Christ Jesus." Phil 4:6,7

In this passage, the Greek word for worry or being anxious is *merimnaō*. The meanings of this word are both obvious and revelatory. It means:

- to be anxious
- to be troubled with cares
- to care for, look out for (a thing)
- to seek to promote one's interests

When we allow the cares of this life to cause anxiety in us, we are not receiving the victory Christ died to give us. We all have problems. Whether we are facing health challenges, financial struggles, relationship issues, or a lack of understanding of our God-created identity and destiny, each one of us will face problems in life. In Matthew 5, Jesus said that the sun rises and the rain falls on the just and the unjust. Both sun and rain can be a huge blessing for crops, warmth, and holding soil together. They can also cause harsh complications through drought, miserable heat, flooding, etc. It is human nature to focus on the problems created instead of the blessings. However, when we focus on problems and how we need to 'get out,' we make the problems bigger in our minds. This creates a lot of stress and self-focus. It's better to admit that "Life happens."

Since we know life is going to happen, how do we prepare ourselves in advance to go to God instead of panicking? I believe there is a three-step process that utilizes the dynamic duo in the title of this chapter: praise and gratitude.

I am a big word lover! Words are powerful currency in life. They can change things; more importantly, they can change you and me from the inside out. Before we get to the steps, let's define and explore the power of these two amazing words.

Before we talk about them, we must add another power word to our discussion. That word is genuine. We have too many faux, or fake things in the world today. My two least favorite are a fake smile on an insincere person's face and fake thankfulness. Y'all know what I mean—those folks that use the magic words please and thank you, but you know by their attitude and the way they treat people that they don't mean them. Being genuine means that in your heart of hearts, you have allowed your Creator to soften you to a childlike amazement of what He has done for you in order to have sweet sincerity in your thanksgiving. I know for myself that without God's love and guidance, I would not be able to keep from being an anxious hot mess! This creates in my soul and spirit true peace and gratitude for all He has done. If this is something you sense is missing in your life, ask the Lord to create a pure grateful heart inside of you. He loves to answer this kind of request and will help you on the path to being genuine in your praise and gratitude.

What is praise? Any believer who goes to church knows we call the songs in the service praise and worship time. We also have praise services that are mainly music. Does this mean praise always includes music? No. The word praise is mentioned in the Bible 237 times. There are more than 10 Hebrew and Greek words used for our English word praise. Here is a compilation of the meanings:

- Confess the name of God
- Shoot out thanks like an arrow
- Laud
- Give thanks
- Praise
- Adorn and beautify
- Dwell and keep at home
- Hymn of praise
- Shine forth
- Boast, commend
- Make a fool of oneself in action of praise
- Adulate
- Sing hymns
- Honor and commendation
- Recommend
- Splendor in judgment
- Magnificence and majesty noted

Let's consider all these meanings and make a cohesive praise statement. Praise can be singing, but it's not always musical. Praise is loud and exuberant sometimes, and at other times it's a matter of dwelling in an attitude of adoring God, which in turn adorns us with thanksgiving. We need to praise in private and in public. When we praise, we shine forth for the Lord and recommend and commend Him to others. Given all of this, I believe a good praise statement is:

We praise God by having an all-in, no-holds-barred, at all times and all places attitude that shines forth His beauty through genuinely, and relentlessly thanking Him for all. We keep our homes filled constantly with His praise in song and word. We also do so in ourselves as His habitation on the earth in attitude and adoration.

Did I capture it all? Feel free to write out a statement yourself with what the Holy Spirit gives you as you consider just what praise is.

Next, we need to define gratitude. This may surprise you, but the word gratitude is not found in Scripture. To understand biblical gratitude, we will look at the words grateful, thankful, and thanksgiving. Variations of these words appear 36 times in the Bible. Some of them are the same Hebrew words we looked at above for praise. This simply shows how linked praise and gratitude are. There are two additional words in Hebrew and one main root word in Greek used in various types of speech (noun, verb, and adjective). The meanings of these words are:

- Confession of God's goodness
- Sacrifice of thanksgiving
- Praise
- To feel thankful
- To give thanks

This one is simpler to define. True gratitude is the combination of speaking out, feeling, and giving thanks to God (or to others), which sometimes is a sacrifice and always recognizes His sacrifice for us. The easiest and most obvious way to see the sacrificial part is in the very English transliteration of the Greek root word for thanksgiving. It is eucharist. Many Christian denominations use this term for communion. Remembering what Christ sacrificially did for us on the cross in itself is a celebration of thanksgiving!

Now that we have a clear understanding of our terms, let's outline the three-step process God gave us in Philippians.

The first step is to choose a lifestyle of praise. Every day, morning and night to offer up energetic praise to our God. This is very different from praising when you discern something good has happened, or simply praising for the first 20 minutes of a church service. I am talking about every waking moment of every day being ready to praise or actively praising. Like a soldier in the military is trained to be on alert and jump into action any moment needed to protect our country, we must train ourselves to be ready with words of praise and thanksgiving for our amazing God. If this is not your current lifestyle it will take some forethought and adjustment. Once you are in the habit it will come naturally to you. It doesn't have to always be a huge hour-long praise and worship singing session. Sometimes it may be. What matters is your heart turned towards Him in adoration. Let me give you a few examples from my own life to help you understand if this sounds foreign to you.

When I wake up in the morning, before I put my feet on the floor, I lay in bed and say something like this: "Good morning, Lord. I love you, and I want to thank You for today. Thank You for the breath in my lungs, for renewing my youth and strength like the eagles (Ps 103), and for the gifts You have placed in this day (Ps 68). Help me to recognize and receive them. Please work in and through me to will and do of Your good pleasure (Phil 2). Thank You in advance for every good thing, sign of Your favor, and answered prayer that I will encounter today, and thank You for the wisdom to deal with each situation and person I will encounter, amen."

The second comes from a dark period in my life. I was in a debilitating car accident 6 ½ years ago. This came directly after spending 3 years getting healthy. I had lost 127 lbs, was working out with folks half my age about four times a week, and felt the best I ever had. After the accident, I was in a lot of pain. Instead of working out for an hour, it took me that hour to get out of bed, crawl to the bathroom, use the toilet, and shower. Then I would have a 30' crawl to the kitchen to get something to eat so I could take at least 800mg of ibuprofen and a slight muscle relaxer (I don't take narcotics. That's another story). In one moment, I went from feeling like the energizer bunny to not wanting to move at all so I could feel the least amount of pain possible. I went to a few doctors for help and was told basically to accept this as my life. That I would need back surgery, and I would never be the same. In my bed on an ice pack one day, I had this thought, "Well, dang, I didn't just go through 3 years of self-sacrifice and investment to lay down and die!" I needed to fight back and recover my health, but how with all the professionals telling me such bad news? I prayed and asked God how. He reminded me that once a woman had spoken this word over me, "Your song and dance of praise is your powerful weapon." I wasn't in any shape to dance, so I sang. In my off-key, shaky voice, I sang many praise songs. After that, another idea came to me. Praise Him for what is working. This one took some creative thought since I was daily barraged with pain, a smaller income on disability, and an uncertain future. Like most new things, I started small. "Thank You, Lord, that my right big toe feels amazing today! Praise God, my left ear lobe is perfect!" Week by week, I thought of more body parts that were working than those that weren't. Within a month, I was told about a back institute in Fort Worth, TX, that might be able to help me. I met a great doctor, and he performed two non-surgical procedures on my back, which enabled me to get rid of about 60% of the pain and go back to work with some accommodations. Praise the Lord!! Three years later, after moving to another state, I found a physical therapy place that increased my mobility, and I lost another 20% of the pain. To God be the glory for fulfilling His Word! In addition, I have recently started utilizing light therapy which has helped remarkably. Today, I am thankful to the Lord to report that almost all pain is gone! I have a workout routine at home I've started. I have to regain my muscle strength and lose again a few pounds, but I am confident that He who began the good work in me is faithful to complete it (Phil1)! All of this recovery started with praise.

The third example is prophetic in nature. It is often referred to as declaring. When someone gives you a prophetic word either personally or you feel in your spirit what someone said in a message is for you, it's important to write that down. Also, and of course, primarily, when you are reading Scripture and a particular verse or passage jumps out at you, write that down, too, or highlight it somehow in your Bible. These are promises God is showing you. For me, I have a word both from the Bible and prophecy that I own a home and land that is so beautiful it is a modern-day Eden. When I think about it, plan for it, and pray, I also praise God in advance. This way, I am agreeing with the promise He has given me. "Lord, I praise You for the amazing gift my land and home are. I thank you that it is my Goshen in this world. I praise You that it is paid for, and I have all I need to take proper care of it and accomplish all You intended by giving it to me." I don't have this land as of the writing of this chapter. I don't even know exactly where it is. I know it's mine, and I thank Him as I wait for more information.

In all these examples, I hope you can see that you can voice, sing, dance, and lift up praise to our great God and King all day long, no matter where you are.

Step two is to pray. Big and small things in your life all matter to God. He wants to hear from you regularly, just like those who love you do. You wouldn't go a day without talking to your spouse, would you? Jesus is your Bridegroom, and He wants to hear the sound of your voice all the time. You can pray a quick "Jesus help me with X" prayer or pray longer. He doesn't care if it sounds fancy. He wants you to know you can talk with Him and ask for His help about anything. I like to keep a prayer journal so I can record when the answers come. This way I have a record of things to praise Him about.

Step three is to receive His peace. Many sermons talk about people walking down the aisle to pray about something, and then instead of leaving it at the altar, they pick it back up and bring it home with them. If you carry your baggage with you instead of giving it to the Lord, you won't be able to pick up and carry the package of peace He has for you. It's just too big!

After choosing to let go of the problem to receive His peace, keep it. The devil would like nothing more than to cause you sleepless nights, poking at your brain with questions about the issue. Don't let him. In James 4, it says when we draw close to God, we have the ability to resist the devil and he has to leave us alone. It doesn't say he might leave us, or it's possible. It says he will flee! If necessary, pretend your pillow is the package of peace God gave you and cling to it. Say, "Lord, I draw near to You. You gave me peace, and I choose to keep it. I resist the devil and say he must leave me alone. Thank You, Father, that You have rebuked him on my behalf and he is leaving. I don't listen to what he says; I listen to You." It really is that simple. God makes things simple. When people listen to the devil's twistings and lies, people make things complicated.

Choose God's plan for consistent peace. In your process of praising, praying, and keeping His peace, you will have victory in life. As you Pray, Praise, and are Genuinely Grateful, you will be kept from panicking and increase your strength to face any challenge while enjoying more completely all the blessings.

Quennie Marie Rose

Author & Life Coach

https://www.facebook.com/EiramWlions/

Quennie Marie Rose is a devoted single mother of two children, residing in Ontario, Canada. She is a best-selling author in the 2022 anthology, alongside number one motivational speaker in the world, Les Brown and an internationally renowned speaker James MacNeil. As a dedicated Life Coach centered in her brand "Heartfelt Solutions", she is committed to helping, inspiring, and motivating others to discover their true selves and navigate their life's journey with courage and authenticity. In addition to her heart centered approach coaching, she is also helping others achieve their wellness goals through holistic approach. She owns 2 network marketing businesses, "Bella Grace" a brand that offers quick, promising, miraculous and reverse aging results from the inside out. Usana brand also offers the same benefits and extensive products designed for protecting, promoting, healing and maintenance of a healthy body and mind.

Furthermore, she is spirited about empowering teenage boys to foster their personal growth and development through a mindset rooted in heart-centered intelligence. She is crafting a legacy of resilience, strength and vibrancy of being alive, that she hopes to pass on to her children.

Quennie Marie Rose is passionate and dedicated to personal growth and spiritual explorations, aiming to inspire others to feel moved, excited, and happy while living their HeartFULL and Dreamlife now.

For future Heartfelt Solution Life Coaching, Training Workshops and other Services, please email at: avantiqueen938@gmail.com

For Holistic/Natural product:
https://heartfeltsolutions.bellagraceglobal.com
https://queenmw.usana.com

From Grief to Gift

By Quennie Marie Rose

HOW I TURNED GRIEF INTO A GIFT...

Have you ever thought of giving up on everything and everyone or life itself? Have you ever felt like you do not want to care anymore about anything and anyone? Because you're just tired of everything and everyone? Simply because you're fed up with trying too hard, doing all the good things, and making the right decisions just to watch losing everything and everyone you love so much one by one? Have you ever been in that painful situation? Every day is a drag, and every waking moment is an unwillingness to participate in this so-called life. What is the point? The common question you ask yourself every time you try to push again to move forward. The loss of meaning and purpose in life, loss of motivation and inspiration, and loss of drive and excitement are all regarded as the same as DEATH. Just here and existing without any feeling of a joyful life at all. A friend of mine calls it "Hitting rock bottom."

We all have been there, and no one is an exemption. If you have not been there yet or have not experienced it yet, know that I'm not being a pessimist here or not placing fear in you. But be prepared. It will happen. That is just the truth. We're all gonna be given some kind of a test here to learn, grow and expand. As we all know, there ain't no easy and simple test. All kinds of tests are painful, dreadful, and perplexing. We pass the test, we graduate and move on to the next level ... the story goes on for centuries...

Now, how are you going to handle these mixed and difficult emotions and solve this puzzle? How do you get out of this state of consciousness that could be very detrimental to your being? How do you fight this feeling? How do you silence the victim mentality? How can you make that shift and live a happy life again?

When I was experiencing so much loss in one year, I lost a big part of who I am. I lost my spark, my light, my enthusiasm, my drive, my energy, and a lot of my willpower to do things I ought to do and want to do. In July 2022, I got separated from my husband. In the same month, I officially lost my 25-year career in the service business of hospitality. In September, my stepdad had been in and out of the hospital until December. In January 2023, my stepdad passed. His death was like a stab in my back. Then, in October 2023, I got a surprise divorce paper that landed in my mailbox without a stamp, filed last April 2023. All of these happened so quickly and it felt so surreal. From having everything I wanted in life to losing them all in a year. I was not able to feel anything at first. I was totally numbed and was just so occupied with keeping myself together and getting through the day by doing my daily duties as a mother, a job seeker, and so on... I was so busy protecting the well-being of my children. They were my first priority. I was like an AI robot operating my day-to-day duties, roles, and responsibilities on autopilot without any feelings at all... Just going through day-to-day life and getting all things done. Suddenly, November hits me like a very bad knock in the head. For the first time, I felt my reality. I felt all the losses I had never felt before, and that was when I felt I hit the biggest rock at the bottom of the ocean. I felt trapped and had no way out. For the first time, I did not know what to do with my life. It was dark and I was feeling all alone. I wanted to scream and break everything I could. Even that, I was not able to do. I was in a staggering state of paralysis. I was just stuck feeling all the pain. I just allowed myself to feel all the pain, without questioning ever why it all happened. I was just fully accepting everything and in full submission for the greater purpose of all my pain and suffering. I was just acknowledging everything and feeling all the different feelings I was undergoing at that time. I gave myself permission to cry as much as I needed. I took my time to feel all the pain until I could not feel it anymore. I did not rush myself to heal. I took all the necessary steps that were required of me to bring back my spark, my light, my drive, my enthusiasm, my interest in life, and my love for life. I consented myself to just be ... all of these were just part of my existence, my story, my journey, my growth, my expansion, and my experience ... all of these have been written in the stars for me to go through to discover one of my many purposes for being here. It's a force of events that were beyond my control to weave stories for me to tell right now. It was all necessary. All the twists and turns of events were the details needed to make my story like one compelling movie in an action, thriller, drama, and comedy genre. Truly, this has been a journey of self-awareness and personal connections. Through this processing journey of discovering the unknown, I have discovered the formula to the path of resilience and strength. Before I discuss with you my discovered formula, I want to mention a very important insight that I also have learned on my journey. I learned that fear is the deep cause and root of all of our sadness. Regardless of the circumstances. When we face the death of a loved one, we become afraid of being alone. When we lose a job, we fear not having an income to pay for our living. When a relationship breaks down, fear of not being good enough or worthy. When we move to a new location or unfamiliar territory, we become afraid of the unknown. When working on a project, dreams, and goals that take time to manifest, fear starts to arise and feeling afraid of failure. All of these make us feel so sad and bring grief into our lives. It's important that we give compassion and grace to ourselves. Grieving during difficult times takes time, and it is also a process.

Here are the breakthrough formulas I have learned and discovered that really helped me. I hope that it will help you as well.

Three C's Formula to RESILIENCE and STRENGTH

1. CONNECTIONS
2. CALLING
3. CONSISTENCY

1. CONNECTIONS: This is the very first and most important formula. Divine GOD or Christ Jesus connection is everything. This is the spiritual wifi between me and the Lord God. This is the understanding, conversing, and constructing secret language between me and God. This is the 80% part I focus myself on.

   John 14:17-18
   "He is the beginning and the end. The way. The truth."

   The spirit of truth, whom the world cannot receive. Because it neither sees him nor knows him. For he dwells with you, I will not leave you orphans; I will come to you. In fact, my connection is where it all began. Understanding that everything is just a test. My abstruse connections help me sustain my well-being and overcome it.

   Luke 21:36
   "Pray all the time and talk to God all the time for everything."

   Watch therefore and PRAY ALWAYS that you may be counted worthy to escape all these things that will come to pass, and to stand before the SON of Man. I was taught to never question why all the drama, pain, and suffering was happening to me. Instead, ask for strength to get through them and learn not to forget all the lessons learned and wisdom gained. Believe that Divine God is always with me and within me, listening and paving the way for me. Nothing too painful and too difficult to last a lifetime. This is all ephemeral.

   Romans 5:1
   "Therefore, having been justified by FAITH, we have peace with God through our Lord Jesus Christ."

   Focusing on God's words. Learning his purpose for all of our experiences. Accepting the fact that this pain and suffering is for character building, polishing, and perfecting me to the same image as he created me to be. I realized that at this golden age, it is the next chapter of human life and the transition to change. To reinvent myself, be who I want to be, and self-actualize to my highest potential. This is the next level in the course of life to set and achieve new dreams. This is another decade of life to face new goals. I call it the "GOALDEN AGE" of making it or breaking it. The decade that the majority of us are being tested if we're going to grab that second chance and opportunity to dream again, reinvent, and make it happen. The middle age of introspection through those wisdom gained.

I journeyed through the loss of my 25-year career, the loss of my 15-year marriage, and the passing of my stepfather and 6 other close relatives. All that happened in a span of over one year has been a profound and challenging experience. I did not know what to do; no one that I felt safe connecting with, and in a place of tremendous confusion. My safest connection to Divine God became a guiding light during such difficult times. Finding solace in my faith and feeling the presence of God's guidance through signs, synchronicity, and daily miracles truly shows the depth of my spiritual connection. My solid connection made me feel that I was never alone in all of my trials and tribulations and never will ever be.

In moments of confusion and despair, having that unwavering connection to God has provided immense comfort and strength. I prayed for everything, and I prayed all the time. I believed and trusted God, for HE never ever disappoints... It's a miracle how my faith not only saved me but also deepened my understanding of my experiences, which brought me peace and acceptance.

My experiences are a powerful testament to the resilience and transformative power of faith. Embracing the language of signs, symbols, and divine communication has clearly been a source of my confidence and hope for the future. My unwavering connection to

God has been a beacon of light in the darkness, guiding me through the toughest moments of my life. Through my strong CONNECTION, I felt the force that is always within me, the power within me. Discovering gifts of healing. I never knew I possessed the extraordinary gift of transformation. I was so uncertain of the direction of my life.

DIVINE GOD, SOURCE LOVE is irreplaceable, eternal and unconditional. The ending of my marriage made me realize that human love is incomparable to God's love. God will never stop loving me and will never leave me in the seas of darkness. The spirit of my stepfather lives on and carries on with me as a way of God's showing me his unconditional love. The loss of relationships I thought I had lost, was not even a loss after all. For I have gained the most important and beautiful thing. That is my stronger relationship and connection to God. Fearless and unshakeable I have become.

2. CALLING: The important ingredient to healing is having life's purpose and meaning. This is the part where I take 5% purposeful action and meaningful responsibility.

Philippians 3:14
"I press on toward the goal to win the prize for which God has called me heavenward in Christ Jesus."

1 Peter 2:21
"To this you were called, because Christ suffered for you, leaving an example that you should follow in his steps."

When I was going through all of life's painful tests, I had a conversation with God. I surrendered and laid all my heavy burdens on HIM. I wanted comfort to get me through them and an understanding of what I was supposed to do with all this pain and heartache.

I got my answers. I'm called to do His will for me, to use my HEART to share all the knowledge I learned and the truth I have discovered in the process of my self-healing and self-discovery. To use all my gained wisdom from all this incredibly painful experience to help others realize their inner strength and inner power. During meditation, I had a revelation of my calling to serve others through the power of words and deliver my message that's coming from our Divine Source Love. The message of "Turning Grief into a Gift" focuses on that purpose. A life well lived, with purpose and meaning each day, shall heal and ease all of heart's trouble, pain, and suffering. Through challenges, sorrows, sufferings, and grief, we grow and expand to new heights of understanding, and new levels of consciousness, and gain a new perspective in life. To me, that is truly a GIFT. Breaking through and becoming resilient overcomers is a must. I decided to listen to the CALLING OF OBEDIENCE AND SERVICE. Obedient to get up, stand up, and rise up. Obedient to believe and trust. Serve through showing up and living life with all the love and light I can give. Serve through circulating the power of words of wisdom. The calling to abide and serve through writing and speaking. By listening to my deepest core heart of heart, I heard my calling that led me to my healing, growth, and transformation. Shifting my focus on my new purpose and deciding to find meaning in my new life have taken me to the path of self-discovery. Living life now with so much excitement, enthusiasm, and earnestness.

3. CONSISTENCY: The process of constant CONNECTIONS and conscious commitment to my CALLING for my healing, growth, and breakthroughs. This is the 15% part that fuels me to be on the right track.

    Hebrews 13:8
    "Jesus Christ is always the same yesterday, today and forever. Consistency is the character of God."

I believe trust is built with consistency. I always say that God never ever disappoints because God is always consistent. We all expect consistency of the fruit of the spirit in every relationship we have. That is exactly the same with our relationship with God. Consistent obedience is the most important act of being an overcomer. MY CONSISTENT CONNECTION TO THE DIVINE AND CONSISTENT OBEDIENCE TO MY CALLING have proven to be my fastest route to healing, coming back to life like a phoenix.

In my experience, I learned to identify Godly grief and worldly grief. How I respond to my circumstances shows and builds my character. Feeling sorrowful for the right reasons and not wanting to disappoint God by accepting His will, no matter how painful, is Godly grief. On the other hand, feeling sorrowful for all the stresses and losses because it is personally painful and not wanting to change the mindset and accept God's better plan is worldly grief. Being able to profoundly assimilate the depth, differences, and nature of my sorrow helps me shake it all off and start a clean slate again to a joyous and blessed life.

In CONCLUSION:

Exploring grief as a gift is a deep and complex topic. Grief, often viewed as a painful and DEPRESSING emotion, can indeed be seen as a BLESSING in disguise. When we experience grief, it means we have PROFOUNDLY loved, DOTED ON moments, and formed SPECIAL connections. Grief IS OUR FEELINGS OF EVIDENCE to the depth of our emotions and the richness of our experiences. It allows us to TREASURE the beauty of life, our breakable existence, and the strength of the human spirit.

Grief as a gift is a concept that challenges us to reframe and RETHINK our WAY OF THINKING about loss, death, pain, and suffering and rewrite our stories. It invites us to ACCEPT vulnerability, to confront our emotions in moving ON. To find SIGNIFICANT purpose in the midst of our pain and suffering. Grief, in its rawest form, can be a REACTANT for personal growth, self-discovery, and esoteric transformation. It teaches us resilience, FEARLESSNESS, TO HAVE THAT FIGHTING SPIRIT OF A WARRIOR, and the importance of carrying the torch for every moment we have.

Moreover, turning grief as a gift INTENSIFIES our SYMPATHETIC awareness of ourselves and others. It opens the THRESHOLD to CONFIDENCE, compassion, and connection with those who are also maneuvering the TUMULTUOUS SEASON of LIFE. We DEEPLY UNDERSTAND the value of friendship and fellowship, the community of support, and shared experiences through grief. A helpful reminder that we are all TOGETHER IN our obstacles and struggles, that grief is a universal human experience that we all share and unites us in our humanity.

Finally, grief challenges us to fully embrace every spectrum of our feelings, to find meaning and lessons in our pain, and to honor the memories of those we have lost. When we view grief through the lens of being thankful for personal growth, it can be our finest life TEACHER, guiding us towards the HIGHEST FORM of healing and acceptance, and deeply treasuring every moment (even the most painful ones) as a precious gift of life.

Anna Barboza Lugo

Pure Tea Love & Pure CBD Love
Business Owner, Author, Mentor, CBD Coach, Leadership Facilitator

https://www.linkedin.com/in/anna-lugo-62746219/
https://www.facebook.com/profile.php?id=61550876111683
https://www.instagram.com/Alohalugo/
https://www.puretealove.com/

My name is Anna Lugo and I Am a Child of God, A Prayer Warrior, A Single Mother, a Sister, a Friend, An Encourager, A Mentor, a Retired I.T. Professional, and a Daughter of the King. I am also a business Owner of Pure Teal Love and Pure CBD Luv. I'm a Tea'V Host on EveryDay Woman TV Network where I have a show called "We Have A Tea For That... Positivi-Tea".

I also manage a Facebook page called "Up2UGod". I organically created this page 10 years ago where I'm dedicated to sharing a word of encouragement on a daily basis. This page recently reached 2.7 millions Souls over a 28 day cycle, I am so blessed that God is using me in this Way. I am also a license plate whisper and have seen hundreds of Spiritual Plates. I post these plates with music on my newly created tiktok page.

My Motto in Life is, "I'm Too Blessed To Be Stressed" and If Its To Be' Its Up To Me'. My goal is to Encourage / Inspire one at least one person a Day!

Everything is "Up2UGod"

By Anna Barboza Lugo

As a Prayer warrior, I always look for ways to stay 'Full'... Hopeful, Joyful, Grateful, Beautiful, Mindful, Peaceful, Thoughtful, and especially Faithful & Spiritual.

Prayer has always been my love language and a second language for me. Friends refer to me as a Prayer warrior, because I will pray for someone for an entire six months and never tell them. I always pray for my C's at 10:00 am (my family and friends who have cancer). For those who have passed on, I still pray for their families. My alarm goes off every morning at 9:50 am to remind me to pray. That alarm has been set every day for many many years. So when I learned of this opportunity to be a part of this book called, *Pray, Don't Panic*, I immediately had to inquire and sign up.

I'm a co-author of a book called *Guide to Living Your Best Life*. I believe that in order to live your best life, you must put God first and let Him orchestrate your calling. The chapter in my first book was inspired by my Tea Company, Pure Tea Love. I also launched a Tea'v show for a short period, called "We Have A Tea for That"... Positivi-Tea! I love being a positive change in a negative world. Inspiring others and bringing positive vibes and positive energy, it's just who I Am.

Over the past several years, I have created and managed several social media pages called Women Inspiring Women, Up2uGod, Thx2.God, Pure Tea Love, Pure CBD Luv, and Alohalugo. The social media pages were created to encourage at least one person a day.

Prayer and spirituality have been a priority as far back as I can remember. Prayer has always been one constant in my life. When we moved from Texas to California, after my daddy passed away, my momma would have us say our prayers before bed. I am extremely thankful my mother instilled this habit, where me and my siblings would kneel every night in prayer. I would pray even though I didn't know or understand what prayer was. I later learned that prayer is simply a conversation between Me and God. They say, train a child in which way to go, and when they are older, they will not depart from it. I never ever want prayer to be my last resort. In fact, prayer has always been my direct connection to my Heavenly Father.

When I first moved to Las Vegas 20 years ago, I ordered my very first personalized "God" license plate. I believe that Everything is up to God, so I ordered plates that read, "Up2UGod", and started seeing God signs and have been blessed to receive hundreds of spiritual messages ever since.

The second license plate I ordered was "BBlessd" because I believe God allows me to truly Be Blessed. Not only am I blessed, but also highly favored. He allows me to be blessed so I can be a blessing to others. I love that when we refresh others, we ourselves feel refreshed. My prayer is that everyone will continue to be blessed and stay blessed. Especially those who are near and dear to my heart. (My BBlessd plate was born in 2014.)

The third customized license plate I ordered was "PlzPray". I remember walking into the hospital emergency room with my daughter and seeing a plate that read JusPray. I knew that was a gentle reminder from God to Pray. I ordered my "PlzPray" license plate shortly after. I'm always open to the signs God himself gives me. I want to be that person who stands in the gap and intercedes in Prayer. Hence, making me a prayer warrior. (PlzPray plate was born in 2017.)

The fourth plate I ordered was "Thx2God" (Thanks to God). Because I am so very Thankful for all my many blessings and answered prayers. I specifically recall the time I begged God to allow my daughter to live after sustaining a brain bleed after being struck by a drunk driver. He was gracious indeed and performed a miracle that day, and I am forever thankful and give Him all Glory. (Thx2God plate was established in 2019.)

My current license plate is "AmenGod" because I give Him a million Amen for the many times He provided my every need. (AmenGod plate was established in 2023.)

I already have plans for my next plate, which will read "Hummble" because I will always humble myself and be selfless before my Lord & Savior.

I am so thankful that God is using me as a messenger to share the hundreds of messages that I receive through signs and sightings. I'm thankful He uses me as a Prayer Warrior to pray for those in need. I find myself constantly thanking Him and praying throughout the day. It's easy to live in gratitude when you have so much to be thankful for. Even in trials, I praise Him. I am truly rich in blessings. When I say, I'm rich, it's not because of material or monetary money, but rather it's being rich with God's Grace, Mercy, Peace, Faith, Hope, and Love.

11 years ago, I launched a Facebook page called "Up2UGod". I made it a daily habit to pray for anyone who commented, shared, or liked my page. It became a daily habit to pray for whoever God would put in my heart. This habit became my morning and evening ritual. I became a prayer warrior developing this habit of praying for those on Facebook and off Facebook. It just feels good to be used by God. He knows my heart and my willingness to lift others up and not tear them down.

I was ecstatic in August 2023, when my Up2uGod page reached 2.7 million souls. I felt like it was finally harvest season after 10 years of sowing and planting seeds, it was finally taking off. Then the following month, on September 9, 2023, I lost all access to my Facebook page. I was just two people shy of six thousand followers. So, of course, I was discouraged for a short while, but decided the devil does not get to win and God still gets all the Glory, so I created a TikTok page called Up2uGod. I now have another way to post my license plate sightings but this time with a worship song attached to each posting. I also have several other Instagram accounts called Thx2.God and Up2uGod, and look forward to creating more in the near future for PlzPray, AmenGod, and HeIsKng.

I am honored to be a license plate whisperer and have been blessed to see hundreds and hundreds of spiritual and God-related plates. God is so Good!! I believe God puts these plates/signs right in front of me on purpose because He has a purpose for me to share His messages. He knows the desire of my heart and my goal is to encourage, inspire, motivate, and pray for at least one person a day. He has by far exceeded my expectations.

During some of the most difficult times in my life, when I could not speak, my prayers would come in the form of teardrops. I know God has seen it all: my pain, my doubt, my heartache, my failures, my setbacks, my depression, he has seen it all. I learned it was better to surrender and turn my worry into worship, my mess into my message, and exchange my weakness for His strength. I needed to stand on my Faith. It's not always easy when you feel defeated and alone. I would fall down seven times but always stand up the eighth time for the sake of my daughter. I learned that my strength comes from the Lord. That I am who God says I Am. I learned to ask for healing. I learned to ask for help. I learned to give it all to God. I did everything to the best of my ability to rebuild my self-confidence and self-worth and became an independent single mother at 7 months pregnant. God entrusted me to be a loving mother to my now 45-year-old baby girl.

I love that God is my strength, and I am blessed that through prayer, I have salvation and can stand strong on His promises.

My Prayer is as follows:

Dear Lord God,

Allow me to be a light for those in the dark. I thank you for being gracious to me and giving me a favor. Thank you, Lord, that your approval is upon me and that you alone give me strength and courage. I thank you, God, that you have promised good concerning me. God, I pray that I will be trustworthy and faithful before you all the days of my Life.

Thank you for listening and hearing me, Lord, when I call on You. Thank you for making me a prayer warrior, thank you for covering over me and defending me and my loved ones. I will always remember who I Am, and whose I Am… I Am a Child of God. I am a masterpiece of God's creation, made wonderfully, beautifully, and fearfully in His own image. The words you put behind your "I Am" are powerful. I believe that all things have been placed under our feet by God. I trust and believe that Everything is "Up2uGod"!

I thank you that your hand is upon me for good. I know you want to repair every broken thing. Even as we are broken, you continue to fix us with your mighty hand. Thank you that your healing hand is upon me, Lord. I pray you continue to heal my heart and everywhere it hurts. I know, God, that your response to my prayers is in your time, and I thank you that your timing is always perfect.

God, you know the desire in my heart: to help those who are lost, lonely, broken, hungry, and sick. Let me be a compassionate servant for You, Lord.

Let Your will be done, Lord, and let me do what You ask me to do. Let me be still when you ask me to Be Still, and let me move when you ask me to move. Let Prayer be my lifeline to You, Lord. Sometimes, all it takes is one prayer to change everything. I believe in the power of Prayer.

I know, Lord, that victory is sure to come. Please give me a favor in the sight of everyone I meet. Let me have a heart, which's willing to do your will at all times. Thank you that you love me and help me in the midst of my suffering. Thank you that my life is in your hands. I know that you are in the middle of the suffering that threatens to defeat me. I will trust and wait on You, Lord. I pray, Lord, that when my enemies come against me, God, that you will frustrate their purpose so that I can continue to do the tasks you have given me. Let me have people in my life who will faithfully and spiritually be by my side and support me in good times and bad.

Sometimes, even the people closest to us do not understand our struggles, our suffering, our pain, our dreams, or our calling from you, Lord God. I want to know and understand my purpose and what you are saying to me. Give me answers. Let me learn to trust you, Lord, when I do not understand what's going on in my own life. Thank You, Lord, that you help me grow in faith, wisdom, and discernment.

I believe that you can do all things, and no thought or purpose can be held back. Sometimes, God allows us to to grow through adversity to build and teach us strength. God, I know that you still have the same good plan for me right now that you had the moment I was born. Let me express joy, peace, and laughter. Let me hug the broken, and feed the hungry. Allow me to trust you to lead me into an even better situation because you have a better plan for me and my life and those concerning me. I've learned that trying to do things that are not a part of God's plan for our lives is like trying to force our feet into shoes that are too small or don't fit. I will ask Him to move in every situation because, Lord, only You know my situation, my struggles, my failures, my successes, my challenges, but mostly, you know my heart.

I thank You, God, that your anger lasts only for a moment, but your favor lasts a lifetime. Thank you that weeping endures for only a night, and joy comes in the morning. Let me have so much Joy that the devil gets frustrated with me while I'm having fun in the Name of the Lord.

God, send your light and truth and lead me, let me hear you speak.

I will have faith in you, God, not just once in a while but at all times. I will continue to be the prayer warrior you called me to be. Thank you, Lord, for hearing my burdens and carrying me day by day. God, I will seek you in my life, and I will continually say, "Let God be Magnified". God, you have Magnifying Me and given me Favor. I am overwhelmed with your Love. I give you a trillion Hallelujha's and a million Amen's.

I will hope in you continually and praise you more and more. I will rise above only and not beneath anything or anyone. I thank you, Lord God, that you will always lead me to wise, Godly leaders.

Lord, I pray that I will never be a sheep without a Shepherd. What God knows about us is more important than what others think of us. I will always rely on you, God, in every situation I face with His guidance. I thank you, God, that you fight for me and because you do, I will not fear.

I thank you, God, that you are merciful and NEVER fail me. Thank you, God, that you have chosen me to receive the hundreds and hundreds of God signs. Thank you that You set me apart, and I am special to You, Lord.

Help me, Lord, to always walk in all your ways, to love and to serve you with all my mind, my heart, and all my soul. Thank You Lord, that you go above me, below me, beside me, behind me, and there is nowhere that I go where you are not with me.

I will always live my life knowing that Everything is "UP2UGod".

Amen, God.

Love, Your Child & Prayer Warrior,
Anna

JOIN THE MOVEMENT!
#BAUW

Becoming An Unstoppable Woman
With She Rises Studios

She Rises Studios was founded by Hanna Olivas and Adriana Luna Carlos, the mother-daughter duo, in mid-2020 as they saw a need to help empower women worldwide. They are the podcast hosts of the *She Rises Studios Podcast* and Amazon best-selling authors and motivational speakers who travel the world. Hanna and Adriana are the movement creators of #BAUW - Becoming An Unstoppable Woman: The movement has been created to universally impact women of all ages, at whatever stage of life, to overcome insecurities, and adversities, and develop an unstoppable mindset. She Rises Studios educates, celebrates, and empowers women globally.

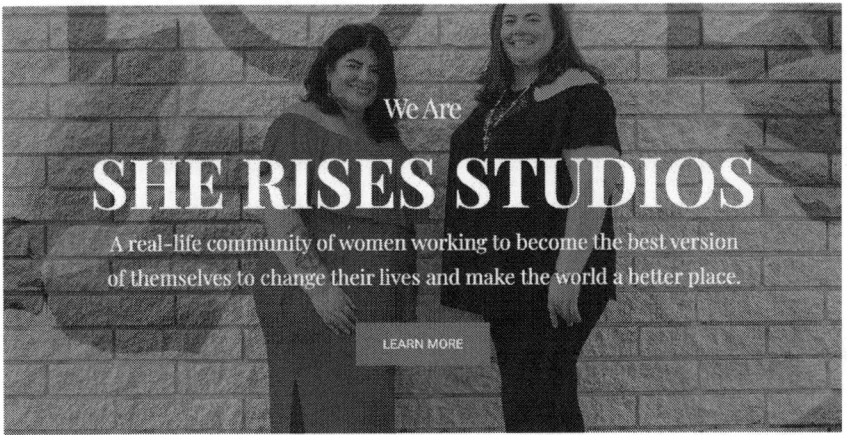

Looking to Join Us in our Next Anthology or Publish YOUR Own?

She Rises Studios Publishing offers full-service publishing, marketing, book tour, and campaign services. For more information, contact info@sherisesstudios.com

We are always looking for women who want to share their stories and expertise and feature their businesses on our podcasts, in our books, and in our magazines.

SEE WHAT WE DO

OUR PODCAST   **OUR BOOKS**   **OUR SERVICES**

Be featured in the Becoming An Unstoppable Woman magazine, published in 13 countries and sold in all major retailers. Get the visibility you need to LEVEL UP in your business!

Have your own TV show streamed across major platforms like Roku TV, Amazon Fire Stick, Apple TV and more!

Learn to leverage your expertise. Build your online presence and grow your audience with FENIX TV.

https://fenixtv.sherisesstudios.com/

278 | Stories of Transforming Fear into Faith for a Fulfilling Life

Visit www.SheRisesStudios.com to see how YOU can join the #BAUW movement and help your community to achieve the UNSTOPPABLE mindset.

Have you checked out the *She Rises Studios Podcast?*

Find us on all MAJOR platforms: Spotify, IHeartRadio, Apple Podcasts, Google Podcasts, etc.

Looking to become a sponsor or build a partnership?

Email us at info@sherisesstudios.com

Made in the USA
Columbia, SC
28 May 2025